The *Bakke* Case

LANDMARK LAW CASES
&
AMERICAN SOCIETY

Peter Charles Hoffer
N. E. H. Hull
Series Editors

Titles in the series:

HOWARD BALL

The *Bakke* Case

Race, Education, and Affirmative Action

UNIVERSITY PRESS OF KANSAS

Published by the University Press of Kansas (Lawrence, Kansas 66049), which was organized by the Kansas Board of Regents and is operated and funded by Emporia State University, Fort Hays State University, Kansas State University, Pittsburg State University, the University of Kansas, and Wichita State University

Library of Congress Cataloging-in-Publication Data

Ball, Howard.

    The Bakke case : race, education, and affirmative action / Howard Ball.

      p. cm. — (Landmark law cases & American society)

    Includes bibliographical references and index.

    ISBN 0-7006-1045-6 (cloth : alk. paper) ISBN 0-7006-1046-4 (pbk. : alk. paper)

    1. Bakke, Allan Paul—Trials, litigation, etc. 2. University of California (System). Regents—Trials, litigation, etc. 3. Discrimination in medical education—Law and legislation—United States. 4. Affirmative action programs—Law and legislation—United States. 5. Medical colleges—California—Admission. I. Title. II. Series.

    KF228.B34 B35 2000

    344.73'0798—dc21

                                         00-041163

British Library Cataloguing in Publication Data is available.

FOR MY FIRST GRANDCHILD,

LILA JULES BERNHARDT

CONTENTS

EDITORS' PREFACE

There are some law cases so complex in their nature and sweeping in their consequences that even the wisest judges cannot easily resolve them. Such a case is *Regents of the University of California v. Bakke*, the subject of Professor Ball's challenging and learned book. In its simplest terms, *Bakke* asked whether a state educational system could weigh past racial discrimination in the scales when its professional schools made admissions decisions. Was the United States Constitution in the 1970s so averse to any distinction based on race that it barred states and their agencies from attempting to right lingering racial injustices, provide professional services to economically disadvantaged areas, or train minority role models? Could the judges of the land fashion an exception—called "benign discrimination"—to the war on racism?

This book is a model of fast-paced narrative and subtle legal interpretation that fits the case into its own time and place, and then goes beyond the 1970s to examine the impact and future prospects of *Bakke*—for the affirmative action issues the case presented divided the court in 1978 and continue to divide judges, legislatures, and ordinary Americans today. Indeed, as the fragile consensus that Justice Lewis Powell of the United States Supreme Court forged, linking the opposing views of two groups of justices, seems to be collapsing, Professor Ball's book becomes all the more valuable to anyone interested in the controversy.

Using published and unpublished sources, including interviews with the justices, Professor Ball reveals the deep cleavages within the High Court on the case. These paralleled the climate of opinion in electoral politics. Although Presidents Lyndon Johnson, Richard Nixon, Gerald Ford, and Jimmy Carter had all supported affirmative action programs of some kind, presidential candidate Ronald Reagan ran against affirmative action. When he became president, he attempted to dismantle some of those programs, with dramatic and lasting consequences for the future of affirmative action. President Reagan's and President George Bush's appointments to the courts affected this process. Professor Ball documents these shifts in personnel and ideas with clarity and force, linking the political to the legal realm.

Mention affirmative action in a group, and in a flash there will be a felt tension followed by an immediate debate and division, often quite irrational and very emotional, among generally reasonable people. Since the late 1960s, affirmative action has been one of America's most controversial public policies, one that instantly triggers emotional defenses and criticisms.

Affirmative action as governmental policy (both federal and state) is a brand-new phenomenon—except for the preferential programs (such as the Freeman's Bureau aid programs) passed by the Reconstruction Congress from the late 1860s into the 1870s to assist the former slaves in the South. Other than that example, there are no historic precedents for the affirmative action programs, in business, contracting, employment, and higher education, that were created beginning in the mid-1960s.

For over three centuries African Americans, other minorities, and women were excluded from the "privileges and immunities" of citizenship. During that time, the U.S. Constitution was *not* color-blind; race, color, gender, and ethnicity were taken into account by legislators, executives, and almost all U.S. Supreme Court justices.

Only after formal equality for African Americans was finally reached, in the 1960s, did political leaders conclude that the formality of equality did not correlate with substantive equality. And it was at this time, especially during the administration of Lyndon B. Johnson (D, 1963–1969), that America turned to the transitory affirmative action remedy to create equal opportunity for disadvantaged racial and ethnic minorities. Beginning in 1965, the controversial concept of occupational and educational proportionality emerged as the key element in preferential affirmative action programs.

Allan Bakke was a thirty-two-year-old Caucasian Vietnam marine veteran when, in 1973, he challenged the University of California at Davis (UCD) Medical School's dual admission program. UCD's was one of many attempts by college and university officials to admit minorities to professional schools that had not admitted them in the past because of their poor performance on standardized tests needed for admission. High scores on these threshold tests were critical for admission because there were not enough seats for every qualified applicant for medical and law schools.

Bakke argued that of the one hundred seats annually filled by first-year med students, the medical school had set aside sixteen solely for minority applicants. Such a preferential quota system, his lawyers argued, was in violation of the Fourteenth Amendment's Equal Protection Clause as well as Title VI of the 1964 Civil Rights Act.

The California Supreme Court agreed with Bakke's lawyers, ordered Bakke admitted to the medical school, and ordered the medical school to cease implementation of its dual admissions process. However, the court delayed implementation of the order pending a final appeal to the U.S. Supreme Court.

The loser in the state court, the Board of Regents of the University of California, immediately appealed to the U.S. Supreme Court. They maintained that both Constitution and statute allowed a public institution to devise preferential admissions procedures in order for the university to diversify its student population. There is a difference, they argued, between a discrimination that prevents a group from entering a university and, in Bakke's case, an admissions policy that allows members of a formerly discriminated against group to enter the university.

The lawyers for the university knew that they were caught between a rock (the Fourteenth Amendment's demand that a state provide all persons with the equal protection of the laws) and the hard place (Title VI of the 1964 Civil Rights Act, as amended, which prohibited discrimination based on race, religion, national origin, or gender, by any public institution receiving federal financial aid). They knew that the UCD admissions programs would be validated only if the Court accepted their premise about the need to admit minority applicants. They also knew, from a case heard three years earlier, the *DeFunis* case, that the Court was split on the question of the constitutionality of preferential affirmative action programs in higher education.

Allan Bakke's litigation, formally called *Regents of the University of California v. Allan Bakke*, was heard, deliberated, and decided by the U.S. Supreme Court during the 1977–78 term. The *Bakke* opinion, eagerly awaited by a public sensitized to the issue of affirmative action in education by the national media, was in reality six opinions. None of them commanded a majority of five. The 156 pages of judicial writing in *Bakke* showed how controversial the issue of affirmative action was to the members of the High Bench. The message presented by the divided Court was a complicated, complex one. First, Allan Bakke was ordered admitted to the medical school. Second, racial quotas such as the UCD set-aside of sixteen of the one hundred first-year seats in the medical school for disadvantaged minorities are unconstitutional. Third, although preferential racial classifications are inherently suspect "and require the most exacting scrutiny," they are not unconstitutional in all circumstances.

The focus of this study of *Bakke* is to examine the law and the politics of affirmative action in a fair, even-handed manner. Both sides of the debate will be presented. The core arguments of pressure groups who participated as "friends of the Court" will be discussed. The brethren's once-secret *Bakke* conference session discussions and memos are presented so that the reader can better understand the dynamics of Supreme Court decision making in controversial litigation. The goal is to enable the reader to draw conclusions about what the dynamics of Supreme Court decision making are; whether affirmative action has value in higher education; whether affirmative action has led to significant changes in democratic diversity on college campuses across America; and whether affirmative action should continue as a viable social policy in twenty-first-century America.

———

Many persons have helped me in the preparation of this book on the *Bakke* litigation. The librarians and the excellent staff in the Library of Congress Manuscript Division, Madison Building, Washington, D.C., provided all the aid I needed when going through the documents in the files of Justices William J. Brennan

Jr., Thurgood Marshall, William O. Douglas, and others who were involved in the debates on the constitutionality of affirmative action programs in higher education. Seven justices, including Justices Powell, Blackmun, and Brennan, were kind enough to speak with me about the *Bakke* case and others involving the Fourteenth Amendment's Equal Protection Clause as well as discussing the dynamics of decision making in the Court.

The librarian of the U.S. Supreme Court allowed me to review all the amicus briefs filed in both *DeFunis*, 1974, and *Bakke*, 1978.

Mike Briggs, senior editor at the University Press of Kansas, was once again an invaluable guide, cheerleader, and friend. I thank him for all his help. I also appreciated the critical observations of an outstanding legal scholar and professor of law, Mark Tushnet. I also want to thank the two editors of this series, Professors Peter Hoffer and Natalie Hull, for their insightful and substantive comments, which helped me so much.

A number of colleagues in the Department of Political Science at the University of Vermont also provided me with ideas and information in a very timely manner. They include Phillip Cooper, Robert Kaufman, and John Burke. In addition, personnel at the Heritage Foundation, the Americans United for Affirmative Action, and the ACLU provided additional enlightening information on their respective positions on affirmative action.

In addition, I want to thank Associate Dean Donna Kuizenga, Arts and Sciences (and her committee), for timely financial support. I also appreciate the university's grant of a Fall 1999 sabbatical that enabled me to finish the manuscript in a timely manner.

The book is dedicated to my first grandchild, Lila Jules Bernhardt, the daughter of my middle daughter, Sheryl Lisa, and her husband, Dr. Jay Bernhardt. I was there at Lila's birth, and it was a most beautiful event.

I cannot conclude without thanking my two other daughters for their love and friendship: Sue Gabrielle, the actress, and Melissa Paige, the animal lover, along with her husband, Patrick Dolan. I thank my wife, Carol, for her love and friendship over almost four decades. Finally, there are our three dogs—Casey, Maggie, and Sam—and our quarterhorse, Stormin' Norman, who always give me absolute love and affection.

CHAPTER I

Affirmative Action
in Higher Education

Dawn, October 12, 1977: hundreds of people lined up at the U.S. Supreme Court building, waiting to hear the oral arguments in the case of *Regents of the University of California v. Allan Bakke.* For NBC-TV news correspondent Carl Stern, it was a case that "may be the most important civil rights case since segregation was outlawed in the 1950s."

That evening, all three television network anchors led off the news with comments about *Bakke.* Walter Cronkite on CBS news: "The Supreme Court heard arguments in a controversial case that could produce its most important civil rights ruling in two decades." On ABC news, anchor Harry Reasoner began: "Good evening. One of the most important civil rights cases in two decades, the Allan Bakke reverse discrimination suit, was argued before the Supreme Court today." At NBC, anchor David Brinkley called the *Bakke* case "one of the most difficult the Court has had in years."

The three anchors then turned to other newsmen for additional information. ABC's Tim O'Brien commented on the presence "of an overflow crowd for what could be one of the most important civil rights cases ever." CBS's Eric Severeid said that "today's *Bakke* case was as inevitable and is as significant as the school desegregation cases of the early 50s." On NBC news, John Chancellor spoke to the possibility of *Bakke* entering "the Hall of Fame of great cases which changed the interpretation of the Constitution; cases like . . . *Brown v. Board of Education,* which changed the face of integration in this country."

For millions of Americans watching television that night, it would be difficult not to grasp the fact that an extremely important event was taking place in the Supreme Court. When the *Bakke* decision was announced, their lives could be affected—positively and negatively—by what a Supreme Court majority said about affirmative action policies in education.

With massive television, radio, press, and news magazine coverage of the *Bakke* case, the public was inundated with terms such as "preferential treatment," "affirmative action," and "reverse discrimination." By the time the decision of the U.S. Supreme Court was announced, on June 28, 1978, most Americans had a perception of the controversial public policy called affirmative action.

Polling data collected by the Gallup Poll and other organizations showed that most Americans opposed preferential treatment for racial and ethnic minorities. At the time of oral argument in *Bakke*, October 1977, the Gallup Poll indicated that 83 percent of Americans were opposed to any preferential treatment not based on merit.

In 1978, the American National Election Studies (NES) polling results indicated that most Americans polled believed that university admissions committees should admit applicants solely on ability (78 percent). Only about 11 percent of those polled supported preferential treatment for minority applicants. When polled by the race of the respondent, 52 percent of whites strongly supported university admission based on ability, while only 28 percent of African Americans agreed with the use of that measure. Only 2 percent of the white cohort supported preferential admissions processes for minority group members, while 24 percent of African Americans strongly supported affirmative action.

Through the end of the 1990s there was a fundamental difference between whites and African Americans when polled by the NES and other polling operations: Over this time period, the NES and the Gallup polls indicated that more than four-fifths of the whites polled opposed preferential treatment for minorities, with the greatest opposition (91 percent) coming after 1994. Data from African-American cohorts polled over this same period indicated that a majority of blacks in almost every poll supported preferential treatment for minorities, ranging from 74 percent in the 1990 NES poll to a bit over 50 percent in the 1994 NES and Gallup polls.

Percentage Opposed to Preferences						
Year	1986	1988	1990	1992	1994	1996
Whites	85	87	82	87	91	88
Blacks	31	35	26	44	50	38

For all the parties in the 1970s *DeFunis* and *Bakke* litigation, the polls were a harbinger of the future conflicts, in the White House, Congress, the U.S. Supreme Court, and the larger society.

The Divisive Social and Political Issue

In 1954, in a watershed opinion, *Brown v. Board of Education*, the U.S. Supreme Court unanimously concluded that in the field of public education, the doctrine of "separate but equal" has no place. "Separate educational facilities are inherently unequal. . . . Any language in *Plessy v. Ferguson* contrary to this finding is rejected." With *Brown*, the Supreme Court ended almost six decades of constitutionally protected separated facilities that effectively discriminated against African Americans. By 1954, equal educational opportunity had become a bedrock social value in American society. In the eyes of the unanimous Court, education was the primary gateway to equal employment and educational opportunity in America.

However, a decade later, there was still massive elementary and secondary school discrimination in almost one dozen Southern states. And colleges and universities were still overwhelmingly white. At the time of *Brown*, only 4.9 percent of college undergraduates were African-American; in 1965, the figure was the same. For many minority students, this was an intolerable condition that could be remedied only by direct, radical actions.

Their argument for radical change in college and university admissions standards took note of the real world in which African Americans had lived since the first slaves were brought to shore in coastal Virginia in 1619 by the slave traders. In an ideal world, equality is a lodestar for society. In such an abstract world, all persons are judged on their intellect, their skills, their integrity, and their character, not on irrelevancies such as race, color, gender, national origin, and religion.

Minority students, however, knew that America did not exhibit these ideal societal characteristics and values. They lived in the real world of America, a world where until the middle 1860s African Americans were chattel property with no standing in federal courts of law and where they had no formal education. Until well into the twentieth century they were denied fundamental rights of citizenship, and their morbidity and mortality figures, compared to those of white persons in America, were dreadful.

The real world had been so unfair, so cruel and brutal, and had stigmatized the African-American community (and other minorities, including women, Native Americans, and Jews) for hundreds of years. It would be, as a justice of the U.S. Supreme Court said in *Bakke*, "the cruelest irony" to turn to the idealistic view of equality: a "color-blind" equality where people succeeded based on their innate, and fully developed, strengths. If that principle was implemented, if racially blind college and university admissions practices continued in American higher education, there would be the continued exclusion of virtually all minority applicants from the best undergraduate, professional, and graduate schools.

In the middle to late 1960s minority students across America demanded that university officials address this fundamental unfairness. On the University of Washington campus in May 1968, Larry Gossett and other members of the newly formed UW Black Student Union (BSU) stormed the office of the university's president, Charles Odegaard. They demanded that UW admit more minority students. Of the more than thirty thousand students at UW in 1968, there were two hundred African Americans, twenty Native Americans, and about ten Mexican-Americans.

Odegaard promised to respond positively to their demands. He created a committee to find ways "to arouse the interest of Negro students in the university." He sought funds to provide financial aid for new minority students. In the summer of 1968, the UW affirmative action policy was implemented. Initially, UW officials as well as BSU members traveled across the state to encourage minority students to seek admission to the UW. Odegaard created the Equal Opportunity Program (EOP) to handle admissions for minority students as well as those who were "educationally and economically disadvantaged."

What happened at the University of Washington that year was happening at hundreds of colleges and universities across the nation: dynamic and militant minority students were marshaling their small numbers to demand of white administrators that there be greater diversity in the staff, the faculty, and the student population. Their demand: end "institutional racism" by diversifying the campus community—staff, faculty, administrators, and students. Their tactics: sit-ins, takeover of buildings on campus, and protest marches, in order to articulate their demands.

By the end of the 1960s, there were only 211 African-American medical students attending predominantly white medical schools. For the first time in American higher education, students' applications to enter law and medical schools exceeded the number of available seats. By 1970, there were 43,000 applicants for only 13,000 medical school seats and 76,000 applicants for 45,000 law school seats.

The ratio of applicants to available places in the UW's school of law was more than five to one by 1970 (1,600 applicants for 300 seats). At the UCD medical school there were 3,700 applicants for only 100 seats in the medical school. To continue to use the traditional color-blind admission policy, with its emphasis on grades and standardized test scores, would further erode the university's efforts to bring minority students into these programs.

Given the reality of this emergent enrollment explosion, with its adverse impact on the acceptance of minority applicants, UW's President Odegaard, the UCD faculty, and other university officials and faculty across the nation realized that educators had to take more aggressive actions to promote fairness and equality of opportunity in college admissions. Aggressive recruitment was simply not enough to diversify the university's student population.

In one of the many ironies of the controversy over affirmative action in higher education, Odegaard and other university administrators seized upon the language in Title VI of the 1964

Civil Rights Act to justify their development of preferential admissions programs enabling minority students to attend undergraduate and graduate schools in greater numbers. Title VI stated: "No person in the United States shall, on the ground of race, color, or national origin, be excluded from participation in, be denied the benefits of, or be subjected to discrimination under any program or activity receiving federal financial assistance."

In the minds of university administrators across the nation, past discrimination against minorities led to exclusion of racial and ethnic minorities from participating in higher education. They compensated for this history by rapidly, affirmatively, hiring and promoting minorities and women—groups who had been traditionally underrepresented and underpaid. The equal employment opportunities section of Title VI was used as the justification for this new, more flexible manner of hiring and promoting.

UW's Equal Opportunity Program (EOP) administrators developed a separate admissions process for minority students. Even though by 1974 the UW moved to a minimum 2.5 grade point average for admission, the EOP standards for admitting minority students were lower.

The EOP justification for such an admissions program: to achieve diversity at the UW, affirmative action, not race neutrality, was needed. Affirmative action effectively promoted equal opportunity by providing qualified minorities with a college education. With such a higher education, graduates had a good chance to achieve success in life—based on their intelligence and training as well as the content of their character, as one African American, Shelby Steele, wrote at the time. As one of President William J. Clinton's lawyers said, in a July 1995 report to the President that reviewed all affirmative action policies in place in the federal government, a fair chance to achieve success is a "bedrock value in our culture."

Quickly, affirmative action in higher education led to admission of minority applicants who otherwise would not have been accepted at these universities and colleges. As a consequence, Marco DeFunis, Allan Bakke, Cheryl Hopwood (who successfully challenged the University of Texas Law School's affirmative action program in the 1990s), and many other white applicants to professional schools who had been denied admission argued that they were the innocent victims of reverse discrimination. And they sued on the grounds that both the Fourteenth Amendment's Equal Protection Clause ("Nor shall any state . . . deny to any person within its jurisdiction the equal protection of the law") and Title VI of the 1964 Civil Rights Act—the very same Title VI used by university administrators to justify preferential admissions—prohibited such race-based preferential admissions procedures!

Affirmative Action and the Clash of Values

For all observers, the 1978 *Bakke* case epitomized the societal clash—political, moral, legal—between the values of meritocracy and race neutrality and those of racial balance and equality of opportunity. It was the ideal notion of equality versus the need to provide members of minority groups with an educational boost so that they could enter areas of employment formerly denied them. The heart of the dilemma is the preferential use of race and ethnicity in these affirmative action higher education admissions programs.

A corollary problem, overshadowed by the controversy over preferential admissions of minority students into colleges, was the matter of retaining the entering minority students. Since affirmative action began, there had been significant numbers of admitted minority students who had dropped out of undergraduate college and professional schools. The stated reason, as UW BSU activist Gossett said decades later: "There were no social, cultural, academic, and financial structures necessary to keep us there."

Responding to this problem of getting into college and then staying in and graduating led to the creation of the BSU and other minority campus organizations, at both the undergraduate and the graduate and professional school levels. Their arguments and their demands, then and now, were ironic: To actualize the ideal of equality in the future, American society must first deal with present group inequalities, vestiges of past racism. In higher education, that meant the creation of preferential affirmative action admission and scholarship programs. About this time, the U.S. Commission on Civil Rights defined affirmative action programs as "any measure, beyond simple termination of a discriminatory practice [against a group], adopted to correct or compensate for past or present [group] discrimination or to prevent [such group] discrimination from recurring in the future."

———

President John F. Kennedy's 1961 Executive Order 10925 is considered the beginning of the affirmative action era. His EO created the President's Committee on Equal Employment Opportunities. It was charged with ensuring that "affirmative steps" were taken to diversify the government's work force. Government contractors were not to engage in employment discrimination based on race, ethnicity, or national origin. The contracting firm had to agree "to take affirmative action to ensure that applicants are employed and treated fairly."

In the administration of Democratic President Lyndon Baines Johnson, 1963–1969, the federal government's commitment to affirmative action policy fully emerged. His 1965 Executive Order 11246 called for each federal agency to "establish and maintain a positive program of equal employment opportunity for all civilian employees and applicants for employment." In this effort, the use of "numerical goals and timetables" is appropriate for an institution to employ. An agency must show a "good faith effort" to diversify; to include groups that historically have not been included due to racial, ethnic, or religious discrimination.

Between 1961 and 1981, affirmative action was implemented as a national and state public policy, in employment, contracting, and education areas, by Republican presidents (Richard M. Nixon, 1969–1974, and Gerald Ford, 1974–1977) as well as Democratic chief executives (Kennedy, Johnson, and Carter, 1977–1981). From 1981 to 1993, two Republican presidents, Ronald Reagan, 1981–1989, and George Bush, 1989–1993, did all they could to end affirmative action programs. However, Democratic president Bill Clinton, 1993–2001, continued the federal government's support of these programs.

Because of America's past racial discrimination, affirmative action programs had to move "beyond simple [race-neutral] non-discrimination," of the type initially undertaken by UW administrative officials in the late 1960s, toward a more aggressive plan that would lead to diversity on campus. Such a proactive plan meant providing preferential treatment to members of certain identified racial groups. It also meant rejection of the concept of a color-blind U.S. Constitution.

There have been at least three kinds of affirmative action programs created by colleges and universities. One group of affirmative action admissions policies is modeled after the Harvard admissions program. The college's admissions committee seeks out qualified minority applicants who will provide diversity to the incoming class of students. And the race of an applicant is a positively weighted factor in the admissions decisions of the college committee.

A second group focuses on the ethnicity of its applicants in order to enroll a small number of minority students in each entering class, whether undergraduate or graduate and professional schools. The dominant weight in the admissions process is given to the traditional numerical scores, standardized test results, and grade point averages. However, university administrators create minority recruitment "goals" to diversify the campus student population; for example, admissions committee members are given a "goal" of 5 percent minority admissions. Consequently, the admissions committee recommends minority applicants who score in the average range but who are considered the most qualified minority applicants. Implicit is the understanding that the "goal" may not be met because the admissions committee members could not identify qualified minority applicants.

A third group of affirmative action college admission programs sets aside a fixed number of seats for minority applicants and employs a dual admissions screening process. Called a quota or set-aside program, this affirmative action plan differs from the second because it fills every one of the seats set aside for minority applicants to the university.

The Defenders and Critics of Affirmative Action

Such preferential treatment for members of identified and targeted "disadvantaged" groups (by race, ethnicity, sex, and disability) raises significant questions about the nature of fundamental rights—and fundamental fairness—in American society:

1. Does the Fourteenth Amendment's Equal Protection Clause prohibit all governmental public policies that rest on group-based racial or ethnic "neutral factors"?
2. Can the Constitution be read and interpreted by the justices of the U.S. Supreme Court to allow minority preferences in order to overcome the effects of past racial and ethnic discrimination in America?
3. Is the Fourteenth Amendment's Equal Protection Clause an absolute barrier against preferential treatment for minority groups at the expense of others?
4. Is Title VI of the 1964 Civil Rights Act an absolute barricade against affirmative action?

Defenders of affirmative action answer no to the first question, yes to the second, a loud no to the third and fourth questions. Group preference is the only practical strategy for overcoming centuries of discrimination in the real, not the ideal, world of America. For hundreds of years, policy makers used race and ethnicity negatively: denial of citizenship and exclusion from schools and most vocations. From 1619, race discrimination was embedded in America's social, legal, economic, and political fabric.

After the Civil War and the constitutional amendments that followed in its wake (the Thirteenth through Fifteenth Amendments, 1865–1870), the separation of the races emerged and was legitimatized by the U.S. Supreme Court majority in the 1896 case of *Plessy v. Ferguson*. That case involved the constitutionality

{ *The* Bakke *Case* }

of a Louisiana statute that required separate rail cars for African-American and white passengers. The Court said that a state or local subdivision could separate the races in all kinds of social activities, from birth to death, so long as the separated facilities were equal. The sole dissenter in *Plessy*, John M. Harlan, argued, vainly, that the Constitution was color-blind. Statutes and local customs and practices that excluded members of racial groups from the rewards of equal opportunity were therefore unconstitutional.

The contemporary affirmative action policy was aimed at overcoming the consequences of the Court's 1896 legitimatization of a color-conscious Constitution. The realization of formal legal equality for African Americans in the 1950s and 1960s (due to Supreme Court decisions and to civil, housing, and voting rights legislation passed by Congress and implemented by presidents) did not erase the consequence of three centuries of racial and ethnic inequality. Affirmative action was introduced to enable African Americans and other insular minorities to attain full citizenship in America's economic and educational arenas.

A decade after the watershed 1954 *Brown v. Board of Education* decision of the Supreme Court, race discrimination in education still flourished. Disparities of all kinds, called "the badges and incidents of slavery," in the areas of health, employment, education, housing, and civil and voting rights still existed between African Americans and whites. Clearly, the goal of equal and fair opportunity for all persons had not been met. Thurgood Marshall, the first African American to serve as an associate justice of the U.S. Supreme Court, noted the unfair inequities that existed in 1978 between the races: black life expectancy shorter by more than five years than that of a white child; black mothers over three times more likely to die of complications in childbirth; black infant mortality rate twice that of whites; percentage of blacks who live in families with incomes below the poverty line four times greater than that of whites.

In a memorable speech to the graduating class at Howard University, broadcast to the nation in June 1965, President Lyndon B. Johnson defended the need for affirmative action. He said that affirmative action is necessary because "you do not wipe away the scars of centuries by saying: 'Now, you are free to go where you want, do as you desire, and choose the leaders you please.' You do not take a man who for years has been hobbled by chains, liberate him, bring him to the starting line of a race, saying 'you are free to compete with all the others,' and still justly believe you have been completely fair." Americans must proactively respond to the distributive inequities that existed in the nation in the 1960s, said the president.

Defenders of affirmative action as the primary but temporary means to achieving success in life argue that implementation of an affirmative action plan was justified for two reasons. It would (1) remedy past centuries of discrimination against racial minority groups in America, and (2) effectively promote inclusiveness, thereby benefiting men and women of all races and ethnicities in educational and economic pursuits.

Going "beyond simple [race-neutral] non-discrimination" meant that, as a temporary solution to the problem of racial and ethnic discrimination, the affirmative action plan had to "provide preferences based explicitly on membership in a designated group" that had historically been discriminated against by society. This fundamental characteristic of an affirmative action program—benefiting persons on the basis of membership in a discriminated-against minority group—is a prime factor in the clash of values over affirmative action.

In an affirmative action program, membership in a designated protected group (determined by a university board of regents, administrative regulations, presidential executive orders, or the Congress) meant preferential treatment for all members of that group in order to compensate members for past societal discrimination. Such affirmative action programs, the U.S. Commission on Civil Rights has argued, are the only device that can effectively "overcome 'group wrongs' that 'pervade the social, political, economic, and ideological landscape' and become 'self-sustaining processes.'"

Additionally, defenders of affirmative action programs maintain that the color-blind admissions process, incorporating an applicant's college grade point average (GPA), Law School Admissions Test (LSAT) scores, and other race-neutral factors,

{ *The* Bakke *Case* }

does not produce an accurate estimate of the quality of the minority candidate. The literature on standardized tests, one of the linchpins of color-blind admissions decisions, clearly shows that those tests are inaccurate indicators of future student success.

At bottom, supporters of affirmative action programs in higher education believe that they provide "democratic diversity" on college campuses. The university is the one institution in America that seeks out diversity for its inherent benefit to the university community of students, faculty, and staff. Supporters point to the 225 percent increase in minority enrollment since 1965 in America's colleges and universities as clear evidence of the growth of such democratic diversity in higher education. For them, as Chief Justice Warren said in his opinion in *Brown*, a quality education is the very foundation of good citizenship. It is the principal instrument in awakening the students to society's bedrock cultural values. These defenders argue that colleges and universities hold a unique position and that racial segregation is intolerable in that setting.

Public colleges and universities, wrote Akhil Reed Amar and Neal Kumar Katyal in a law review article, should be places where people from different walks of life and diverse backgrounds come together to talk with, to learn from, and to teach each other. To enhance this learning process, each student's unique background and set of life experiences should be examined by members of the college's admissions committee. Amar and Katyal claim that there has emerged an American tradition of treating education specially because it teaches Americans about America's heterogeneous, pluralistic, melting-pot scheme of democratic self-government.

For democracy to flourish, college students have to be able to interact with other students who are different from them, whether in race, color, national origin, religion, or gender. For supporters of affirmative action in education, absolute color-blindness is not required by the Constitution or by congressional statutes. If the university was forced to return to racially blind standards for admission and for scholarship awards, America's university system would once again be a nearly all-white enclave.

Critics of the policy argue that affirmative action does away with the principle of color-blindness in America: individuals, not anonymous members of racial or other groups, have rights that must be protected equally without regard to race or ethnicity or other personal characteristics. The U.S. Constitution, they argue (drawing upon Justice Harlan's *Plessy* dissent) is "color-blind" and does not countenance a "good or benign" discrimination based on race. Such group preferences, based on past discrimination against members of those groups, seriously disadvantage whites who had nothing to do with past racial and ethnic discrimination. Affirmative action programs are a form of "reverse racial discrimination" prohibited by the Fourteenth Amendment's Equal Protection Clause.

Critics of affirmative action argue that higher-education admissions officials must base their admissions decisions on one standard merit review of all individuals as individuals, not as members of a group. The quality of an individual's prior academic record determines whether that applicant will be admitted or rejected. Standardized admission test scores, high school or undergraduate grade point averages, extracurricular work record, and the quality of the high school or college attended should be the key factors in determining whether a student enters a particular university. Race and ethnicity are "neutral factors"; they are not relevant factors in a university admissions process.

This argument says that to deny a white person rights guaranteed by the U.S. Constitution or by legislation passed by Congress, to treat a white applicant for admission differently than an African-American applicant for admission because of race or ethnicity, is to discriminate against that applicant in violation of the Constitution and congressional civil rights statutes. The Constitution is color-blind, and affirmative action plans are a fundamental discrimination based on neutral factors such as race and ethnicity.

Alexander Heard, the chancellor of Vanderbilt University, said: "To treat our black students equally, we have to treat them differently." For the critics, however, such counting by race in the admissions process means that unqualified students enter the university. Critics such as Terry Eastland and William Bennett maintain that *Bakke* was "supremely a conflict between two ideas of equality, one the idea of numerical equality, as represented by the academic institution, the University of California, and the other the idea of moral equality, as represented by the individual, Allan Bakke." For these and other critics, moral equality was the most important way in which men and women could be equal. The Constitution's Fourteenth Amendment underscores the primacy of moral equality. The Equal Protection Clause makes all racial classifications unconstitutional per se. So, too, do congressional statutes such as the 1964 Civil Rights Act.

As soon as admissions processes are implemented that make the opportunity to attend a university dependent on race, moral equality is replaced by its opposite, numerical equality. That equality has a negative impact on learning and on America's traditional values. For the critics, the subordination of merit, conduct, and personal character to race and ethnicity means that moral considerations are subordinated to statistical ones. They insist that the use of preferential programs to overcome serious educational disadvantages of minority students will destroy the quality of higher education in America. For them, a commitment to affirmative action is a threat to the moral vibrancy of American society, a society committed to the concept of a color-blind Constitution.

———

How Does a Judge Determine Whether Affirmative Action Programs in Higher Education Are Constitutional?

Cases dealing with affirmative action in higher education came to the attention of the U.S. Supreme Court in the early 1970s. To understand what the Court did, one must understand a few basics about Supreme Court actions. There are a few threshold questions the U.S. Supreme Court must answer positively if they are to hear a case.

First, the litigation must fall within the jurisdiction of the Court. *Jurisdiction* is the authoritative power of a court, any court, to hear cases. Judges cannot hear any case they like. All judges, state and federal, including the justices sitting on the U.S. Supreme Court, are given their jurisdiction in statutes and, in the case of the U.S. Supreme Court, Article III of the U.S. Constitution.

The Supreme Court's jurisdiction consists of both appellate and original jurisdiction. Its appellate jurisdiction is outlined in Article III of the Constitution, which states, in part, that the Court can hear all cases and controversies "arising under the Constitution." In addition, as one of the many checks and balances built into the Constitution, in Article III the Congress was given the power of adding to or reducing the Court's appellate jurisdiction.

Almost all the Court's case load is appellate; that is, the Court reviews questions of law that have emerged from trial courts' and intermediate appeals courts' judgments. Almost all of its work comes from the Court's granting of a writ of certiorari. Certiorari is one of a small number of extraordinary writs of equity created in Great Britain in the early Middle Ages and transported to the American colonies. *Certiorari* means literally "to be informed." In the legal context, when the Court grants the writ, it means that the justices will be formally informed of the case history by having the full record sent to the Supreme Court. In 1978, then–Rule 17 (now Rule 10) of the Court's formal rules, stated that the granting of the writ of certiorari was not a right but a matter of "sound judicial discretion."

The second threshold issue is whether the Court majority thinks that it can provide a meaningful remedy to right the perceived legal wrong. The term used to describe this second threshold matter is *justiciability*. As the Court said in an early-twentieth-century case, justiciability means that the Court majority thinks the "case is appropriate for judicial determination." Put baldly, a case is justiciable if four or more justices believe that it falls within the Court's jurisdiction and that it can be successfully resolved by the Court.

Justiciability, as Chief Justice Earl Warren wrote in a major case that broadened the term's meaning, *Flast v. Cohen*, 1968, is an "accordion-like" concept. Depending on who is sitting on the Court at the time, the granting of certiorari can be extremely limited because a majority wants to avoid "hot potatoes." However, if an activist Court majority, either conservative or liberal, is sitting, it can grant certiorari in cases earlier Court majorities would not have taken. If the U.S. Supreme Court decides that it has the jurisdiction and believes that the case is justiciable, then the case passes from the threshold to Court deliberations and decision on the merits.

The anatomy of a significant constitutional dispute such as *Bakke* must include an examination and an understanding of just how judges evaluate that contested public policy in light of limits placed on all governmental action by the American Constitution. That fundamental law of American society provides a conceptual map describing both the powers and the limits of governmental power as well as the alienable and inalienable rights, liberties, and obligations of persons living in the society.

Any judge, when hearing an affirmative action case, must employ (1) a consistent definition of *equality* as well as (2) a measurement tool that has transformed the definition so that the judge can evaluate, analyze, and, finally, answer the question: Is this contested affirmative action program before this court constitutional? In this area of constitutional litigation—as in other areas—it has been the U.S. Supreme Court that has, over the generations, created sets of standards to answer such questions in equal-protection litigation that comes before the judiciary.

Tucked away in a footnote in the non–civil rights case of *United States v. Carolene Products*, 1938, were three paragraphs that had dramatic impact on future equal-protection litigation in the Supreme Court. It was a case that upheld Congress's authority to ban the shipment of "filled" milk in interstate commerce. Chief Justice Harlan F. Stone's majority opinion announced that the Court would no longer carefully scrutinize economic and social legislation passed by Congress. Henceforth, he wrote, the justices would assume that such legislation rested on "some rational basis," and unless the party bringing suit could show that the legislation was irrational, or capricious, or arbitrary, the Court would defer to the legislature's judgment.

At that point in the opinion, Stone inserted his now-famous footnote 4: The justices would carefully scrutinize legislation that affected the "fundamental rights" of persons or that "discriminated against particular minorities based on race or color" and other "discrete and insular minorities." Such legislation, he thought, must be "subjected to more exacting judicial scrutiny under the general prohibitions of the Fourteenth Amendment than are other types of legislation."

Unlike economic or social legislation, where the justices' presumption was the existence of a "rational basis" for the challenged statute, when legislation discriminated on the basis of religion, race, or national origin or curtailed fundamental rights, the Court would apply "strict scrutiny" and demand a "compelling" justification from the government for its challenged action.

Ironically, the Court first applied the "strict scrutiny" standard in a case that upheld the incarceration of more than 120,000 Japanese Americans (mostly American citizens) during World War Two. In *Korematsu v. U.S.*, 1944, Justice Black wrote for the majority that "all legal restrictions which curtail the civil rights of a single racial group are immediately suspect. That is not to say that all such restrictions are unconstitutional. It is to say that courts must subject them to the most rigid scrutiny." Given the total war being waged by America and its allies against the Japanese in the Pacific theater of war, removing the Japanese residing in America from the West Coast's industrial centers was an important security measure; their exclusion served a compelling national purpose, he concluded for the six-person majority.

By the end of World War Two, the U.S. Supreme Court had developed and implemented a two-tier standard to help them determine whether a challenged state action was justified or was an invidious, capricious, and hence unconstitutional, discrimination. If the discrimination was against what the Court over the years came to call a *suspect class* of citizens, that is, members of historically persecuted, politically powerless racial, ethnic, religious, or insular groups (African Americans, Jehovah's Witnesses, Japanese Americans, Japanese aliens, and Native Americans, for example),

{ *The* Bakke *Case* }

then the standard used by the Court in judging the validity of the discrimination against such classes of persons would be what became known as the *strict scrutiny* standard.

Because a member of a suspect class is discriminated against does not make the discrimination automatically invalid. In such litigation, the "heavy burden" is on the state or the federal government to show "compelling" reasons for the racial discrimination. If, in the judge's estimate, no compelling reasons are presented for discriminating against suspect classes of persons, then the governmental action is unconstitutional. However, if the lawyers for the government can show convincing evidence that there were compelling reasons, then the discriminatory action is a valid one.

Obviously, if one is discriminated against, one wants to show membership in a suspect class or, alternatively, argue that one's particular class of persons should be added to the "suspect class" category. (Women, the aged, and the poor, for example, have argued before the Court—unsuccessfully—that they should be considered members of suspect classes.) Whether one is successful in this effort to convince the justices depends on the validity of the argument and the makeup of the Court when the argument is made.

What if, as seen in all the affirmative action cases brought before the U.S. Supreme Court since 1971, the person allegedly discriminated against was not a member of a suspect class but a member of the majority group in America, a Caucasian plaintiff? As will be seen, some of the justices, because of their view that the Constitution was color-blind fundamental law, argued that the strict scrutiny standard was the only basis for decision making in these cases.

Another group of justices, led by Justice William J. Brennan Jr., argued that strict scrutiny was necessary when a case involved a racial discrimination that demeaned and stigmatized a particular group. In the affirmative action education litigation, there was a "benign" discrimination used to overcome the vestiges of three hundred years of slavery and racial discrimination. The white plaintiffs in these cases, unlike African-American plaintiffs who came to the Court a generation earlier, were not humiliated, stigmatized, or brutalized by arbitrary and capricious university affirmative action programs. Therefore the justices had to use a different standard, called the *intermediate standard.* The justices using it had to determine whether the challenged policy was valid because the state showed that the policy served "important," but not "compelling," state goals.

In the affirmative action litigation, the justices of the U.S. Supreme Court had to determine just what kind of scrutiny was necessary when evaluating and adjudicating cases challenging a college's preferential treatment of some classes of persons over others. Some used strict scrutiny, while others used the rational basis standard or the higher intermediate scrutiny standard.

The individual judge's definition of *equality* has determined the standard that the jurist has employed in affirmative action litigation over the past quarter century. As will be seen in the anatomy of the *Bakke* case, given the judges' varying perceptions about the concepts of equality and of equal opportunity, both the state and the federal courts—all the way up to the men and women who sit on the U.S. Supreme Court—battled over what was the appropriate standard to use. In these battles, there were no judicial deadlocks. Who sat on the Court at a particular time determined what standard was used to decide these questions.

———

In the litigation that emerged in the 1970s, unlike the secondary school segregation cases of the 1950s and 1960s, the injured litigants were Caucasian male applicants who were denied admission to law school (Marco DeFunis) and to medical school (Allan Bakke). Prior to these cases, the injured plaintiffs in education discrimination litigation had always been African Americans and other racial or ethnic minorities.

DeFunis and Bakke entered the swirling affirmative action controversy reluctantly. Both had been denied admission twice—by the University of Washington for DeFunis and by the University of California at Davis for Bakke. Only after their repeated efforts to enter the schools failed did they turn to the legal sys-

{ *The* Bakke *Case* }

tem to seek a remedy for what they termed unconstitutional "reverse discrimination." The lawyers for both men argued that the Fourteenth Amendment's Equal Protection Clause prohibited the universities from using preferential admissions policies to admit less-qualified minority students over DeFunis and Bakke.

What follows is the "anatomy" of a major constitutional decision, *Regents of the University of California v. Allan Bakke*, handed down in late June 1978. It is an account of the legal, social, and political events that emerged when these two determined and goal-oriented white men argued that they had been unjustly discriminated against by university officials and unconstitutionally denied admission to law and medical school. They ushered in a debate, at all times very heated, about the meaning of equality in both the U.S. Constitution and congressional statutes. It is a dispute that shows no signs of ending soon.

CHAPTER 2

Marco DeFunis Seeks Admission to the University of Washington School of Law, 1971–1974

Allan Bakke was not the first plaintiff who challenged the constitutionality of affirmative action programs in higher education. Almost four years earlier, Marco DeFunis argued that the University of Washington's law school's preferential admissions policies violated both the U.S. Constitution's Fourteenth Amendment's Equal Protection Clause and Title VI of the 1964 Civil Rights Act.

Marco DeFunis is a lifelong resident of Washington State. (In 1999, he was practicing law in Seattle, Washington, with David Balint—DeFunis and Balint, P.S., Attorneys at Law.) He comes from a Sephardic Jewish family, and he attended the University of Washington (UW), where he graduated magna cum laude, with a Phi Beta Kappa key, in 1970. He had a grade point average of 3.6 (out of 4.0) and received no grade less than A– during his last two years at the UW. During his undergraduate years, he worked twenty to forty hours a week for the Seattle Park Department. He taught Sunday School at his synagogue for that period of time.

After graduation, DeFunis applied to a number of law schools. He was accepted at two public law schools, Idaho and Oregon, as well as at two private law schools. However, he was rejected by two other schools, the University of California, Berkeley (Boalt Hall), and the UW School of Law. DeFunis, for personal, financial, and family reasons, wanted to go to law school in his home state and practice law there. He reapplied to the UW in 1971 but was rejected again. It was at that point that DeFunis sought legal counsel to pursue his goal of entering UW's law school.

Marco DeFunis's Efforts to Attend UWSL

By the time DeFunis applied to UWSL in 1970 and again in 1971, the school had established a new, affirmative action, admissions process. UW President Odegaard had led the academic community in the development and implementation of an admissions policy that took race and ethnicity into account. UW, he said, was "in pursuit of a state policy to mitigate gross under-representation of certain minorities in the law school and in membership of the [Washington State] bar."

Three general criteria were employed in the new law school admissions process. Its admissions committee consisted of five professors and administrators and two students. These seven examined each of the applications in light of the three guidelines:

1. The applicant's past academic performance as a predictor of performance in law school: the standardized Law School Admission Test (LSAT) score (averaged if taken more than once, as was the case with DeFunis), the undergraduate grade point average, the quality of the undergraduate institution attended, grades in difficult courses, and grades in the junior-senior year were accorded a single predicted first year average (PFYA) score;

2. The applicant's ability to make "significant contributions to law school classrooms and the community at large"; and

3. The applicant's "social or ethnic background," considered as one factor in the admission committee's assessment of the likelihood of the applicant's successfully graduating from law school.

The PFYA score was used to assist the admissions committee as it examined every applicant's file. The highest score possible was an 81. To be automatically admitted, an applicant's PFYA had to be 77 or higher. If an applicant had a PFYA score of 74.5 or less, that person was rejected. Two groups, however, were treated differently: (1) returning military veterans who had at one time been admitted but were then called for military service and (2) applicants from one of four identified minority groups: African

American, Hispanic American, Native American, and Philippine American.

Two pools of applicant files were examined by the committee. The files of white and non-preferred minority applicants were randomly distributed to individual members of the committee. Using the PFYA index as the major guide, the individual members returned the files, for final determination by the full committee, with a recommendation to admit, reject, or hold for possible placement on a wait list.

The applicant screening process provided special treatment for the preferred minority applicants. Their files were also considered separately, but not randomly, by the committee members. African Americans' files went to an African-American law school student and a faculty committee member who had worked in a special university program for disadvantaged college students. Minority applicant files from individuals in one of the other preferred groups were also sent to selected members of the committee.

After the files returned to the full committee, with recommendations, the seven members reviewed the special minority applicants separately, attaching less weight to the PFYA than they did for white applicants. The reviewers compared the minority candidates to each other, rather than to the entire cohort of applicants. The white and non-preferred minority students who scored below 77 and above 74.5 were re-examined competitively within that particular applicant pool. The law school also established a goal of between 15 percent and 20 percent minority student admittees. This goal was established to achieve a "reasonable representation" of minority law school students at the UW.

When Marco DeFunis applied a second time in 1971, he was one of 1,600 applicants for UWSL, which had only 150 seats available for first-year law students. Although he had a PFYA of 76.23, DeFunis was placed on a wait-list and then rejected by the admissions committee in late July 1971. Of those in the special category that year, 48 percent of the minority applicants were admitted, although most scored below the 74.5 cut-off point for non-minority applicants. Although minorities were only 4 percent of the applicant pool, of the 150 applicants admitted to the law school, 44 of them were minority students.

DeFunis had a better PFYA than 74 applicants who had been admitted, including 38 special minority students. (Additionally, 22 veterans, and another 16 who had other factors in their files that mitigated their low PFYAs, were admitted to the first-year law school cohort.) Although it does not appear in the briefs filed in state and federal courts, there were also 29 white applicants with PFYAs higher than DeFunis's who were denied admission to the UWSL.

By the end of July 1971, DeFunis and dozens of other applicants were sent rejection letters. Marco then sought out counsel, Josef Diamond, to appeal the judgment of the UW admissions committee. A lawsuit charging the UWSL with reverse discrimination in violation of the Fourteenth Amendment was filed in the summer of 1971.

———

The Questions of Law Raised by DeFunis and by the University of Washington in the State Courts

DeFunis's lawyer, Josef Diamond, argued, in state courts and before the U.S. Supreme Court, that UWSL's special treatment of applicants from the four minority groups was a racial classification prohibited by the Fourteenth Amendment's Equal Protection Clause. He insisted, using the words of Justice John M. Harlan in his 1896 *Plessy* dissent, that "the Constitution is color-blind and neither knows nor tolerates classes among its citizens."

For Diamond, race could not be the determinative factor in the decision to admit or to reject an applicant. UWSL's use of that neutral factor called for strict scrutiny by the courts to determine whether there was a compelling interest served by operation of the affirmative action program. Diamond argued that a careful review of the challenged UWSL practice would lead to its invalidation. Preferential treatment of some minority groups violated DeFunis's right to the equal protection of the laws.

Furthermore—and this was a very important point made by counsel for DeFunis and by critics of affirmative action—there was no record of the UWSL's ever deliberately discriminating against racial and ethnic minorities. Therefore there was no compelling interest warranting the use of racial goals in the law school admissions process. It was clearly in violation of the U.S. Constitution as well as the 1964 Civil Rights Act's Title VI.

The state attorney general, Slade Gorton, for the University of Washington, rebutted this argument. He maintained that the UW could constitutionally give special preference for targeted minority applicants because there was a compelling state interest in overcoming the consequence of centuries of racial and ethnic discrimination across America: less than 2 percent of lawyers practicing law in 1970 were African Americans. The UW's admissions goal was to end the vestigial "badges of slavery" that still attached to African Americans. There was no violation of the Constitution.

Gorton argued that the policy was a constitutionally benign form of discrimination that let formerly excluded groups into law school. There was a compelling interest in diversifying the law school population and the legal profession as well. The Constitution prohibited only invidious discrimination, and the UWSL's benign discrimination did not rise to that level—it was not arbitrary and capricious.

Diversity in higher education was also a democratic value of the first order, and the UWSL admissions process gave life to the norm of democratic diversity. In the U.S. Supreme Court, Gorton also argued that reliance on Title VI of the 1964 Civil Rights Act was an improper argument because DeFunis had not raised the statutory argument in the Washington State courts.

Both sides did agree on a number of legal points:

1. Invidious discrimination was prohibited by the Constitution.
2. Race and ethnicity could be factors, among others, in the decision to admit a student to the UWSL (but the parties differed on the weight given to race and ethnicity).
3. Racial or ethnic classifications could be either negative or positive, or benign (but the parties differed on whether the Four-

{ *The* Bakke *Case* }

teenth Amendment categorically barred benign racial classifications).

4. The Fourteenth Amendment's Equal Protection Clause en-
compassed an individual's claim to fair treatment by an agency
of the state.

At the core, the DeFunis legal battles raged over the question
of what kinds of positive, or benign, racial and ethnic classifications—if any—passed constitutional muster. Could there be a
valid difference drawn between negative racial discrimination
(which excluded African Americans from an activity) and positive
racial discrimination (which would attempt to end the "badges of
slavery" worn by African Americans)?

Judgment in the Washington State Courts,

1971–1972

A short time after DeFunis received the second rejection letter,
Judge Lloyd Shorett of the Washington Superior Court for King
County upheld DeFunis's claim that he had been denied equal
protection of the laws when UWSL denied him admission. In his
oral decision, Judge Shorett concluded that DeFunis had been
denied his Fourteenth Amendment rights. Shorett quoted from
the watershed 1954 *Brown v. Board of Education* opinion: "Public
education must be equally available to all regardless of race."
After *Brown*, the judge concluded, "the Fourteenth Amendment
could no longer be stretched to accommodate the needs of any
race. . . . The only safe rule is to treat all races alike." The remedy for the wrong DeFunis received was his immediate enrollment in the 1971–1972 law school academic year. Judge Shorett
ordered that Marco DeFunis be admitted to UWSL for the class
of 1974, beginning September 22, 1971.

The University of Washington reluctantly admitted DeFunis
into its law school. However, because a very important constitutional issue was at the core of the case, Gorton was able to bypass
the state appeals court and appeal directly to the Washington
Supreme Court. The case was argued in the state supreme court

in mid-May 1972; almost a year later, on March 8, 1973, the court rendered its verdict. By a vote of 6 to 2, the court reversed Shorett's order.

The majority accepted the state's argument that positive, or benign, racial and ethnic discrimination is not negative or invidious discrimination (which is barred by the Fourteenth Amendment). The denial of benefit to DeFunis was not, in and of itself, a violation of the Fourteenth Amendment's Equal Protection Clause "if the racial classification is used in a compensatory way to promote integration." The court majority maintained that racial classifications may be used for either or both of the purposes of (1) remedying past national discrimination and (2) promoting the integration of the races. For UWSL to act to "prevent the perpetuation" of past racial or ethnic discrimination is not invidious nor violative of DeFunis's right to equal protection of the laws.

The state supreme court also held that Judge Shorett misinterpreted the *Brown* precedent: that opinion invalidated racial classifications that "stigmatize a racial group with the stamp of inferiority." Using the strict scrutiny standard suggested by DeFunis's lawyers, they found a "compelling" case made by UWSL for the preferential program: ending racial imbalance in the legal profession. "Where the purpose is to promote integration," they wrote, "and to undo the effects of past discrimination it is not per se violative of the equal protection clause." The two dissenters accepted DeFunis's "color-blind" Constitution argument. "Racial bigotry," they argued, "will never be ended by exalting the political rights of one group or class over that of another. The circle of inequality cannot be broken by shifting the inequities from one man to his neighbor."

Because his continuation in law school was at the pleasure of UWSL administrators, DeFunis, after the state supreme court denied him a rehearing, appealed to the U.S. Supreme Court a few months later. As the Court was in its summer recess, Associate Justice William O. Douglas, whose circuit-riding duties throughout the year covered appeals from the state of Washington, issued a *stay of action* pending final Supreme Court resolution of the matter. This meant that Judge Shorett's order placing De-Funis in the law school class of 1974 remained in effect until the full U.S. Supreme Court reviewed the briefs and decided whether to decide the constitutionality of affirmative action programs in education.

The U.S. Supreme Court "Ducks the Issue,"

1973–1974

Josef Diamond, DeFunis's lawyer, filed an appeal with the Court on August 3, 1973, less than five months after the Washington Supreme Court opinion was announced. The brief requesting the Court to hear the petitioner's case is called a jurisdictional brief. The lawyers for the petitioner argue that the issue is a very substantial one, that the Court's opinion will impact many thousands of other persons, and that the Court should hear the legal issue presented because it is timely and because the nation needs resolution of the matter.

On behalf of the petitioner, DeFunis, Diamond raised two critical and related questions that he felt the U.S. Supreme Court had to answer:

1. "Is the affirmative action program in violation of the 'Equal Protection' clause because preference is given to certain racial minorities?"
2. "Is Title VI of the 1964 Civil Rights Act violated because white applicants must meet different and more stringent standards than are persons of certain other races in obtaining admission?"

The Anti-Defamation League of B'nai Brith (ADL) and the Jewish Rights Council (JRC) filed amicus briefs supporting De-Funis's argument. For the ADL, categorically opposed to restrictive quotas or "goals," the substantive question was "whether, consistent with the Fourteenth Amendment's 'Equal Protection' clause, [UWSL] may extend a preference for admission solely on the basis of race to a certain number of persons who are concededly less qualified than applicants of other races?"

The JRC argument for the Court's hearing the case also reflected the historic legacy of anti-Semitism in American higher education. Until the 1950s Jewish applicants had run into severe problems when they tried to enter certain undergraduate schools and many professional graduate schools of law and medicine. These schools included in the admissions process a quota that limited the number of Jews admitted. Having experienced generations of religious quotas designed to keep Jewish applicants out of college, most Jewish organizations at the time of *DeFunis* were unable to accept the idea of a positive, or benign, racial quota that let formerly excluded applicants into law or medical school.

For the JRC, *any* racially preferential criteria for admission to a state law school violated the Fourteenth Amendment because there were better qualified, meritorious students who were not accepted. "The merit system of admissions to institutions of higher learning has been one of the keystones for the success of the Jew and other minorities in America," noted their brief. While not opposed to affirmative action efforts by colleges and universities to recruit qualified minorities, they were opposed to an admissions process that used quotas, goals, or set-asides.

They argued that the Court should hear the case because the Washington Supreme Court's majority opinion "substantively misreads and misapplies . . . prior decisions of this Court and of other courts concerning the use of racial classifications [as well as] distorts the remedial device of affirmative action. . . . By so distorting the remedy of affirmative action, the decision below threatens to destroy its utility."

Slade Gorton prepared the respondent's brief in opposition. It was filed in the U.S. Supreme Court on October 19, 1973. It maintained that the U.S. Supreme Court should either dismiss the case or affirm the Washington Supreme Court. However, if the Court granted certiorari, the sole question for the justices to answer was this: "May UWSL constitutionally take into account, as one element in selecting from among qualified candidates for the study of law, the race of applicants in pursuit of a state policy to mitigate gross under-representation of certain minorities in the law school, and in the membership in the bar?"

The *DeFunis* case was now in the Court's hands. After discussing the case in its October 19, 1973, conference session, the Court instructed both parties to submit supplemental briefs on the question of whether the case was moot. Since DeFunis was in his final year and was expected to graduate in the spring of 1974, four of the justices—Chief Justice Warren Burger and Associate Justices William Rehnquist, Harry Blackmun, and Potter Stewart—would have remanded the case because of mootness. A fifth jurist, Lewis F. Powell Jr., was leaning toward remanding on mootness but was interested in hearing both sides in the dispute before making up his mind.

Both parties responded quickly. They argued that the case was not moot and that the Court had to decide the important constitutional question raised by the litigants. Although DeFunis was in the last year of law school, he was attending only because of the state trial court judge's injunction. UWSL earlier had said that it would "reconsider" DeFunis's application if the injunction was lifted and would probably allow him to continue his studies.

DeFunis's brief argued that the uncertainty of the UW response to DeFunis's continuing if the Court lifted the injunction "does not make that injunction moot." Further, the case would not be mooted if DeFunis graduated because of the "continuing controversy [because] the law school will continue its policy and it will certainly affect others even though it may no longer matter to DeFunis. Thus, under the broad rule of mootness, as employed in *Roe v Wade*, 1973, the abortion case, this question would not be moot."

On November 9, 1973, Justice Douglas's law clerk made a convincing argument to his boss about the case. He wrote to Douglas that the case wasn't moot because the "controversy will continue and is a recurring one." If the Court dismissed the case as moot, he concluded, "I think it would be fairly obvious that all the court is doing is ducking the issue."

Ten days later, in the Court's November 19, 1973, conference session, the Court voted to grant the writ of certiorari in order to examine the question of preferential affirmative action on the merits. Voting to grant were Associate Justices William O. Douglas, William J. Brennan, Thurgood Marshall, and Byron R. White.

A look at the votes in conference clearly indicates that the Court was very split on whether or not to even hear the constitutional question. Four wanted to remand for mootness; four wanted to hear and decide the case on the merits. One justice, Lewis F. Powell, was still open to listen to arguments on both sides. He did not cast his vote with the other three Nixon appointees and Potter Stewart. However, he did not vote to grant certiorari. He would be, as he was to be in the *Bakke* litigation, the pivotal jurist in this case.

When the Court agrees to hear a case, the petitioner and the respondent submit longer briefs "on the merits" that contain their respective legal positions on the substantive questions of law before the Court. On December 29, 1973, the Court received the petitioner's brief. DeFunis raised and then answered two questions: (1) "Whether equal protection is violated when UWSL gives preference, solely on the basis of race, to certain persons to the exclusion of others in competition for limited spaces available in the law school," and (2) whether UWSL's admission policy for whites employed "more stringent criteria" than those used when reviewing the applications of "persons of color" and was therefore in violation of the Fourteenth Amendment.

DeFunis's brief presented arguments in support of his view that the Fourteenth Amendment prohibited UWSL's affirmative action admissions policy. The lawyers focused on the meaning of "equal protection of the laws" in the Fourteenth Amendment: "Equality is the touchstone" for all Fourteenth Amendment equal protection cases. It is the result "that has to be attained to give [persons] equal protection of the law." Racial or ethnic preferences in an admissions process void the "equality" concept, and these preferences are unconstitutional. Finally, they maintained that "Individual rights cannot flagrantly be sacrificed in the interest of achieving racial balance. Past inequities are not remedied by creating new inequities to be visited upon individuals in the non-minority groups."

The respondent's brief arrived shortly after. Gorton maintained that UW's use of race was an affirmative factor and therefore did not violate the equal protection of the law. "Since 1866," he argued, "the Constitution has been color conscious," and "objec-

tions to the use of race [in a positive manner] are without merit."
Arguing that there was a difference between negative racial discrimination and the positive, affirmative action, discrimination involved in the case, Gorton said that the UWSL admission process
was valid—regardless of what test the Supreme Court used—because "its purpose and effect are to improve the education [of mi-
norities], diversify the Bar, and the Bar's service to the public,
including members of majority as well as minority races."

According to the brief, UWSL had "an affirmative duty to
maintain a racially integrated student body." The brief closed
with the following observation: "All law classifies and all law discriminates, but only that law which classifies or discriminates in-
vidiously offends the 'equal protection' clause of the Fourteenth
Amendment."

In addition to the briefs on the merits filed by the two parties,
in many cases, especially controversial ones, amicus briefs are
filed in support of the petitioner or the respondent. When a
group believes that a case before the U.S. Supreme Court will
have an impact on its members, it can file a *brief amicus curiae*, a
"friend of the court" brief, with the permission of both the petitioner and the respondent. (Lacking permission from one or
both parties, it can ask the Court to grant the organization leave
to file an amicus curiae brief.)

In 1973, when DeFunis asked the U.S. Supreme Court to review the issue, many pressure groups participated in the legal
battle before the Court. Affirmative action split the liberal community into two irate and contentious camps. Groups that had
marched side by side in the deep South on behalf of civil rights a
decade earlier were now on opposite sides of a more complex
civil rights struggle: Martin Luther King's Southern Christian
Leadership Conference and the NAACP were now adversaries of
the Anti-Defamation League (ADL) of B'nai Brith. Some Jews
were opposed to affirmative action programs that employed quotas and "goals." Indeed, Jews were opposing other Jews, for in
the *DeFunis* litigation, ironically, some Jewish groups supported
the UW affirmative action plan. (By the time of *Bakke*, four years
later, *all* Jewish amici supported Bakke's argument.)

Over 120 groups and individuals, in 22 briefs amicus curiae filed in the U.S. Supreme Court, supported the UWSL position on affirmative action. They represented a wide spectrum of organizations, including the legal profession, the medical profession, universities, governments and governmental agencies, civil rights organizations, and a variety of racial, ethnic, and women's organizations.

Legal amici included the Center for Law and Education, Harvard University; the Council on Legal Education; the Group of 70 Law School Deans; the National Conference of Black Lawyers; the Legal Aid Society and NAACP; the American Indian Law Students and American Indian Lawyers Association; the American Association of Law Schools; the Lawyer's Committee for Civil Rights under Law; the Mexican American Legal and Educational Defense Fund, the Puerto Rican Legal and Education Defense Fund, and twelve other minority groups; the American Bar Association; and the Law School Admission Committee. Their common assertion was that affirmative action programs such as the UW's were the only mechanism available for overcoming America's continuing discrimination against African Americans and other racial and ethnic minorities.

Medical, university, and education amici included the American Association of Medical Colleges; Harvard College and the Massachusetts Institute of Technology (joint brief); University of Massachusetts; Rutgers University; Antioch School of Law; the National Education Association; and the National Organization for Women (NOW) Legal and Educational Defense Fund. Their position was identical to that of the legal associations who defended the UW policy.

Government amici included Seattle, Washington; the State of Ohio; and the U.S. Equal Employment Opportunity Commission. These groups, under intense pressure to diversify governmental work forces, saw professional school diversity programs ultimately benefiting them by providing these public entities with qualified minorities. For them, the UW affirmative action program was a "significant contribution to the community."

Civil rights amici included a joint brief from eighteen groups, including the Children's Defense Fund, UAW, the National Council of Jewish Women, the United Farm Workers, Americans for Democratic Action, the United Negro College Fund, the Southern Christian Leadership Conference (SCLC), and the Japanese American Citizens League; the NAACP and NOW (joint amicus brief with NEA). Concerned about the continuing discrimination against minorities—in business, housing, employment, and education—these organizations aggressively sought to present arguments that justified affirmative action programs.

The thrust of the almost two dozen amicus curiae messages was that constitutional color-blindness in America is a fiction, that the Constitution allows reasonable uses of racial classifications. The UW program was an appropriate and constitutional effort to remedy "the effects of long-standing racial discrimination in the legal profession." There is, they all concluded, a compelling state interest in overcoming America's history of racial discrimination. In the joint brief Marian Wright Edelman prepared were words used throughout the legal debates in the Supreme Court and borrowed by Justices Blackmun and Marshall in the *Bakke* litigation: "Color-blindness has come to represent the long-term goal. It is now well understood, however, that our society cannot be completely color-blind in the short term if we are to have a color blind society in the long term."

The briefs also maintained that standardized tests such as the LSAT are racially biased and therefore invalid and that "academic grades showed a zero relationship to measures of [legal] performance."

Only one organization, the Center for Law and Education, pointed out that the enrollment data showed that DeFunis would not have been admitted even if there had been no preferential affirmative action admission process. There were white applicants with PFYAs higher than his who were not admitted to the UWSL (and who did not challenge UWSL's decision). And the NAACP was the only organization that emphasized, in its brief, that all the minority applicants admitted under the special admissions procedure were qualified for the study and practice of law.

Siding with DeFunis were only six organized groups: the

American Jewish Congress, the Advocate Society (consisting of Polish-, Italian-, and Jewish-American groups opposed to preferential admissions affirmative action programs), the AFL-CIO, the ADL, the U.S. Chamber of Commerce, and the National Association of Manufacturers.

All of them maintained that the use of race to determine admission to law school was contrary to the language and the meaning of the Fourteenth Amendment. They argued that the Constitution is a color-blind document that bars all discrimination based on the color of one's skin or one's national heritage. The UWSL preferential admissions process was an unconstitutional racial "quota." There was only one exception to this principle of color-blindness, the ADL brief noted, and that was when preferential admissions programs were used "as a specific remedy for specific [past or present] unconstitutional or illegal racial discrimination [by that institution]." A state agency may not "command that any person be [preferred] simply because he was formerly the subject of discrimination, or because he is a member of a minority group. The Constitution forbids 'discriminatory preference for any group, minority or majority.'" Lacking this factual basis, there is no compelling state interest that would allow the UWSL to practice a form of "reverse discrimination."

The AFL-CIO brief noted that there was a difference between employment and educational affirmative action realities. Given the centuries-old history of bellicose, negative discrimination in employment, "the range of affirmative action [programs] open to enable 'minority' Americans to meet performance related rules of selection is, and should be, all but unlimited." Education was different, the labor brief argued. There was the need to rely solely on the merit of the applicants when selecting the first-year law school class. Any criterion beyond merit was not "open" to the university to use when admitting students. Similarly, the Chamber of Commerce brief argued that race can be a consideration only in "voluntary efforts to improve employment opportunities of under-represented groups."

After granting certiorari and after reviewing the briefs filed on behalf of the petitioner and the respondent, the justices of the Court are ready to meet in conference to talk about the case and to cast initial votes as to its disposition. However, before their meeting in conference to discuss and vote on Case Number 73-235, *DeFunis v. Odegaard*, there was the matter of oral argument before the full Court.

In the 1970s, scheduled oral arguments before the Court occurred the first two weeks of every month from the first Monday in October, when the Court's term starts, through the month of April. The Court met in open session for four hours, from 10 A.M. to noon and then from 1 P.M. to 3 P.M., for three days. At a minimum, then, there were fourteen weeks of scheduled oral argument, or a little less than 170 hours annually, to hear arguments in the cases they decided to decide on the merits. When the Justices heard the *DeFunis* and *Bakke* cases in the 1970s, they met on Fridays to determine what actions the Court would take on the cases heard earlier that week.

Oral argument was scheduled in *DeFunis* for February 26, 1974. The day before, Burger received a letter from Diamond telling the Court that DeFunis had just registered for courses "for his final quarter in law school." When the oral arguments began the following day, it was clear to all the justices that DeFunis would complete his studies and graduate in a few months. The issue of mootness was uppermost in the minds of at least five of the justices: the four Nixon appointees and Justice Potter Stewart.

Each of the parties was given thirty minutes to make their arguments to the justices. Given the oral argument process, once the clock begins, the justices often interrupt repeatedly with questions to the lawyers and with remarks to other brethren through questions and views ostensibly directed to the befuddled lawyer.

Most attorneys who appear before the Court argue only that one case. Few attorneys are noted for their frequent appearances before the Court. To help the first-time lawyer prepare for this very unusual process, *The Guide for Counsel in Cases To Be Argued before This Court* was prepared by the present clerk of the U.S.

Supreme Court, William Suter. For example, counsel are cautioned to "never under any circumstances interrupt a Justice who is addressing you." Rather, "give your full time and attention to that Justice—do not look down at your notes and do not look at your watch. If you are speaking and a Justice interrupts you, cease talking immediately and listen."

On the lectern there are two lights, white and red. When the lawyer has five minutes left, the white light goes on. "When the red light comes on," the *Guide* instructs, "terminate your argument immediately and sit down unless you are answering a question from a Justice, in which event you may continue your answer and respond to any additional questions from that Justice or any other Justice." Do not argue facts with a justice; "avoid emotional oration and loud, impassioned pleas." Don't try to humor the justices during your argument: "Attempts at humor usually fall flat." Do not, under most circumstances, "'correct' a Justice unless the matter is essential"; if "a question seems hostile to you, do not answer with a short and abrupt response. It is far more effective to be polite and accurate."

The Supreme Court's courtroom was filled to capacity for the arguments in the *DeFunis* case. The *New York Times* reported that dozens of lawyers and students stood outside in the Great Hall, unable to get seats to hear the arguments. Counsel for the petitioner is first up before the brethren. DeFunis's lawyer rose to introduce arguments that amplified but did not repeat the arguments made in the written briefs. Diamond began by presenting the overarching picture: under the UWSL admissions process, an applicant received "special privileges" if the person "checked off one of four minorities on the application form." There were two classes established by the UWSL admission process: (1) minorities and (2) whites and orientals. Sixty percent of minority applicants were admitted, while only 10 percent of whites and oriental applicants were accepted.

DIAMOND SAID: "You've got to treat everybody alike and not set up two classes, minority students and nonminority students. Otherwise, you're violating the Fourteenth Amendment and the civil rights laws."

JUSTICE WHITE INTERRUPTED: "Is this a class action?"

DIAMOND ANSWERED: "No, it is not a class action, and we're not concerned about that."

He continued with his presentation, only to be interrupted again and again.

REHNQUIST: "Should the law school admit the top 150 applicants?"

ANSWER: "No, sir. I'm not saying that. I am saying that they have to treat everybody alike, and they're not going to set up two classes, one minority and one non-minority."

POWELL ASKED: "Would DeFunis have been admitted except for the special minority program?"

DIAMOND ANSWERED, INCORRECTLY: "Yes, Mr. Justice, he would have been admitted but for the special minority program."

These interruptions went on throughout Diamond's half hour of oral argument. He tried to use them to return to the essential point he wanted to make that day: The "special privilege" minorities received in the admission process was essentially a racial quota that was prohibited by the Fourteenth Amendment's Equal Protection Clause and the civil rights statutes.

After the red light went on, Diamond sat down and Slade Gorton, the Washington State attorney general, strode to the lectern for his presentation to the justices. Almost as soon as he began, Justice Rehnquist asked a question: "Hadn't DeFunis made Law Review" (an honor bestowed on the very best law students)?

GORTON ANSWERED: "DeFunis is not Law Review, Mr. Justice Rehnquist. He's roughly in the middle of his class."

Brennan asked what would happen if UWSL was forced to end the special admissions program.

THE RESPONSE: "The UWSL, which has never engaged in racial discrimination by force of law, only produced twelve black law school graduates out of 3,812 [who graduated] between 1902 and 1969."

Burger then asked why the special admissions program was needed if the UWSL never discriminated against minorities.

ANSWER: "Mr. DeFunis will be better prepared to practice law in a pluralistic society [because his law school class had nineteen African Americans], the result of an admission program designed to promote qualified applicants from racial minorities."

THE FOLLOW-UP QUESTION: What would happen if you had to follow the guidelines proffered by the petitioner?

GORTON SHOT BACK: "We would have an absolutely white law school."

JUSTICE DOUGLAS THEN ASKED: "Are you promoting proportional representation?"

ANSWER: "I am not. We do not operate a pro rata system, and we are not asking you to validate such a system."

ANOTHER HARD QUESTION: Does the UWSL "impose a racial quota?"

GORTON: "[The admissions committee] has to arrive at a ratio, they have to make a determination, call it what you please."

Douglas then asked whether DeFunis would have been admitted had there not been the special admissions process.

ANSWER: "DeFunis ranked 290th in a group of 330 applicants [who were reviewed a second time]. There was no assurance he would have been admitted in the absence of any minority program. A number of white applicants above him were denied admission, a number of people below him were given admission. The UWSL was looking for 150 students to meet other valid social values."

JUSTICE DOUGLAS, ONCE AGAIN: Was there any finding that "those so-called tests (LSAT) had a built-in racial bias?"

ANSWER: "There is no finding in this record, Mr. Justice Douglas, because neither party wished even to bring that subject up. . . . Although you might very well, in a proper case, find that the PFYA had a built-in racial bias."

Gorton was able to answer the questions the justices peppered him with during his half hour. He also successfully reinforced the state's position that UWSL's preferential affirmative action program was constitutionally viable because it addressed the consequences of centuries of racial discrimination and segregation.

The hour of oral argument passed very quickly as the justices hit both attorneys with a barrage of questions. As the *New York Times* reported the next day, both lawyers "were interrupted frequently by questions from the bench. All nine Justices participated in the discussion, several of them repeatedly." That Friday, the nine brethren met in their secret conference session.

The conference session is where the justices for the first time meet as a group to discuss the merits of the cases heard that week, explaining how each would resolve the questions of law raised. There are no formal votes taken; however, as each justice states his views, starting with the chief justice, followed by the eight associate justices (in order of seniority), the other eight are listening—and taking notes on their docket sheets—and are able to determine how the justice talking comes down on the questions of law that have to be answered by the Court.

After all nine have spoken, the chief justice tallies "votes." Usually, there is general consensus at that moment about the direction the Court will go in the written opinion assigned to one of the justices in the majority. The opinion assignment is done by either the chief justice, if he is in the majority, or the senior associate justice, if the chief justice has come down with the minority.

This action is the necessary starting point for Supreme Court decision making because the conference outcome demarcates the divisions on the Court on the question of law the case raises. However, while the discussion and the tallying of "votes" is a necessary Court activity, it is not a necessary and sufficient one. Supreme Court decision making is a fluid process. Often, over the course of three to seven months of reading and writing and circulating six or seven or more revisions of opinion drafts, what starts off as a majority position turns into a dissenting opinion— and vice versa.

In the conference session* on No. 73-235, on March 1, 1974, four days after oral argument, the brethren were very divided on two grounds: (1) whether the issue was moot and (2) whether the UWSL preferential policy violated the Fourteenth Amendment. If there was a Court majority (five or more) favoring dismissal on the grounds of mootness, there would be no answer to the substantive question. If that was the final judgment, then Americans would not have an answer to one of the most controversial questions related to race relations that had come to the public's attention. But if, instead, a majority favored deciding *DeFunis* on the merits, then there would be a resolution of, or at least an answer to, whether racial preferences and quotas were constitutional.

Justices Brennan, Marshall, and White spoke in favor of deciding the constitutional question on the merits by validating the Washington State Supreme Court decision. Justice Douglas also expressed the opinion that the case should be decided on the merits, but disagreed with his three brethren on what were the merits in this affirmative action case.

Burger started the discussion. He began by stating that "so far we have never allowed a person to be excluded because of his race." Gorton's premise, for the university, was that "because blacks suffered oppression, there's a duty to redress the harm." He disagreed with the argument, stating that there was "no 'compelling' [state] need for this [redress]"; however, it was a moot issue.

The next speaker, the senior associate justice, Douglas, passed after saying, "I'm suspicious of tests."

His colleague William J. Brennan Jr. spoke next. *DeFunis* "probably is not moot even if he graduates in June," exclaimed

<hr />

* A cautionary note: The following paragraphs disclosing the justices' views expressed in the secret conference session are based on the author's reading of the conference notes of three justices (William O. Douglas, William J. Brennan, and Thurgood Marshall), which are a small part of their files in the Library of Congress. As there is no transcript extant of these conference discussions, there is no way of validating the accuracy of the quotes. This cautionary note is appropriate throughout this book whenever the justices are quoted in the conference sessions held in *DeFunis* and in *Bakke*. It should also be noted that there was general accord in the notes of the trio regarding the comments of their brethren.

Brennan. On the merits he believed that UWSL had the right "to form a law class in light of a racial component." What the law school had done was to "right a wrong done to blacks." The Fourteenth Amendment "does not bar this, the [Civil Rights] Act does not. I would affirm."

Potter Stewart, next in seniority, said that the case was moot. "It was not a class action and not remotely akin to *Roe v. Wade*." Marco was in his third year, in the middle of his class "and he will graduate. If he was a first year student then the case would not be moot."

Byron White spoke next. He said that the case was not moot and that on the merits he was close to Brennan. Thurgood Marshall said the same thing.

Harry Blackmun was the next discussant. He agreed with the chief justice that the case was moot. However, he expressed worry as to whether he should participate further in the case or recuse himself because "for twenty years, he interviewed Harvard applicants and he may be biased." Blackmun, however, noted that there "were good arguments on both sides on the merits." (Blackmun did participate, strongly encouraged by his longtime friend and best man at his wedding, his "Chief," Warren E. Burger.)

Had Blackmun not participated in the final judgment, the Court ultimately would have deadlocked, 4 to 4. That would have meant that the last judgment in the *DeFunis* litigation, the Washington Supreme Court's affirmation of the UWSL plan, would stand. In the end, he did not recuse himself and joined the "remand for mootness" majority of five.

Lewis Powell then spoke. He acknowledged that the case was "probably moot." However, he spoke to the merits, arguing that "courts have no business limiting in any significant way admission policies of graduate schools so long as there is no clear racial discrimination. . . . Race is a factor that can lawfully be considered." According to Brennan's notes, Powell tentatively affirmed the decision of the state Supreme Court.

Rehnquist, the "freshman" jurist, spoke last. Since all points had been made by the others, he did not say much other than that *DeFunis* was moot and that the Court need not reach the merits. The conference adjourned to await Powell's further reflections on the issue. Within two weeks he had reached a decision. After "more mature consideration on my part," he decided to join with those who argued mootness.

While troubled that the Court, "as an institution, will be taking a course of action which will be viewed by many as a means of avoiding a truly 'sticky wicket,'" he nevertheless concluded that "if the case was substantially moot when we granted certiorari, it certainly is today." "Accordingly," he wrote, "I have decided—although with great reluctance under the circumstances —to vote . . . that the case is moot."

The chief justice then assigned the task of writing the short, unsigned opinion—called a *per curiam opinion* of the Court—to Justice Potter Stewart. In it, the Court majority of five remanded the case because of mootness. However, there were four justices who disagreed with the majority's response, and consequently two dissenting opinions were written.

Brennan, writing for the four dissenters, criticized the majority for "straining to rid itself of this dispute." Arguing that "there is no want of an adversary contest in this case," he chastised the Court majority for "sidestepping" this controversial and very emotional issue. "Few constitutional questions in recent history have stirred as much debate and they will not disappear. They must inevitably return to the Federal courts and ultimately again to this Court. [The Court majority] clearly disserved the public interest."

Douglas also dissented separately. All told, he wrote thirteen drafts of his dissenting opinion before he was satisfied with it. He agreed with some amici that the LSAT was an inappropriate determinant of future success in law school because it measured only "the dimensions and orientation of the 'organization man.'" On the merits, his opinion rejected the use of racial preferences in a university's admissions process. He argued, applying strict scrutiny, that the UWSL admissions process was unconstitutional because it used race as a classification. The Fourteenth Amendment's Equal Protection Clause required that race "not militate against an applicant or on his behalf." Rather than using race or ethnicity in the decision to admit a student to law school, give preferences instead to applicants who were "a poor Appalachian white or a second-generation Chinese in San Francisco" as well as to other "would-be lawyers with limited backgrounds."

On April 23, 1974, the U.S. Supreme Court announced its judgment in Number 73-235, *DeFunis v. Odegaard*. The next day's headline in the *New York Times* captured the essence of the decision and the certainty of further litigation: "High Court Avoids Ruling on Quota for Law School: Refusal to Decide on Constitutionality of Preferential Treatment for Minorities Is Considered Only Postponement." The paper's observation was correct. At the very moment the *DeFunis* non-decision came down in April 1974, thirty-four-year-old Allan Bakke was embarking on his legal crusade against the University of California, Davis, Medical School's preferential admissions policy.

CHAPTER 3

"Let Me In!": Allan Bakke's Plea to the University of California, Davis, Medical School

Allan Paul Bakke is presently practicing medicine at the Mayo Clinic in Rochester, Minnesota. He has been there since his graduation from the University of California, Davis (UCD), School of Medicine in 1982, when he was almost forty-two years old. Bakke was born in February 1940 in Minneapolis, Minnesota, to parents of Norwegian ancestry. His father was a mailman and his mother a school teacher. After moving to Florida for a time, he returned to his native state to attend the University of Minnesota. He graduated in 1962 with a degree in mechanical engineering. His overall grade point average was 3.51 (out of 4.0), and he was elected to the national mechanical engineering honor society. Because Bakke needed funds to attend the university, he joined the naval ROTC campus unit. After a year of graduate work, he honored his military obligation by serving as an officer in the U.S. Marine Corps from 1963 to 1967. He served a combat tour in Vietnam. Captain Bakke left the service in 1967.

Immediately upon separation from the Marines, Bakke began work as a research engineer for the National Aeronautics and Space Agency (NASA) Ames Research Center south of San Francisco, California. He quickly became assistant chief of the equipment engineering branch at the center. He continued his education, receiving a master's degree in mechanical engineering in June 1970.

After 1971, because of his interest in medicine that developed while he was in Vietnam, Bakke attended night classes at San Jose State University and Stanford University. He took all the undergraduate chemistry and biology prerequisites for admission to medical school. He also volunteered for emergency-room work at El Camino Hospital in Mountain View, California. As he said in his application for admission to the UCD medical school: "I have an excellent job in engineering and am well-paid. I don't wish to change careers for financial gain, but because I truly believe my contribution to society can be much greater as a physician-engineer than in my present field. . . . More than anything else in the world, I want to study medicine."

A friend noted that Bakke was "the perfect engineer, . . . [who was also] cursed with a logical mind." He knew that his four years' service in the military and his six years with NASA posed a serious problem for him as an applicant for admission to medical school. He was very concerned that his age would be a negative factor for him in the admissions process. He was thirty-two years old when he first applied to the UCD medical school for admission in 1972.

Bakke raised the age issue frontally when, in 1971, he inquired of almost a dozen medical schools about their policy on age. He was told by the UCD admissions committee, in reply to his query, that "when an applicant is over thirty, his age is a serious factor which must be considered. . . . The Committee believes that an older applicant must be unusually highly qualified if he is to be seriously considered."

After being rejected twice by the UCD medical school, Bakke, like DeFunis, sought legal counsel to continue his effort to gain admission to that medical school. During this time, he evidenced some of his mordant humor when he wrote to a friend: "If this [the legal action and the appeals] takes much longer, I may be the first person to retire from engineering to study medicine."

When he began his legal battles, he was living with his family in a comfortable home in affluent Los Altos, California, forty miles south of San Francisco. He drove to work in a mustard-colored Volkswagen beetle. The *New York Times* described him as a six-foot, "fair-skinned, blond haired, daily jogger, . . . a husky baldish father of two [who has] a personal obsession to become a physician. . . . [He became involved in the litigation] because of an almost religious zeal to fight a system that he felt was unfair, which treated whites less equitably than members of minority groups."

A member of the UCD administration said that Bakke "struck me as a character out of a Bergman film—somewhat humorless, perfectly straightforward, zealous in his approach—an extremely impressive man with a determination to become a physician." The *Washington Post* noted, similarly, that after one met Bakke, what "emerges is a portrait of an extraordinarily determined man fully convinced of the rightness of his position."

The first part of Bakke's journey to practice medicine was not to end until June 29, 1978, five years later, when the Supreme Court announced its decision in *Bakke*. When Marco DeFunis graduated from law school in May 1974, in California Bakke had just received his second rejection letter from UCD. The next two months saw Bakke's lawyer, Reynold H. Colvin, file a complaint with the regional HEW Office of Civil Rights and bring suit in California Superior Court to have Bakke admitted to the UCD medical school. Although the HEW office did not respond in a timely manner to the complaint, Colvin was more successful in superior court.

There were a few significant differences between the *DeFunis* and the *Bakke* litigation. For one, DeFunis was ordered admitted to UWSL by Judge Shorett of the Washington Superior Court at the very beginning of the litigation. He attended law school while his case slowly wound its way to the U.S. Supreme Court. Bakke had been twice rejected and was not enrolled in the UCD medical school until after the Court's opinion came down.

Unlike UW's procedures, the UCD medical school admissions process had two subcommittees. They examined different medical school applicant pools: one subcommittee reviewed minority applicants, the other, white applicants. Additionally, sixteen of the one hundred first-year med school seats were set aside for minority applicants.

The major issues in *Bakke* were whether the Constitution's Equal Protection Clause or Title VI of the 1964 Civil Rights Act prohibited a public university from using set-asides or quotas for minority applicants. Colvin asked the court: Was the medical school's admissions effort to do "something more" for minority students an action that disregarded the Constitution and federal statutes?

The UCD Medical School's
Preferential Admissions Policy

In 1970, there were only about eight hundred minority students attending medical school in America. Almost 80 percent of that number were attending the two predominantly African-American medical schools: Howard University's medical school in the District of Columbia and Meharry Medical School in Nashville, Tennessee.

As was the case with law school applications at this time, there was the geometric growth in the numbers of students interested in attending medical school. America's medical schools did not have nearly enough seats to provide all qualified applicants with a medical education. Accompanying this extraordinary increase in applications for admission, most of the schools established a variety of preferential admissions policies in order to increase the number of qualified minority students attending their predominantly white medical schools. That led to more regular applicants being rejected in favor of admitting special applicants.

The medical school at UCD opened in 1966 with forty-eight entering students. It was one of five medical schools in the University of California system. The four other medical schools were located at Irvine, Los Angeles, San Diego, and San Francisco. There were no system-wide admissions standards; each medical school established its own admissions standards and procedures.

For four years, the UCD medical school had no preferential affirmative action admissions program. During that time only 3 percent of its applicants were minorities. The administration, concerned about the lack of diversity at UCD, established a special preferential admissions program in 1970. The general objectives of the program, said the board of regents' lawyer in the brief filed with the Court, were to "enhance diversity in the student body and the profession, eliminate historic barriers for medical careers for disadvantaged racial and ethnic minority groups, and increase aspiration for such careers on the part of members of those groups."

Sixteen percent, or eight out of fifty of the seats for admitted first-year med students were set aside for minority applicants. (Between 1970 and 1974, UCD's medical school admitted almost no African-American or Hispanic-American applicants who were not "disadvantaged.") In 1971, when the medical school was able to admit a first-year class of one hundred students, the number of set-aside seats for minorities doubled. Since the special admissions program began, not a single disadvantaged white applicant had been admitted by the special admissions committee.

The UCD admissions process was two separate processes. There was the regular admissions committee of fifteen persons (twelve faculty and three students) for non-minorities and non-disadvantaged minority applicants (eighty-four seats), and a special admissions subcommittee to examine the files of those applicants who identified themselves as members of an "economically and/or educationally disadvantaged" minority group. By the time Bakke sought legal remediation, there had been 132 candidates selected by the special-admissions committee: 50 Chicanos; 46 African Americans; 33 Asian Americans; 1 Native American; and 1 Asian Chicano.

Under the regular selection process, if an applicant's GPA was less than 2.5, there was summary rejection. Of those applicants who had better than a 2.5 GPA, 40 percent were invited to the campus for interviews. Admissions committee members served as the interviewers. They examined the applicant's personality, motivation, and other non-statistical characteristics. Afterward, the interviewer's responsibility was to review the entire file and to grade the applicant, using a 1–100 scale. All the interviewers based their scores for each applicant on the following: the interview, the overall GPA, the scores on the Medical College Admission Test (MCAT), letters of recommendation, and extracurricular experiences. Four (five in 1974) other committee members then reviewed the file, and each of them rated the applicant on the same 1–100 scale. The five scores were tallied and averaged, producing the "benchmark score." In 1973, the maximum score possible was 500; in 1974, it was 600.

To be considered for admission through the special program, an applicant had to be an "economically and/or educationally

{ *The* Bakke *Case* }

disadvantaged person." At the time of Bakke's first rejection, UCD had adopted and used a national medical school application form that asked students if they "wish[ed] to be considered as a minority group applicant?" If an applicant chose to be reviewed under this program, the file was sent to a special subcommittee of the UCD admissions committee, consisting primarily of white and minority faculty members and minority medical students. In 1973, for example, when Bakke first applied to UCD's medical school, there were five white and two Asian-American faculty on the committee. They were joined by eleven minority medical students.

The committee initially had to determine whether the applicant was personally "economically or educationally disadvantaged." Was the application fee waived for the applicant? Did the applicant work while completing undergraduate studies? Did the applicant interrupt studies and take a leave of absence because it was necessary to work a full-time job because of economic disadvantage? Was the applicant a participant in an equal educational opportunity program at the undergraduate institution? What did the applicant's parents do for a living? If the committee determined that the candidate was not so disadvantaged, the file was sent to the regular admissions committee for their review and judgment.

In 1974, however, when Bakke applied to UCD a second time, there was a new general application form. It now asked whether the applicant wished to be considered as an "economically and/or educationally disadvantaged" person in one of four enumerated minority groups: "Black, Chicano, Asian, and American Indians." Through 1974, there had been no white applicants accepted in the special admissions process. In 1973, 73 whites who claimed economic or educational disadvantage had applied under this program. None were reviewed by the subcommittee. In 1973, the number of white applicants for special admissions more than doubled to 172. None were reviewed by the subcommittee.

The special committee reviewed the files the same way the regular admissions committee did. However, the standard of review was different: there was no minimum GPA requirement for minority applicants. There was also no comparison of the cohort admitted in the regular process with the cohort recommended under special admissions.

These realities led to highly significant statistical differences between those admitted under the two programs. In the two years Bakke unsuccessfully sought admission as a regular applicant, 1973 and 1974, the differences were stark between regular and special admittees to the UCD medical school:

MCAT	MCAT	MCAT	General	GPA
Science (percentile*)	Verbal (percentile)	Quantitative (percentile)	Information (percentile)	
Regular/ Special	R/S	R/S	R/S	R/S
83/35	81/46	76/24	69/33	3.5/2.6
Bakke:				
97	96	94	72	3.44

*For all, Regular, Special, and Bakke, percentiles are the two-year average.

UCD medical school administrators and legal counsel acknowledged this extremely skewed quantitative statistic. They said that even though the special admittees' quantitative scores were not nearly as high as those of the regular admittees, it was because the tests were biased against disadvantaged applicants. Furthermore, these minority admittees were qualified to do the work demanded of med school students. Dr. George Lowery, associate dean and chair of the admissions committee, insisted that no one was admitted to the medical school who was adjudged unqualified. The special admittees were qualified for medical school education; they were, however, just less qualified than the regular admittees.

When Bakke applied, in 1973, to the medical school at UCD, the application packet contained his MCAT scores; transcripts from other schools he had attended; community and extracurricular activities information; work experiences; two letters of recommendation; and his personal statement explaining why he wanted to become a physician. In 1973, Bakke's application was one of 2,464 received by the UCD for only one hundred seats. The following year saw 3,737 applicants seeking one of the one hundred seats.

The Questions of Law Presented and Argued

Bakke's lawyer, Reynold Colvin, then fifty-seven years old, was a well-established lawyer in San Francisco. Bakke began his relationship with Colvin in January 1974, about the time that DeFunis's lawyer was preparing for oral argument before the U.S. Supreme Court. Colvin had been an attorney in the city since 1941. He was also an active member of the city's Jewish community and was the president of the city's chapter of the American Jewish Committee. He also filled the city's "Jewish" seat on the city's board of education, serving a stint as its president.

Colvin's elemental strategy did not focus on the enormous quantitative disparities between regular and special admittees or on Bakke's qualifications, which were categorically better than most of the admittees, whether minority or non-minority. Instead, he argued that the setting aside of sixteen seats for minority applicants was an illegal, unconstitutional racial quota, prohibited by both the Fourteenth Amendment's Equal Protection Clause and Title VI of the 1964 Civil Rights Act.

He argued, again and again, one theme: racial quotas, however laudatory their rationale, were nevertheless unconstitutional. Whether it was called a special program, or an affirmative one, or benign, or remedial, or a compensatory program, at bottom they all used an illegal racial quota. And the Fourteenth Amendment barred the use of such color-conscious admissions mechanisms.

Donald Reidhaar, the general counsel for the University of California nine-campus system, was self-effacing, sort of boring, and very taciturn, contrasting with Colvin's down-home gregariousness. Born in Iowa, Reidhaar moved to California after law school and practiced law in a small private firm. In 1973, he was appointed general counsel for the University of California system. When the *Bakke* litigation began, he pulled together a three-person legal team to help him prepare the defense of the UCD preferential admissions process.

He argued that there was nothing illegal or unconstitutional about UCD's creation of a preferential admissions program for minorities. Indeed, when race was used as a positive factor to overcome the vestiges of slavery and race discrimination, the racial preferences were constitutional. Reidhaar always maintained that the 16 percent figure was a UCD admissions "goal," not a "quota." (He didn't explain to the state courts how UCD selected the 16 percent UCD medical school goal.) If there were fewer qualified candidates in a given year, Reidhaar noted, then the unfilled seats reverted to qualified regular applicants. However, it was a goal that had always been met by UCD since its inception in 1970. In any event, Reidhaar argued, Bakke had no "standing to sue" in court because in both years he had fallen short of the minimum scores necessary for admission to the medical school.

Allan Bakke Appeals to the State Courts for Redress

In 1973 all eleven medical schools Bakke applied to rejected him. The rejections came from Minnesota, Stanford, UCD, UC Los Angeles, San Francisco, Bowman-Grey, Cincinnati, Georgetown, Mayo Clinic, South Dakota, and Wayne State medical schools. Bakke's age was given as the major factor in their decisions not to admit him. For example, although Bakke did quite well in his 1973 interview at UCD, Dr. Theodore West, the interviewer, wrote that Bakke was "a well-qualified candidate for admission whose main handicap is the unavoidable fact that he is now 33 years of age."

Bakke's overall score was 468 out of a possible 500 points. He had applied late because of his mother-in-law's serious illness, and UCD used a rolling admissions process and had already sent admission letters to 123 applicants; 470 was used as the de minimus line for admission at that late date. On May 14, 1973, Allan received his rejection letter from UCD.

Toward the end of May, Colvin prepared a letter for Bakke to send to George Lowery. It requested that Bakke be placed on the wait-list and that he be allowed to register for fall 1973 and to take courses until slots became available. Receiving no answer, Colvin, on behalf of Bakke, prepared and then sent another letter to Lowery. This letter addressed what was to be the basic question raised by Colvin in both the state and the U.S. Supreme Court: Was the special admissions program an illegal racial quota?

In mid-July 1973, Lowery asked his assistant, thirty-year-old Peter Storandt, to invite Bakke to campus to discuss his rejection and to offer advice and counsel to him. Storandt encouraged Bakke to reapply for admission and to seek "early admission." Furtively, Storandt informed Bakke of Marco DeFunis's efforts to end the preferential admissions program at UWSL and urged the engineer to continue his research and, if he was rejected again, to challenge the special admissions program in court.

Clearly, the UCD staffer acted in an unprofessional manner, but Storandt was very concerned about the legitimacy of UCD's special admissions program and encouraged an impatient and angry Allan Bakke. It was a very serendipitous and symbiotic meeting of two men, almost the same age, concerned about a lack of fairness in the admissions procedures at UCD's medical school.

A few days later, Bakke sent Storandt a thank-you note. "Our discussion was very helpful to me in considering possible courses of action. I appreciate your professional interest in the question of moral and legal propriety of quotas and preferential admissions policies; even more impressive to me was your real concern about the effect of admissions policies on each individual applicant."

Bakke applied in August 1973 for early admission to UCD's medical school first-year class of 1974. There were over 3,100 non-minority applicants for the eighty-four available seats. His total score after the admissions committee reviewed his file was 549 out of a possible 600 points (six persons reviewed the files to create the 1974 medical school student cohort). After Bakke's interview, the student interviewer gave him a score of 94 (out of

100). Dr. Lowery, coincidentally, was the second interviewer, and he gave Bakke the lowest score Lowery recorded that year: an 86.

He had developed a less than positive view of Allan Bakke's character. His evaluation of Bakke after the interview was critical. He wrote that "I found Mr. Bakke to be rather limited in his approach to the solution of the difficulties in improving the delivery of medical care. . . . He is a rather rigidly oriented young man who has the tendency to arrive at conclusions based more on his personal impression than upon thoughtful processes using available sources of information."

In late September 1973, Bakke was informed that he was not admitted under the early-decision process. Nor was Bakke placed on the alternate wait-list. (Twelve other non-minority applicants with scores higher than Bakke's did not make the alternates list. Thirty-two non-minority applicants with scores higher than Bakke's were also not admitted to the UCD medical school). On April Fool's Day 1974, he was informed that he was again rejected by the UCD medical school.

That fall, Colvin filed Bakke's complaint with the regional office of HEW's Office of Civil Rights. It alleged that Bakke was "the victim of racial discrimination in medical school admissions in 1973" because UCD had implemented a "16% racial quota" and that because of these minority set-asides, Bakke had "missed acceptance by only two points." Over five months later, the HEW-OCR answered his letter. However, by this time Colvin and Bakke had committed themselves to bring the issue of "racial quotas" into court. On June 20, 1974, just before the *DeFunis* non-decision came down, Colvin brought suit on behalf of Bakke in Yolo County Superior Court. Judge F. Leslie Manker, a sixty-seven-year-old former Superior Court judge, was asked to come out of retirement in order to hear the case, because the two sitting judges were swamped with cases.

Colvin's legal complaint requested that Bakke, like DeFunis, be admitted to the UCD medical school because the medical school's special admissions program had "reduced the number of places" for which Bakke could compete. Bakke was excluded because of his race. That being the case, the UCD special admissions process was in violation of the U.S. Constitution's Fourteenth Amendment, the California constitution's article I, section 21, and Title VI of the 1964 Civil Rights Act. (Interestingly, from the fall of 1973 to at least the brief amicus curiae filed by DeFunis in the U.S. Supreme Court in the fall of 1977, Allan Bakke was in communication with Marco DeFunis. For example, in a December 1973 letter to Peter Storandt, Bakke wrote: "I have heard from Mr. DeFunis, and expect to receive some helpful information from him.")

UCD's legal counsel filed a cross-declaration with the court. It asked the judge to issue a declaration that the special admissions program was constitutional and not in violation of Title VI .

The burden of proof fell on Colvin and his client. They had to argue that Bakke would have been admitted to the UCD med school had there been no special admissions program in place. They also had to show that the special admissions process was arbitrary, capricious, and fraudulent.

Colvin requested relief from the court in the form of an order to compel UCD's medical school to admit Bakke. Reidhaar, the university's counsel, filed a cross-claim, asking the court to issue a declaratory judgment that the UCD's special admissions program was constitutional.

For the judge, there were two questions he had to answer: Was the special admissions preferential program constitutional? If it was not, should Allan Bakke be admitted to the UCD medical school by court order?

In late November 1974, Judge Manker ruled that the special admissions program operated as a racial quota and ran afoul of the Fourteenth Amendment, the state constitution, and Title VI. "The use of this program did substantially reduce plaintiff's chances of successful admission to medical school for the reason that, since 16 places . . . were set aside for this special program [in 1973 and 1974], the plaintiff was in fact competing for one place, not in a class of 100, but in a class of 84, which reduced his chances for admission by 16%." Concluding, he said that "No race or ethnic group should ever be granted privileges or immunities not given to every other race."

However, Manker did not order UCD to admit Bakke (because of the UCD argument that Bakke would not have been accepted even in the absence of the sixteen set-asides). Instead, Manker ordered the UCD admissions committee to consider Bakke's application again without regard to his or any other applicant's race.

In March 1975, Manker modified his earlier judgment. First, judicial involvement was warranted when an alleged unfairness, based on racial discrimination, rises to the level of arbitrariness or capriciousness. Second, Manker said that the burden of proof had shifted to the UCD and that they must produce evidence substantiating their claim that Bakke would not have been admitted in any scenario. Finally, although not admitting Bakke to the medical school, Manker issued an injunction prohibiting UCD from using, in the future, the race of any applicant as a factor in the admissions process.

The university's lawyer, Donald Reidhaar, immediately appealed Manker's ruling to the California Supreme Court in May 1975. A month later, that court agreed to hear the case. Bakke's lawyer also appealed because Judge Manker did not issue the requested order calling for the UCD medical school to enroll Allan Bakke. At this time, the California Supreme Court was perceived as being the most liberal appellate state court in America. Those groups who formally supported the UCD affirmative action process felt that the California Supreme Court would overturn the Yolo County judge's ruling. They were very mistaken.

The following year, in March 1976, oral argument took place in the state supreme court. Nine organizations filed amicus briefs with the state supreme court: six groups, civil rights organizations such as the NAACP, supported the UCD position. Three sided with Bakke (the ADL, the American Jewish Congress, and the American Federation of Teachers [AFT]). The latter organizations were still gravely concerned about the possibility of the court's validating the use of quotas in higher education admissions processes.

As in the *DeFunis* litigation but much more sharply, the battle lines were drawn: civil rights groups and the medical (and legal)

{ *The* Bakke *Case* }

profession on one side of the issue; on the other side, Jewish organizations, a few ethnic groups, teachers' unions, and some labor organizations. The court itself outlined the question of law: "Whether a racial classification which is intended to assist minorities, but which also has the effect of depriving those who are not so classified, of benefits they would enjoy but for their race, violated the constitutional rights of the majority."

Colvin argued that the Fourteenth Amendment, article I, section 21 of the California constitution, and Title VI were colorblind; a public university could not discriminate, either negatively or positively, on account of race, ethnicity, or other "neutral factors." Reidhaar argued that a benign, remedial discrimination was constitutional. There was a difference between programs that helped minority students and those that discriminated against them. Besides, Reidhaar maintained, Bakke would not have been admitted had there not been a special admissions process used by the UCD medical school admissions committee.

A half year later, in mid-September 1976, in a 6 to 1 vote, the highest state court answered the question posed to them by both parties. The forty-eight-page majority opinion affirmed Manker's ruling that preferential admissions policies violated the Fourteenth Amendment. The opinion concluded that the challenged program was in violation of the Fourteenth Amendment's Equal Protection Clause: "The Equal Protection clause applies 'to any person,' and its lofty purpose, to secure equality of treatment to all, is incompatible with the premise that some races may be afforded a higher degree of protection against unequal protection than others." It overturned UCD's special admissions program. It was, the court concluded, at bottom an illegal racial quota that violated Bakke's Fourteenth Amendment rights. Though the majority believed that the program was "laudable," there was no compelling state interest served by the special admissions program. Additionally, the UCD racial quota policy was not the most "narrowly tailored" approach to the substantive problem of diversifying the student cohorts attending America's medical and law schools.

The chief justice of the court, a well-known and highly respected jurist, Stanley Mosk, authored the six-person opinion.

For him, "this was a case of racial discrimination, and it was our feeling that discrimination against a person of any race is just bad." Mosk and the five other justices greatly feared the revival of a quota system in education if UCD's preferential program was ruled constitutional. And so he concluded the majority opinion with the judgment that the UCD preferential admissions process violated Bakke's Fourteenth Amendment rights "because it affords preference on the basis of race to persons who, by the University's own standards, are not as qualified for the study of medicine as non-minority applicants denied admission."

That the UCD special admissions program was a voluntary one made no difference to the court majority. Mosk wrote that "there is no merit in the assertion that there is some undefined constitutional significance to the fact that UCD elected to adopt the special admission program and was not compelled to do so by court order." All race-based admissions programs are unconstitutional! No notice can be taken of the applicant's race and color, for the Constitution is "color blind." Mosk continued: "To [decide for UCD would be] to sacrifice principle for the sake of dubious expediency."

Furthermore, because Bakke's Fourteenth Amendment constitutional rights were violated, the burden of proof was on UCD to show why Bakke should not be admitted. The Court ordered the medical school to prove Bakke would not have been admitted. If UCD could not meet that burden of proof, then Bakke had to be enrolled in the medical school.

The solitary dissenter, Justice Mathew O. Tobriner, wrote a fifty-seven-page dissenting opinion. He noted that all minority applicants accepted by the UCD in the two-year period "were fully qualified for the study of medicine."

He maintained that the UCD program did not violate the Constitution and that there was a reasonable relationship between the program and the goals of the state. "Two centuries of slavery and racial discrimination have left our nation an awful legacy, a largely separated society, in which wealth, educational resources, employment opportunities—indeed all of society's benefits—remain largely the preserve of the white-Anglo majority."

He concluded the dissent by noting the supreme irony of the majority ruling: "It is anomalous that the Fourteenth Amendment that served as the basis for the requirement that elementary and secondary schools be 'compelled' to integrate should now be turned around to forbid graduate schools from voluntarily seeking that very objective."

The majority opinion remanded the case back to Judge Manker to determine whether Bakke would have been admitted in either year without the special admissions program. The medical school administrators could not provide the data requested by the state supreme court. In his response, Reidhaar stipulated that "it cannot be clearly demonstrated that the special admissions program did not act to deny Mr Bakke admission in 1973 because he came extremely close to admission . . . even with the special admissions program being in operation." This unsatisfactory answer led the California Supreme Court to amend its earlier ruling. It ordered Bakke's immediate entry into the UCD medical school.

That order, however, was stayed by U.S. Supreme Court Associate Justice William Rehnquist in November 1976, pending the outcome of the petition for a writ of certiorari to be filed by the Regents of the University of California to the U.S. Supreme Court in December 1976. The regents had decided to ask the High Bench for review on the merits because "[Davis and other professional schools] have a strong interest [in finding out] whether the special admissions program at the Davis medical school and other similar programs are, as held by a majority of this [California Supreme Court], unconstitutional."

CHAPTER 4

Asking the U.S. Supreme Court
to Review *Bakke*

Thousands of litigants annually petition the U.S. Supreme Court to hear their cases. All lost their legal arguments in the lower federal courts or, as in the case of the University of California, in a state supreme court. The primary method, as already noted—almost the only method available to 98 percent of litigants—is to ask the Court to grant a writ of certiorari. For *Bakke* to be heard in the U.S. Supreme Court, the University of California's lawyers had to claim that (1) the UCD medical school had a right, consistent with the Fourteenth Amendment and with the 1964 Civil Rights Act, to develop a preferential affirmative action admissions plan, and that (2) the California Supreme Court erroneously rejected that argument.

————

Very few petitions for certiorari are granted by the U.S. Supreme Court. The Court will grant certiorari to hear what is to at least four of them an important question of law. In a 1949 address to a state bar association, Chief Justice Fred Vinson said that certiorari was granted only in "those cases which present questions whose resolution will have immediate importance far beyond the particular facts and parties involved."

In addition to the Formal Rules, there are informal norms that guide Supreme Court behavior. One informal norm is that the justices' law clerks review all the petitions for certiorari and prepare short summaries for each of their "bosses" to read prior to the conference session vote on whether to grant certiorari. For example, in the *Bakke* case, Allan Taylor, one of Justice Thurgood Marshall's three law clerks, on January 7, 1977, wrote that "this is the case in which the California Supreme Court held unconstitutional (on federal grounds) the preferential admissions program of the state medical school [sic]. The opposing cert [brief] presents no reason not to grant. The order of the California Supreme Court has been stayed by this Court. GRANT."

Marshall wrote, on the top right hand corner of the note, "Join 3 ??," which meant that if three other justices voted to grant the writ of certiorari, then he would join them and the writ would be issued. His notation pointed to a core informal norm: "the vote of four."

If in the conference session four of the nine justices believe that a case should be heard "on the merits" and recommend the granting of certiorari, the parties to the dispute are so notified by the clerk of the court. The case is placed on the Court's "plenary" calendar for briefs on the merits, oral argument, and plenary decision making. Between 97 percent and 99 percent of the cases do not receive the "vote of four" in conference. Thereafter the petition is denied, and the clerk's office sends each petitioner a very brief letter informing the parties of the Court's decision. No reasons are ever given for the denial of certiorari.

The University of California's Petition for a
Writ of Certiorari from the U.S. Supreme Court

UCD is one of nine public universities that made up the University of California system. Overseeing them was the board of regents of the University of California, a group of Californians selected by the governor and the legislators of the state. One of their many tasks was to determine whether or not, in the *Bakke* case, there would be an appeal from the California Supreme Court to the U.S. Supreme Court.

Donald Reidhaar, the board's chief counsel, urged this action because the university system (as well as the other major multicampus unit of higher education in the state, the California state university system) had developed and was implementing a wide variety of preferential affirmative action programs on all campuses.

It was necessary for California educators as well as higher education educators across the nation to find out whether or not these preferential programs were constitutional. A few months after the California Supreme Court ruling, the regents approved the filing of a petition for certiorari.

The constitutional question posed by the regents in their petition went to the core of the controversy over affirmative action in higher education: "When only a small fraction of thousands of applicants can be admitted, does the Fourteenth Amendment's "Equal Protection" clause forbid a state university professional school faculty from voluntarily seeking to counteract the effects of generations of pervasive discrimination against discrete and insular minorities by establishing a limited special admission program that increases opportunities for well-qualified members of such racial and ethnic minorities?"

Colvin's brief for the respondent urged the Court to let the California Supreme Court's decision stand and to therefore deny certiorari. For him, "the primary issue in this case is Allan Bakke's right to be admitted to the medical school . . . as well as the constitutionality of the petitioner's procedure for selecting students to attend the medical school." He argued that the Court should deny certiorari in *Bakke* because (1) the plaintiff's petition "distorted the holding of the California Supreme Court," (2) the "alleged conflict between the California Supreme Court and other state Supreme Courts is not a true conflict meriting resolution by this Court," and (3) the California Supreme Court correctly decided *Bakke* "and did so by way of a reasoned application of this Court's prior constitutional decisions."

Four briefs amicus curiae were filed with the Court when the petitioner asked for the writ of certiorari. Two called for the issuance of certiorari and the overturn of the state court decision. If not, then "the movement of minority groups toward meaningful representation in the profession[s] will virtually cease." Two others urged the Court to grant certiorari for a different reason: to stem the tide of the "rampant" spread of reverse discrimination in higher education. They labeled Colvin's argument against certiorari "weak and specious." Certiorari must be granted so that the U.S. Supreme Court could establish a national prohibition against such emergent and uncontrolled reverse discrimination.

A very important amicus brief came from A Group of Fifteen [Civil Rights] Organizations (including the National Urban League, NOW, the National Bar Association, the National Conference of Black Lawyers, La Raza National Lawyers Association, the Mexican-American Inc Fund, and the Puerto Rican Inc Fund). Their brief urged the Court to deny certiorari because "the record of the [*Bakke*] case was deficient and thus was not a good vehicle for deciding such an important issue."

While they supported the UCD medical school affirmative action plan on the merits, their amicus brief reflected concern and trepidation. They feared the impact of an adverse Supreme Court decision in *Bakke*, one that validated the California Supreme Court decision. Such a decision would have an "adverse, dramatic, and long-term impact on civil rights and race relations for future decades." The *Bakke* case was not a good one for the Court to review for a number of reasons.

First of all, Manker's opinion illustrated a lack of a true "case or controversy," one of the basic jurisdictional necessities if the Court was to decide a case. The trial judge had written that Bakke "would not have been accepted for admission to the class entering Davis medical school [in 1973 and 1974] even if there had been no special admissions program." Second, other cases were more suitable for review by the Court because there was a "fully developed record."

They argued that there was "just not enough" of a record to warrant constitutional adjudication by the brethren. There was not sufficient evidence presented by UCD to warrant their initial request for summary dismissal in the state trial court. Nor was there any factual evidence presented to the state supreme court.

The amicus brief showed examples of evidence that had not been submitted and therefore could not now be used if the Court were to grant certiorari. These were important omissions, ones that created dilemmas for these civil rights groups. For example, the board of regents claimed that there was an important patient-doctor relationship that would be enhanced if UCD graduated more African-American doctors. "But the [*Bakke*] record contains no evidence to justify this proposition." There was also the claim, unsubstantiated, that the affirmative action admissions program at the UCD medical school was "the only method whereby the school can produce a diverse student body."

Furthermore, there was no evidence of past discrimination presented by UCD's lawyers. Without such evidentiary data, the California Supreme Court ordered the admission of Bakke and invalidated the affirmative action program because it "deprives a member of the majority of a benefit because of his race." Lacking evidence presented in the record, the state supreme court, in its own words, "must presume" that UCD has not engaged in past discrimination.

The brief pointed out that UCD presented no evidence of the racial bias of the MCAT examination that all medical school applicants had to take. Did taking the MCAT have a racially disproportionate, adverse impact on minorities? Not presenting evidence, one way or another, to answer this question was a "striking" omission because of the Douglas dissent in *DeFunis*. He had urged remand in that case precisely in order to have UW present evidence as to whether the LSAT was racially biased! But the *Bakke* record was absolutely silent on this critical issue. UCD had an "obligation to demonstrate the validity [or invalidity] of the MCAT."

In addition, "the record is devoid of evidence to prove that the State of California, through its educational system, has discriminated against minorities in numerous ways that have deprived them of an equal opportunity to gain admission to medical school." Furthermore, "closely related is the absence of any evidence relating to the omnipresent influence of racial discrimination that mars this Nation's history."

The final amicus brief, filed by three civil rights organizations (the National Conference of Black Lawyers, the National Lawyers Guild, and the California Rural Legal Assistance Inc Fund) just days before the Court made its announcement, asked the Court to remand the *Bakke* case to the California Supreme Court for its disposition on the ground that the California constitution had been amended since the earlier decision "in a manner which may provide an adequate state ground [rather than the Fourteenth Amendment and the 1964 Civil Rights Act, Title VI] as a basis for decision."

It wasn't really a surprise that the Supreme Court granted certiorari. As the four *DeFunis* dissenters and Justice Powell had maintained four years earlier, affirmative action in higher education litigation was an issue that the Court could no longer avoid. However, the brethren who voted to grant certiorari were not the four dissenters in the *DeFunis* case. Only Justice Byron White from that cohort voted to grant certiorari in *Bakke*. Justices Brennan and Marshall felt that the record in *Bakke* was poor and did not vote to grant. In addition to White, there were two Nixon appointees, Justices Rehnquist and Powell, joined by Justice Stewart and the newest member of the Court, Justice John P. Stevens, appointed by President Gerald R. Ford in 1975 (upon the retirement of liberal Justice William O. Douglas).

In its December 14, 1976, conference session, the Court first broached the question of whether to grant certiorari in the *Bakke* case. However, because of Justice Harry Blackmun's absence due to illness, it was relisted. There were discussions on January 24, 1977, and again on February 18, 1977. At that last discussion, the Court voted 5 to 4 to grant certiorari in *Bakke*. The quintet who voted to grant were Justices Potter Stewart, Byron R. White, Lewis F. Powell, William H. Rehnquist, and John P. Stevens. The four who voted to deny certiorari were Justices William J. Brennan Jr. and Thurgood Marshall, and two men appointed by President Richard Nixon, known as the "Minnesota Twins," Chief Justice Warren E. Burger and Associate Justice Harry A. Blackmun.

A report that appeared in the February 23, 1977, edition of the *New York Times* noted the Court's announcement of the grant of certiorari in the *Bakke* case the preceding day. "Setting the stage for a landmark decision on what is often called 'reverse discrimination,' the U.S. Supreme Court agreed to review the California Supreme Court decision that invalidated the minority admission program of the University of California's Medical School at Davis."

Major stories appeared in the press, from the *New York Times* to the *Los Angeles Times*. In a page-one story, the *New York Times* noted that the issue raised in *Bakke* "is one of the most controversial and difficult in civil rights today. The Court's decision to consider it sets the stage for a landmark ruling—both on the permissibility of the preferential university admissions policies, and also, perhaps, on the broader issue of voluntary affirmative action programs in general."

The *Los Angeles Times* headline was: "Supreme Court to Rule on UC Minority Admissions." It was noted that there had been a great deal of controversy in the months preceding the Supreme Court's decision to grant certiorari and hear the *Bakke* case. The clashes occurred between university administrators, civil rights groups, religious groups—especially Jewish civil rights organizations, business, labor, educators, and lawyers.

By this time, February 1977, Allan Bakke was almost thirty-eight years old. His last hope for admission into UCD's medical school and for the resolution of the moral, political, and legal issue of racial quotas now rested with the nine men who sat in Washington, D.C. With the grant of certiorari, the Court announced that it would, in its 1977–1978 term, hear, discuss, debate, and then decide whether or not preferential admissions processes based on race and ethnicity were constitutional.

The Briefs on the Merits Filed with the Court

To help the Court reach a decision, the parties to the dispute file new briefs with the Court. These briefs present arguments on the substantive questions raised in the appeal for review. Under the Court's rules, the University of California lawyers had to file forty copies of the brief on the merits. The legal team for the board of regents now included two big guns, former U.S. solicitor general (and the initial special prosecutor in the Watergate break-in investigation, fired by Nixon in 1973) Archibald Cox and University of California, Berkeley, law professor Paul Mishkin, a highly regarded and experienced civil rights advocate.

Both had argued many cases before the U.S. Supreme Court, and their expertise was needed by Reidhaar and the other California attorneys working on the *Bakke* appeal.

For Cox, who was the chief architect of the petitioner's brief on the merits, the "legacy of pervasive racial discrimination cannot be undone by mere reliance on formulas of formal equality. Educators have recognized the necessity of employing race-conscious remedies as a means to achieve true—and compelling—educational opportunity."

"The outcome of this controversy," concluded the university's brief, "will decide for future generations whether blacks, Chicanos and other insular minorities are to have meaningful access to higher education and real opportunities to enter the learned professions, or are to be penalized indefinitely by the disadvantages flowing from previous pervasive discrimination." If the Court affirmed the California Supreme Court decision, "it would be a return to virtually all-white professional schools." Reversal of the state court decision, what the petitioner was asking for, "would permit continuation of admissions programs, like the one at Davis, fashioned by educators who have agreed that 'the greatest single handicap the ethnic minorities face is their under-representation in the professions of the nation.'"

The "race-conscious plan for minority admissions" is the only affirmative action program that actually works to enable "qualified applicants from disadvantaged minorities to attend medical schools, law schools, and other institutions of higher learning in sufficient numbers to enhance the quality of the education for all students," concluded the Cox brief.

Colvin had thirty days after receipt of the petitioner's brief to file his response. On August 5, 1977, it was filed. For Colvin "the case presents a constitutional conflict in which this Court must decide whether the right to equal protection, granted by the Fourteenth Amendment to 'any person,' does indeed extend to individuals such as Allan Bakke or, instead, applies only to protect certain racial and ethnic groups."

The brief argued that the UCD special admissions program violated Bakke's Fourteenth Amendment rights. A "rigid racial quota" was employed by the admissions committee at UCD, one that in effect substituted group rights for individual rights. The Fourteenth Amendment right, however, is a personal right, and Bakke's personal right to the equal protection of the laws was violated because of the special admissions program. Colvin concluded by arguing that the California Supreme Court decision was correct; he requested that the U.S. Supreme Court affirm the state court's decision.

––––

The nation's largest and busiest pressure group in the federal courts is the federal government itself. Legal advocates work for the hundreds of independent federal regulatory agencies and a similar number of bureaucracies in the executive branch of the national government. Their task is to implement the public laws passed by Congress and signed into law by the president. The litigators include (1) the U.S. attorneys and their legal staffs (there are ninety-four U.S. attorney's offices across America [including four offices in the American territories], with at least one U.S. attorney in every state in the Union); (2) the advocates for agencies such as the Food and Drug Administration, who argue cases and file appeals on behalf of their "clients"; (3) the many hundreds of lawyers in the various divisions of the U.S. Department of Justice (DOJ); and, with regard to federal government appeals and petitions for certiorari to the U.S. Supreme Court, (4) the U.S. Office of the Solicitor General (SG) in the DOJ.

At the time of *Bakke*, the SG's office had a dual responsibility. As a political appointee, the "General," as the solicitor general is called, had a responsibility to the political leaders of the administration, that is, to the president and to the General's "boss," the attorney general (AG). As the advocate for the federal government in the U.S. Supreme Court, however, the General has a significant responsibility to the Court. Over the generations, the justices have come to rely on the good judgment of the SG, regardless of political party, in fulfilling certain basic litigation-management tasks that relieve the Court from performing them.

All federal government losses in the lower federal and state

{ *The* Bakke *Case* }

courts are reviewed by the SG and a staff of about two dozen lawyers. The great bulk of requests for Supreme Court review are rejected. As former solicitor general Erwin Griswold (Nixon administration) said: "The Solicitor General does most of the screening which is done in other cases by the Supreme Court, for he tries to take to the Court only cases which he thinks the Court will accept."

Fewer than one in six cases involving the federal government ever lead to petitions for a writ of certiorari. The one case in six filed with the Court by the solicitor general exhibits clean facts and a good trial record. It can make good law, and it is an issue the Court is willing to discuss on the merits. Furthermore, because five of six are not sent to the Court, that one in six stands an excellent chance of being heard by the justices on the merits. The success rate of the SG is truly phenomenal. In the *Bakke* era, when more than 95 percent of the thousands of petitions for the writ of certiorari were denied, the General's success rate for the granting of "cert" ran—as it still does—between 70 and 80 percent!

The second major function of the SG's office involves the brief amicus curiae. If the federal government is not a party to the litigation, it can, if it chooses (as was the case in *Bakke*) or if it is requested to by the Court (as the Court did in 1953 in the school desegregation cases), file a brief amicus curiae. At the time of the *Bakke* litigation, the SG's office was filing amicus briefs in 20 to 25 percent of the cases heard by the Court on the merits.

According to the rules of the U.S. Supreme Court, the SG's office is the only interest group that need not request permission to file an amicus brief. The SG's office is permitted to participate in oral argument even when the federal government is not a major party in the legal dispute. The Court's own rules treat the SG's office significantly differently than all other interest groups that bring suit or file briefs amicus curiae.

The impact of the SG as amicus brief presenter is dramatic. If the SG's office files such a brief, it carries great weight. For example, in litigation where a state or local subdivision is a party, until very recently, the chance of winning the case was about 15 to 20 percent. However, if the SG filed an amicus supporting that governmental entity, the success rate rose to a phenomenal 85 percent.

In the *Bakke* litigation, the U.S. government was not a direct party. However, the Carter administration believed it was appropriate to file an amicus brief in support of affirmative action. Carter's campaign promises to minorities included support for affirmative action programs. Just one month after Carter took his presidential oath of office, the Supreme Court granted certiorari in the *Bakke* case. Shortly thereafter, the Carter administration made the decision to file an amicus brief. It was not to be an uneventful drafting of a government amicus brief.

Jimmy Carter's order to his DOJ to prepare a *Bakke* amicus brief led to an intense political struggle between the White House staff and the Department of Justice and between personnel in the DOJ itself over just what position the U.S. government would take on the question of affirmative action.

In 1977, Carter's friend (and former campaign manager when Carter ran for governor in Georgia) Griffith Bell was the attorney general and participated in the discussions. Wade McCree Jr. was the U.S. solicitor general. He was only the second African American in that appointed post; the first African American to serve as "General" was then sitting on the Supreme Court: Thurgood Marshall. McCree had been the first African American elected to a state judgeship in Michigan. In 1961 President Kennedy selected McCree to be a federal district court judge, and in 1966 President Johnson appointed McCree to the federal court of appeals.

Another, younger (thirty-five years old), African-American lawyer, Drew Days III, was the assistant attorney general, Civil Rights Division, the first of his race to head a division in the DOJ. Days was born in Tampa, Florida, and moved to New Rochelle, New York, when he was in junior high school. His father ran an insurance company, while his mother was a school teacher. He experienced the pain of state-ordained, blatant racial discrimination, and drew upon those bad memories once he became an attorney.

He attended Hamilton College in Clinton, New York. Given the political upheavals and protest of that era (antiwar, black power, civil rights), he was quickly transformed into a radical activist on campus. The law, not medicine, became his career goal. Days attended Yale Law School, where his concentrations were constitutional law, civil liberties, and race relations. (Days was one of only five African Americans in a class of almost two hundred law students.)

"It was a strange atmosphere," Days recalled of his law school days. For the first time in his life, Days was in a cohort that included some students "who were the truly rich." The gulf between Days's background and that of most of the white students was striking. He recalled an incident that illuminated the yawning gap between the two groups of students. In his first year, Days (like all other law school students) took the required contracts class. During his first examination he answered a question incorrectly. His comments about that incident speak volumes about the environment minorities found themselves in when they attended formerly all-white professional schools. "A question did not turn on whether the contract was signed, but I answered it that way because I didn't recognize the short-hand signature for signed, /s/. The Professor just assumed that everybody was familiar with it, though it had never been part of the course. He must have gotten a real laugh at my answer."

McCree and Days worked closely to define the position of the Carter administration on affirmative action, although McCree asked Days to take the lead in the preparation of the brief. Days then found himself in a role reversal. Until January 1977, when Carter asked him to head the Civil Rights Division, Days had been one of the sharp young lawyers working in the NAACP's Legal and Educational Defense Fund, Inc.! He was now an advocate for the United States, not the NAACP.

One of the first things Days did was to ask the heads of federal agencies and departments, including the Departments of Health, Education, and Welfare, of Housing and Urban Development, and of Labor, the Equal Employment Opportunity Commission, the Civil Service Commission, and the U.S. Commission on Civil Rights, whether to file an amicus curiae brief in *Bakke*. The word back was an unequivocal yes. Federal agencies had by 1977 implemented numerous affirmative action policies. Their lawyers encouraged the DOJ to prepare a brief that strongly supported affirmative action but also opposed rigid racial quotas.

For AG Bell, *Bakke* "was the most significant civil rights controversy to come before the [U.S. Supreme Court] since the school desegregation cases of 1954." He wrote that "clearly, the issue was both crucial and timely in the development of civil rights law, and the federal government would want to lend its assistance in the form of an . . . amicus brief." After Bell called for the amicus brief, he then "made perhaps my greatest mistake with regard to the power centers at the White House." His "mistake was in taking a copy of the draft amicus brief with [him] to the White House when [he] went to tell the President what position [they] were developing." Bell told the president that the brief would state that the "government would stand for affirmative action but would oppose rigid quotas to carry out affirmative action programs, a position that meant that Bakke would have to be admitted to the medical school."

Carter's key political advisors included Vice President Walter Mondale, domestic chief Stuart Eizenstat, and Bob Lipschutz, the president's counsel. They found themselves at odds over the draft. Except for Eizenstat, the Jewish members of Carter's White House staff supported the draft. Others, Vice President Mondale, chief of staff Hamilton Jordan, and Joseph Califano, the secretary of the Department of Health, Education, and Welfare, were opposed. They expressed grave concern about the impact on minority groups of a government amicus brief that rejected UCD's special admissions program because it used "rigid quotas" and called for Bakke's admission to UCD medical school. In addition, at this time the Black Congressional Caucus, a group of African-American congresspersons, was pressing the Carter administration for absolute support for the UCD affirmative action plan.

The initial draft prepared by Days was promptly leaked to the press. The resulting firestorm of protest from the Black Congressional Caucus and minority and civil rights organizations was loud and continuous. Chief Justice Burger was so infuriated with these daily stories that he told McCree that "the entire Court was offended by the numerous news leaks of early drafts of the [DOJ] brief [and] that the Justices felt the resultant uproar had subjected them to improper public pressure when they were about to hear oral arguments."

Eizenstat was especially livid when he read the press coverage and heard the reaction from Carter loyalists. He saw the proposed governmental position suggested in the brief as a political disaster, one that would see racial minority groups across the nation break ties with the Democratic president. His policy advisors told Carter that the draft had to be changed in a major way.

The president agreed and told Bell to meet with McCree and have the solicitor general rewrite the brief so that it would categorically support affirmative action. For the policy men in the White House, the instructions were direct: come up with an amicus brief that did not ignore the promises Carter made during the presidential campaign.

Bell provided a summary of the Carter administration's principles on affirmative action and passed that on to McCree and Days. This was followed by a press conference in late July 1977, where President Carter announced that the Department of Justice amicus brief would defend the UCD minority admissions program even though the program might "contravene the concept of merit selection." That was a positive message to the civil rights community.

In early September 1977, the press was having a heyday with the story. Almost daily, there were additional leaks about the goings-on in DOJ and the fights between the lawyers and the policy makers in the White House. The opponents of the initial draft were outraged at the position the U.S. government was preparing to make before the Court and demanded that McCree rewrite the brief. Given these pressures, from Congress, from the civil rights community, from the White House, and from the "principles" statement Bell gave them, McCree and Days reluctantly rewrote the U.S. government's amicus brief.

By mid-September 1977, the new draft took very different positions on affirmative action in higher education. As Bell recounted, "in the [final] brief submitted to the Court, the government supported neither Bakke nor the University." It said that the government (1) strongly supported affirmative action programs based on race and ethnicity, (2) was opposed to "rigid exclusionary quotas," but did not provide any detailed argumentation, and (3) believed that there was an inadequate finding of evidentiary data in *Bakke* (a major contention of the civil rights organizations). Finally, it urged the Court to remand the case back to the California trial court to address the unanswered factual questions associated with preferential affirmative action (the other major argument in the civil rights groups' briefs amicus curiae).

The U.S.'s brief argued that "race may be taken into account to counteract the effects of prior discrimination; minority-sensitive [admissions] decisions are essential to eliminate the effects of discrimination in this country." As public policy, both Congress and federal agencies "have adopted minority-sensitive programs for the purposes of eliminating the effects of past discrimination." UCD "could conclude that a minority-sensitive program was necessary to remedy the lingering effects of past discrimination." Furthermore, California's Supreme Court applied incorrect legal standards in evaluating the constitutionality of the UCD special admissions plan. The brief then noted that "the central issue on judicial review of a minority-sensitive program is whether it is tailored to remedy the effects of past discrimination." Because the lower court record was incomplete, the case should be remanded in order to generate additional evidence not presently in the record. Whether Allan Bakke was wrongfully denied admission to the UCD medical school "should not be decided on the present record."

By October 3, 1977, the day Solicitor General McCree filed the seventy-four-page brief amicus curiae in the Supreme Court (and only nine days before oral arguments in *Bakke* were scheduled), the *Washington Post* accurately noted that Drew Days III was a "harried man in recent months." His former colleagues in the NAACP's Inc Fund sarcastically asked Days, "How's your friend Allan [Bakke] doing?" With the filing of the brief, the pressure was suddenly off him. The next task: prepare the government's oral argument strategy, argued by McCree before the justices on October 12, 1977.

———

The government's amicus brief was the very last of dozens of such briefs filed with the Court after certiorari was granted in *Bakke*. Phrases such as "reverse discrimination," "racial quotas," and "special minority admissions programs" still triggered deep emotions in Americans. The *DeFunis* litigation had led thirty organized groups to present their views in amicus briefs. By 1977, when the U.S. Supreme Court granted the writ of certiorari in *Bakke*, the tumult over racial quotas had greatly increased in volume. Americans had developed fairly definitive views about the legitimacy or illegitimacy of special affirmative action programs in universities. As a consequence, in *Bakke*, as the *Los Angeles Times* reported: "never before in its 189-year history had the nation's highest court attracted so much unsolicited advice in a single controversy as it received in Allan Bakke's case. [There were more briefs] than in a series of cases that led to the Supreme Court's 1954 landmark decision outlawing racial segregation."

A record fifty-eight amicus briefs were filed after the Court granted certiorari in *Bakke*. Forty-two briefs supported the petitioner, while sixteen sided with the respondent. They represented the views of over 160 organizations and individuals—including a lawyer practicing in Seattle, Washington: Marco De-Funis Jr., Esq., who wrote the brief for a conservative group, the Young Americans for Freedom.

In the twentieth century, bringing lawsuits in state and federal courts has become a staple and direct strategy of many American interest groups. Whether liberal or conservative, public- or private-interest, repeat player or single-shot player, these groups seek to achieve their organizational goals through test cases or class-action suits in court. There are hundreds of groups that either bring litigation to the courts or file amicus curiae briefs.

Included in the wide spectrum of such organizations are businesses and corporations, chambers of commerce, the National

Association of Manufacturers, the ACLU, the NAACP, organized labor, Jehovah's Witnesses, NOW, environmental groups such as the Sierra Club and the Environmental Defense Fund, and conservative public-interest groups such as the Pacific Legal Foundation and Citizens for Decency through Law.

A group can participate directly as a litigating party by challenging on behalf of their injured members an action that allegedly violates a state or federal statute or the Constitution. By either filing a test case challenging an action that injures their members in discrete ways or filing a *class action* on behalf of all persons who are similarly situated in the law (whether or not members of that organization), a pressure group can achieve some of its organizational goals—if the U.S. Supreme Court decides to hear the case.

In a two-decade period, the 1930s and 1940s, the Jehovah's Witnesses brought dozens of cases into state and federal court. The group challenged local restrictions on their religious freedom and won a significant number of these cases, thereby expanding the scope of that First Amendment freedom. In like manner, the NAACP, for over forty years, from 1910 through the 1950s, on behalf of its members, brought over four dozen cases to the U.S. Supreme Court, culminating in the watershed *Brown v. Board of Education* (1954). They won most of them, and their goals—quality education and equal voting rights for African Americans—were achieved because the U.S. Supreme Court granted certiorari and, on the merits of these legal disputes, broadly expanded the meaning of the Civil War amendments.

An indirect action taken regularly by these groups is the filing of an amicus curiae brief. A group's leadership takes this course because they feel it is in their members' best interest to support one of the parties in a legal dispute. The Court's Rule 37 describes how a group may file an amicus curiae brief: "If accompanied by the written consent of all parties, or [if a party objects], if the Court grants leave to file." (However there is one exception in the rule: "No motion to file an amicus curiae brief is necessary if the brief is presented on behalf of the United States by the Solicitor General.")

For the past half century, these amicus curiae briefs have proliferated to the point that such briefs are filed in all non-commercial (civil rights and civil liberties) cases. In the more controversial of these types of cases, for example, affirmative action and abortion, it is not unusual to count two to three dozen such friend-of-the-court briefs filed by interested pressure groups. (In *Bakke* almost sixty amicus curiae briefs were filed; in an important abortion rights case decided a decade later, *Webster v. Reproductive Health Services*, 1989, the *Bakke* record was smashed: seventy-eight briefs amicus curiae were filed with the Court, representing the views of over four hundred groups.)

Rule 37 of the Court's own Rules of the Supreme Court of the United States is entitled "Brief for an Amicus Curiae." It lays out in general terms the general role of these briefs: "An amicus curiae brief that brings to the attention of the Court relevant matter not already brought to its attention by the parties may be of considerable help to the Court. [One that] does not serve this purpose burdens the Court and its filing is not favored."

For the pressure group filing an amicus brief, the goal is to persuade the justices to rule on behalf of "their" party in the litigation before the Court. The groups participating as amici are not parties to the dispute. Costs are very reasonable, and the group believes filing such a brief shows the organization's flag. The pressure group files the amicus brief because it furthers that group's goals. A critical question: Does the amicus curiae brief help the justices of the U.S. Supreme Court reach judgment in a case?

Justices Hugo Black, William J. Brennan Jr., Thurgood Marshall, and William O. Douglas, for example, appreciated the briefs: They kept the brethren in touch with the views and the attitudes of many dozens of groups. In a memo written to his colleagues in October 1957, Black said that "most of the cases before this Court involve matters that affect far more people than the immediate record parties. I think the public interest would be better served [by allowing for greater amicus participation] rather than tightening the rule against amicus curiae briefs."

However, there have been other justices who argued vigorously for a rule change that would make it very difficult for a group to file an amicus brief. Justice Black's nemesis, Justice Felix Frankfurter, disagreed regularly with the Alabaman on substantive and procedural issues before the Court, including Black's views of the amicus brief: He objected to having "the Court exploited as a soap-box or as an advertising medium, or as the target, not of legal arguments but of mere assertion that this or that group has this or that interest in a question that ought to be decided."

At bottom, the value of the amicus brief is determined by the particular justice. If one shares Black's belief in its value, then that jurist's clerks will carefully read and mark up for their boss a summary of the arguments. If the justice shares Frankfurter's attitudes, then the brief will be an insignificant factor in the Court's decision-making process. In the past half century, which saw the explosion of amicus briefs, there has emerged a set of generalizations about their success.

Amicus briefs filed by state and local governments seem to have had little effect on the Suprene Court. Briefs filed by other amicus parties have some moderate impact—so long as they are not opposed by the solicitor general in the role of one of the major parties in the dispute or as amicus curiae. The U.S. government has, without question, the greatest impact on the Court, with regard both to granting of certiorari and to getting a favorable decision from the Court on the merits.

The Amicus Curiae Arguments, Pro and Con,
Raised in the *Bakke* Case

In addition to the SG, fifty-seven groups submitted amicus curiae briefs. Four were filed either in support of or in opposition to the Court's granting certiorari in *Bakke*. Fifty-three were filed after the Court granted certiorari. Thirty-eight supported the petitioner's argument, including briefs submitted by the National Conference of Black Lawyers and by Doctors Cobbs and Kahn. While in support of flexible affirmative action programs, these two briefs argued that the trial record in *Bakke* was so "poor and incomplete" that *Bakke* should be remanded by the Court. Wait for a better case, with a complete record, they said; the issue is too important for America for the justices to reach judgment on such a flawed record.

Some civil rights organizations were very concerned that, on an issue of such magnitude, the petitioner in the litigation was not one of their groups. Most of the minority groups had a hard time with the fact that white lawyers representing a predominantly white organization, the University of California, were arguing on behalf of minorities. They believed that the white advocates for the petitioner's case were "unreliable" advocates of their cause. Fifteen amici joined with Bakke, arguing that preferential affirmative action programs based on race and ethnicity were unconstitutional and in violation of the 1964 Civil Rights Act.

Thirty-eight groups urged the Court to reverse the decision of the California Supreme Court, although a very small number believed that the case should be remanded to the state trial court for a new trial. Many had participated in the *DeFunis* litigation as amici, but more groups found it in their constituents' interest to file briefs in the *Bakke* litigation. As with the supporters of the UWSL, the UCD supporters included universities that had been in the forefront in establishing affirmative action programs on their campuses; civil rights groups; professional-school student groups, medical, legal, and other associations; state governments, and testing organizations.

The list of amici groups that filed on behalf of preferential treatment for minority students included colleges and universities such as Antioch School of Law; Rutgers University; Columbia University, Harvard, Stanford, Pennsylvania, and seven other private universities; Howard University; and the University of Washington.

Many civil rights organizations filed briefs, including the ACLU, the ACLU of Northern California, and the ACLU of Southern California; eight Mexican-American organizations; the Equal Employment Advisory Council; the Fair Employment Practices Commission of California; the Lawyers Committee for Civil Rights under Law; the NAACP; the NAACP Inc Fund; and the Puerto Rican Inc Fund. As in *DeFunis*, they filed because they feared the consequences of an adverse Supreme Court decision.

The same reasoning led to the filing of briefs by organized student groups such as the American Medical Student Association; the Black Law Students Association of UCLA and two other organizations; the Black Law Students Union–Yale; the Black Law Students Association–Cleveland State; and five Native-American bar groups in the University of California.

Medical, legal, educational, and other professional associations also filed amicus briefs. They came from the American Association of University Professors; the American Bar Association; the Asian-American Bar Association of the Greater Bay Area; the Association of American Law Schools; the Association of American Medical Colleges; the Bar Association of San Francisco and the Los Angeles County Bar Association; the Council on Legal Educational Opportunities; the Law School Admissions Council; the Legal Services Corporation; the National Association of Affirmative Action Officers; the National Association of Minority Contractors and Minority Contractors of Northern California; the National Conference of Black Lawyers; the National Council of Churches plus twenty others, including Americans for Democratic Action, the AFL-CIO, the American Public Health Association, the Japanese-American Citizen League, the National Education Association, NOW, the National Urban League, and the YWCA; the National Employment Law Project; the National Fund for Minority Engineering Students; the National Medical Association; the National Bar Association; the National Association for Equal Opportunity in Higher Education; the North Carolina Association of Black Lawyers; and the Society of American Law Teachers.

Private individuals also filed briefs: Doctors Cobbs and Kahn, plus twenty-one other medical doctors; Jerome Lackner, director of health, California, and M. J. Woods, director, California Department of Benefit Payments.

Most of these briefs repeated the message presented by the University of California lawyers: The special admissions plan was constitutional; it did not violate Title VI of the 1964 Civil Rights Act. The MCAT was a standardized test biased against minority students. There were "compelling reasons" for the preferential affirmative action (including educational objectives). There was also the need to overcome "pervasive societal racism." Finally, "invidious" discrimination differs from "benign" discrimination; the latter is inclusive and remedial assistance, and not a program to keep group members out.

However, a small number of amicus briefs raised new questions and answers for the justices (and their law clerks) to ponder. The Rutgers University brief, for example, argued that the justices should look at *Bakke* through the Thirteenth Amendment lens: Continued exclusion of minorities from professional schools, because of the application of the "color-blind" constitution standard, constituted a "badge of slavery" prohibited by that amendment.

The ACLU brief, prepared by Ruth Bader Ginsburg (now a sitting U.S. Supreme Court justice) and two other lawyers, argued that Allan Bakke had not suffered "stigmatic injury." There was no violation of the Constitution by UCD. (*Stigmatic injury* was a concept successfully employed by the NAACP in *Brown* to show the courts that minority children suffered psychological harm when segregated by race in secondary schools.)

The Law School Admissions Council (LSAC) argued in its brief that excluded non-minority applicants were not better qualified than the minority students admitted. Where there is a history of racial discrimination in university admissions, numerical figures should not be used. "When a wrong is racial, a racial remedy is essential and there is no need to seek a non-racial alternative means, either for the state here or from Congress. . . . A color-blind requirement would seriously impair the governmental and educational contribution of diversity and the consideration of race or any other 'suspect category' as one factor to be taken into account both positively and negatively in the interests of diversity of viewpoints and experiences constitutes neither an unconstitutional preference, nor a quota."

The American Medical Student Association's brief argued that numerical critera (MCAT scores, the GPA of the applicant) were "inappropriate instruments for admission to medical school. [They] do not predict either success in medical school, or as a physician. [Their use] does insure that minority students are not admitted."

As was the case with the *DeFunis* amici, fewer organizations asked the Court to affirm the decision of the California Supreme Court. Included in the group were religious, ethnic, labor, business, law enforcement, and conservative organizations. Religious groups included the American Jewish Congress (AJC) plus seven organizations, including the Italian-American Foundation and the Ukrainian Congress Committee; ADL plus five organizations, including AFL-CIO and UNICO International; and the Queens, N.Y., Jewish Community Council and the Jewish Rights Committee. Ethnic groups filing briefs included the Order of the Sons of Italy in America; the Polish-American Congress plus two other Polish-American groups. As in their *DeFunis* briefs, these groups condemned as unconstitutional any quota or set-aside admissions system, regardless of the motivation for such a process.

The American Federation of Teachers also filed a brief on behalf of Bakke. Business groups included the American Sub-Contractors Association and the Chamber of Commerce of the United States. The Fraternal Order of Police plus three other law enforcement groups filed an amicus brief, as did a number of conservative groups that included the Committee on Academic Nondiscrimination and Integrity and the Mid-America Legal Foundation; the Pacific Legal Foundation; and the Young Americans for Freedom. Finally, private individuals filed amicus briefs; these included Ralph Galiano; Timothy Hoy; and Congressman Henry A. Waxman.

Like those on the other side, most of the briefs on behalf of the respondent were redundant, repeating the arguments Colvin presented in his brief of the merits. The "color-blind" Constitution prohibits racial discrimination of all kinds and therefore UCD's use of "racial quotas" is invalid. Additionally, there is "no history" of UCD ever discriminating against minorities. The Supreme Court must use the "strict scrutiny" standard to decide the case and must conclude that any reverse discrimination is arbitrary and in violation of the Fourteenth Amendment and Title VI.

The AJC brief maintained that there was no "pressing public necessity" shown in defense of the use of preferential affirmative action programs, while the Order of the Sons of Italy brief criticized the "social engineering" the UCD administrators and faculty had created in order to overcome the centuries of discrimination. Two conservative organizations presented arguments that were not redundant: The Pacific Legal Foundation argued that if the UCD practice was allowed to stand, there would be a resurgence of the *Plessy* separate-but-equal doctrine. Marco DeFunis, for the YAF, argued in part that Bakke had been denied the Fourteenth Amendment protection of the "privileges and immunities" of American citizenship. The University's "position is unfounded: It assumes the majority group is monolithic when in fact it is pluralistic. Jews, Poles, Italians, Japanese, Chinese, are all a part of the 'majority' now. These dissimilar groups have each endured past discrimination. Who but the most sheltered could avoid hearing words such as Kike, Dago, Wop, Polack, Chink, Shanty Irish, and Jap. Yet what protection or special treatment is accorded these groups who have in the past and still suffer the effects of overt discrimination?"

This, then, was the melange sent to the Court by the amici in *Bakke*. Other than the basic premise held by all of them that, ideally, there should be diversity in the college classroom, two stark positions emerged: Either the Constitution is color-blind and prohibits preferential racial discrimination, or the Constitution is flexible enough to tolerate the temporary use of a preferential program that uses race and ethnicity to enable minority students to enter professional schools. All the briefs were asking the Court to choose one or the other.

———

After all the briefs on the merits have been submitted, the Court's brethren—helped by their law clerks—examine the arguments carefully as they prepare for the next stages in the Court's decision-making process: the oral argument, followed a few days later by the conference session.

CHAPTER 5

"Mr. Chief Justice and May It Please the Court": The Oral Arguments in *Bakke*, 1977

During the Court's often heated internal *Bakke* circulations and conference sessions, clashes occurred between allies. Justice William Brennan, the leader of the Court's "liberal" contingent on the matter of affirmative action, "resolved to get Marshall's reaction to [a] problem over lunch one day," Brennan recalled.

> I asked whether if [his son] were a candidate for admission to medical school, he thought it would be proper for school administrators to accord his application special consideration because of his race. Thurgood's asseveration was: "Damn right, they owe us!"

Brennan was astonished at his friend's answer. He refused to acknowledge the validity of that rationale to justify the use of affirmative action in higher education. (Years later, Marshall explained Brennan's amazement: "I think [my colleagues on the Supreme Court] honestly believe that Negroes are so much better off than they were before.")

Another issue that bedeviled the brethren was the level of scrutiny applied by the Court in deciding the constitutional question. Colvin and the Bakke amici urged the Court to use the strict scrutiny test. The petitioner's brief and its many supporting amici argued either that the Court use a less severe test or that, if the Court used strict scrutiny, it conclude that the affirmative action program met a compelling state interest and was narrowly tailored.

Finally, there was yet another major controversial issue that split the Court: Was Title VI of the Civil Rights Act applicable? In the briefs filed in the Court and at oral argument, neither side had discussed the matter, but the justices themselves came to see this question as a very substantive one. As Justice White said, in a memo to the conference written the day after oral argument, "we are at least entitled to consider the statutory ground, . . . I think we should deal with the Title VI argument."

Much like the parties and the amici, the justices of the Court clashed in the at times contentious effort to find meaning in the "spirit" and the "letter" of Title VI and the Fourteenth Amendment's Equal Protection Clause. Ultimately two very divergent groups of justices emerged. There was the quartet led by then Associate Justice William H. Rehnquist (including Chief Justice Burger and Justices John P. Stevens and Potter Stewart), who believed that the UCD affirmative action policy violated Title VI of the 1964 Civil Rights Act.

The pro–affirmative action quartet was led by Associate Justice William J. Brennan Jr. (and included Justices Thurgood Marshall, Harry A. Blackmun, and Byron R. White). They believed that a temporary affirmative action admission plan resting on race and ethnicity is a form of "benign" discrimination permitted by Title VI and not prohibited by the Fourteenth Amendment's Equal Protection Clause.

Since *DeFunis* came down in 1974, there had been a personnel change on the Court. Justice Douglas, the jurist who wrote a stinging dissent in *DeFunis*, one that had been used by Allan Bakke's lawyer and the amici supporting Bakke, had retired in 1975. He was replaced by John Paul Stevens, a federal appellate judge appointed by President Gerald Ford. Meanwhile, the Nixon quartet of Burger, Blackmun, Rehnquist, and Powell had grown closer on a number of constitutional issues, especially those involving the scope of equal protection under the Fourteenth Amendment.

By the time of the scheduled October 12, 1977, oral argument in *Bakke*, then, the justices had privately discussed the issue of affirmative action and were sharply divided. And if they were not convinced of the volatile public feelings surrounding the affirmative action issue, they were reminded just how controversial the policy was when they opened their copies of the *Washington Post* on October 10, 1977. They read that some members of the American Nazi Party, in full regalia and chanting "White Power Now," tried to interrupt over three thousand protesters demonstrating against Allan Bakke. (Dozens were arrested in the ensuing, very brief, battle that took place across the street from the Supreme Court building.)

———

The Oral Arguments in *Bakke*

Oral arguments took place as scheduled on Columbus Day, October 12, 1977. Typically, they hold little public interest and attract very little public attention. Usually the audience consists of persons who have been provided reserved seats by one of the sitting justices, some school and college groups, interest-group representatives, and the general public touring the Court that day. Seldom was the four-hundred-seat (with only one hundred unreserved seats) courtroom filled to capacity.

Because of *Bakke*'s importance, hundreds of would-be spectators lined up in the Court's plaza—some as early as 4 A.M.— hoping to gain entrance to the oral argument. Many who heard the arguments were members of minority groups. Allan Bakke, however, was not in the courtroom to hear the arguments in his case. "He's at work in California," said Colvin. "He considered coming but felt he couldn't maintain his seclusion from the press."

The 400 seats were quickly filled; hundreds were turned away. In the Court's plaza anti-Bakke picketers appeared, chanting: "Defend. Extend Affirmative Action!" The press treated the *Bakke* oral arguments as a major event in American politics. There was a record number of newspaper and broadcast reporters—more than ninety—in the courtroom to hear the oral arguments. The *New York Times* referred to the *Bakke* litigation as "the long-smoldering dispute over whether preferential treatment for minorities can reduce educational opportunities for whites without violating the Constitution."

The *Los Angeles Times* headline trumpeted, "Hundreds Jam High Court to Hear Bakke Arguments." The *Washington Post*

{ *The* Bakke *Case* }

story told of the unusual and very exciting events that took place inside and outside the courtroom. "Not since the court ruled against Richard Nixon three years ago had there been such a scene. People waited throughout a chill October night for a chance at the few public seats inside. They carried placards and banners and cheered as their lines grew and wound down the marble steps and around the corner. And all for an old reason, and an emotional cause—race."

———

The experienced lawyer carefully prepares for the brief time before the justices. One Washington, D.C., lawyer who has argued before the Court said that he locked his law office door while preparing for the oral argument. "I stuffed myself with every bit of fact that I possibly can [*sic*]; to familiarize myself with all of the legal arguments and the lines of argument that might develop, and possibly to play a kind of 'what if' chess game: If I make this move and he makes that move and I counter thataway, what will happen."

Bert Neuborne, a leading ACLU lawyer and an experienced advocate before the High Bench, once spoke about the strategy that a good advocate must develop when arguing in the Supreme Court: "The role of the lawyer going up to the Supreme Court is to assemble a coalition of five votes. . . . All of us are acutely conscious of the voting patterns of the various justices and what we do is to try to plug the case into those voting patterns, to maximize the chance that five of them, based on their past voting records, will vote with us on the case."

In the *Bakke* oral arguments, two of the three advocates, Archibald Cox for the petitioner and Wade McCree for the U.S. government, were experienced advocates. Reynold Colvin was not; *Bakke* was his first appearance before the justices. (His inexperience and his lack of any ascertainable strategy did lead to some exasperated comments from the justices.) Because of the importance of the affirmative action controversy and the fact that the U.S. solicitor general was a participant in the argument, the Court gave each side one hour to present its arguments.

Before the justices enter the courtroom to hear and participate in oral arguments, they too prepare for the dialogue. Typically, that occurs with the reading of "bench memos" prepared by each justice's law clerk, who has worked on that case since the petition for certiorari was received by the Court.

Bench memos are five- to twenty-five-page summaries, prepared by a justice's law clerk, of the salient facts and questions of law posed in a particular case. William J. Brennan's law clerk, Allan Taylor, began his unusually lengthy bench memo: "This memo attempts to summarize the original papers in *Bakke*, to indicate the extent to which the factual assertions of the parties and the findings and factual assumptions of the California courts are supported by the record, and to point out issues as to which the record is silent." Throughout the memo, the clerk prepared possible questions for Brennan to ask Cox, McCree, and Colvin. For example, after presenting information gleaned from the record about the UCD special minority admissions program, there appeared two questions: "How many special program applicants actually matriculated in 1973 and 1974—was it 16 in each year? Record page 69 indicates that only half of those offered admission from that program actually matriculated. Question: How many disadvantaged whites were offered admission in each year and how many matriculated?"

Taylor advised his boss about what issue he should focus on during oral argument. In *Bakke*, he noted that the faculty was convinced that a "special admissions program is the only method whereby the school can produce a diverse student body which will include qualified students from disadvantaged backgrounds, that few, if any, blacks, Chicanos, Indians, or Orientals would be able to get into Davis or any other medical school, without the special or similar programs. The record is barren of any other evidence of availability of alternative means." He concluded by telling Brennan: "Despite the paucity of the record, . . . I hope we can reject the Government's suggestion that we remand for an examination into the reasons for adopting that particular means."

Justice John P. Stevens received his memo on October 8, 1977, from Marc Richman, one of his two law clerks. Richman wrote his boss that "my brief study of this case convinces me that the judgment of the California Supreme Court should be reversed and the case remanded for consideration of whether the special admissions program at Davis violates the Federal Civil Rights Statutes. However, the Court may first wish to direct the parties, and the United States, to brief the question."

Ellen Silberman's bench memo to her boss, Justice Thurgood Marshall, dated September 13, 1977, said: "I suspect it is too late for the Court to choose to not decide this case on the merits, but I feel I should point out a couple of things which make this an unfortunate case for the Court to use to announce its views on affirmative action." She pointed out that the record was very underdeveloped. "It is ludicrous that there is absolutely nothing in the record on the issue [of what other alternatives could have been used by UCD] to achieve diversity in the medical school. Clearly, a much better case for this program could have been made by California." Concluding, she wrote that what *Bakke* "really comes down to is are we going to put an end to all attempts to bring minorities and particularly Negroes out of the lowest level occupations and into the mainstream of America. This short term race consciousness is essential if there will ever be racial harmony in this country."

All the justices in the *Bakke* litigation, even the absent Harry Blackmun, received bench memos from their clerks. Using those documents as their primary data, the justices, except for Blackmun, participated in the two-hour *Bakke* oral argument.

Archibald Cox, at the time a sixty-five-year-old Harvard Law School professor and legal scholar, was a tall, crew-cut, ramrod-straight New Englander accustomed to arguing before the Court "in magisterial tones," noted the *Washington Post*. As U.S. solicitor general appointed by President John F. Kennedy in 1961, Cox had often participated in oral argument before the justices. All told, he had argued dozens of cases before the justices and was at home and assured before the brethren.

A few of the brethren knew him personally because of his prior work in the Court as General. All knew of him as the special prosecutor, appointed by President Richard M. Nixon to investigate the "Watergate" matter, who was fired on Saturday evening, October 21, 1973, by the president because Cox was relentless in his quest for the secret tapes held by the president.

Given Cox's experiences and the fact that he taught at a university that had a "model" admission policy that took race and ethnicity into account in making admission judgments, Reidhaar and the University of California regents asked him to help them prepare the case after certiorari was granted. Because of his prior association with the Court, Cox argued the public university's position before the brethren. (He shared his allotted hour with the U.S. solicitor general: forty-five minutes for Cox and fifteen minutes for McCree.)

Cox started off by presenting the petitioners' central theme once again: "Whether a state university, which is forced by limited resources to select a relatively small number of students from a much larger number of well-qualified applicants, is free, voluntarily, to take into account the fact that a qualified applicant is black, Chicano, Asian, or Native American, in order to increase the number of qualified members of these minority groups trained for the educated professions and participating in them, professions from which minorities were long excluded because of generations of pervasive racial discrimination."

Cox argued that special admissions are the only workable method of increasing minority group enrollment in professional schools to overcome the effects of past national injustice. The reality is that "there is no racially blind method of selection which will enroll today more than a trickle of minority students in the nation's colleges and professions." Almost immediately the questions began.

JUSTICE STEVENS STARTED OFF: "Do you agree, then, that there was a quota of 84?"

COX: "I would deny that it was a quota—"

JUSTICE STEVENS, INTERRUPTING: "And then, why not?"

COX: "This is not something imposed from outside, as the quotas are in employment, or the targets are in employment, sometimes, today. . . . [The UCD plan] doesn't point the finger at any group, it doesn't say to any group, 'You are inferior,' it doesn't promise taking people regardless of their qualifications, regardless of what they promise society, promise the school, or what qualities they have."

POWELL: "Does it really matter what we call this program, a target or a quota?"

COX: "No, the salient fact is that the program does not stigmatize."

Rehnquist then chimed in with a hypothetical: "What if the UCD had decided that, [because there was a dramatic need for minority doctors], they would set aside 50 seats, until that balance were redressed and the minority population of doctors equaled that of the population as a whole."

COX RESPONDED: "So long as the numbers are chosen and they are shown to be reasonably adaptable to the social goal, then there's no reason to condemn a program because of the particular number chosen."

POWELL CONTINUED THE QUESTIONING: "Would you relate the number in any way to the population [23 percent minority in 1977]?"

COX ANSWERED: "As the number gets higher, the finding of invidiousness increases and social purposes are diminished. I'll be quite frank to say that I think one of the things which causes all of us concern abut these programs is the danger that they will give rise to some notion of group entitlement to numbers, regardless either of the ability of the individual or of their potential contribution to society."

Powell commented that, to him, "it was undesirable to link admissions programs to numbers in the population. The danger was that [such a program] would give rise to the idea of group entitlement to a number of seats."

BURGER CHIMED IN: "Is there any evidence on the record that orientals are disadvantaged?"

COX: "No."

Stevens then raised the troublesome issue: the relevance of Title VI of the 1964 Civil Rights Act. "Do we have to consider the Title VI question before considering the constitutional question?"

COX: "No, because Bakke did not press the issue before and may not raise it here."

JOHN P. STEVENS THEN ASKED COX: "What is invidious discrimination?"

COX: "It is primarily stigmatizing [legislation]—classifying a person as inferior."

Burger wanted to know whether there were other alternatives to the use of a "quota"?

COX: "Other alternatives [building more medical schools and better recruitment of applicants] simply won't work."

Cox closed with a return to his opening remarks, comments made before the questions took him up a number of different roads.

I'd like to direct your attention to one important point, and that's again the significance of the number 16. We submit, first, that the Fourteenth Amendment does not outlaw "race-conscious" programs where there is no invidious purpose or intent, or where they are aimed at offsetting the consequences of our long tragic history of discrimination, and achieving greater racial integrity.

On rebuttal, regarding the argument of a few amici as well as the solicitor general, Powell asked Cox: "Is the record inadequate to make a constitutional decision and should be remanded?"

Cox answered: "I do not agree [with the solicitor general]. I disagree. . . . The Court doesn't need a record to determine whether it's permissible to take race into account in the admissions process."

Wade H. McCree Jr., fifty-seven years of age, the Carter administration's General, and a graduate of Harvard Law School (where Cox taught), spoke after Cox. He had been a federal trial judge prior to his appointment as solicitor general after Carter became president in January 1977. In *Bakke*, he had fifteen minutes to present the government's position.

McCree argued that racism was incorporated into the Constitution in 1787, "in the three-fifths compromise, in the fugitive slave provision, and in the provision preventing the importation of such persons prior to 1808. And it continues until the present day, as the overburdened dockets of the lower federal courts, and indeed of this Court, will indicate."

He urged the justices to find constitutional a program designed to help "persons who were held back to be brought up to the starting line, where the opportunity for equality will be meaningful." Race may be employed, he said in his opening statement, to deal with past and present discrimination.

The remedy for the pervasive racism, McCree said, was preferential affirmative action programs. "The interest of the United States as amicus curiae stems from the fact that the Congress and the executive branch have adopted many minority-sensitive programs that take race or minority status into account in order to achieve the goal of equal opportunity."

Affirmative action practice was the only remedy that worked to diversify the professional school population. "If there is discrimination against a minority with a continuing impact, then preferential treatment is justified."

He pointed out that in 1977 in California, almost half of black school children (40 percent) spent their elementary and secondary education in segregated public schools.

REHNQUIST INQUIRED: "Does the U.S. government care whether the decision [to adopt an affirmative action program] is made by the legislature, the Board of Regents, or the faculty?"

MCCREE: "No, [as long as the] result is the same."

Rehnquist continued, this time asking why Oriental-Americans did not receive any of the sixteen set-asides for minority applicants. "What does the record lack with respect to orientals that it does not with respect to other minorities?"

McCree had no answer to that question.

REHNQUIST: "Do you agree with Cox that we should not consider the Title VI question?"

McCree answered in the affirmative. The Title VI case was not argued in the California courts and "this Court has held that a general principle not raised below may not be raised here in support of a judgment."

Chief Justice Burger raised a final query: Has UCD "ever engaged in any exclusion or discrimination on the basis of race?"

MCCREE, QUICKLY: "There is no evidence in the record."

Interestingly, McCree did not pursue one suggestion presented in the amicus brief he filed a few weeks earlier: reverse and remand the case back to the California courts.

Colvin spoke next. Unlike Cox, who never mentioned Bakke, Colvin's "at times impassioned" presentation, according to the *Washington Post* reporter covering the story, focused solely on Allan Bakke's rights, rights that were violated by the UCD medical school's affirmative action program. His inexperience showed, for he spent nearly half his time repeating the facts in the case.

He began by maintaining that Allan Bakke was the victim of an illegal quota that violated the U.S. Constitution's Equal Protection Clause, the "privileges and immunities" portion of the California constitution, and Title VI of the 1964 Civil Rights Act.

It was unconstitutional because it was based on a racial quota "where sixteen of the one hundred vacancies were filled with minority applicants with lower overall ratings than some majority applicants who were rejected."

JUSTICE STEWART ASKED: "You spoke of a right to admission. You don't seriously suggest that [Bakke] had a right to be admitted?"

COLVIN JUST AS QUICKLY RESPONDED: "That is not Allan Bakke's position. Allan Bakke's position is that he has a right, and that right is not to be discriminated against by reason of his race. And that's what brings Allan Bakke to this Court."

He continued in this fashion, presenting data from his brief on the merits, until an exasperated Justice Powell inquired: "We are here, at least I am here, primarily to hear a constitutional argument. You have devoted 20 minutes to belaboring the facts, if I may say so. I would like help, I really would, on the constitutional issues. Would you address that?"

That interjection by the mild-mannered jurist from Virginia signaled the others on the bench to raise the constitutional issues with Colvin.

White then asked for Colvin's response to the university's contention "that it was entitled to have a special program and take race into account. . . . What's your response to that?"

COLVIN: "Race is an improper classification in this system. . . . We believe it is unconstitutional."

BURGER: "Why, because it is limited rigidly to 16?"

COLVIN: "No, . . . because the concept of race itself as a classification becomes in our history and in our understanding an unjust and improper basis upon which to judge people."

Justice Marshall, the first, and in 1977 the only, African-American justice to sit on the Court, asked Colvin's reaction to a hypothetical where there was only one seat set aside for minority applicants: "Would it be constitutional if it was one?"

COLVIN: "No, whether it is one, one hundred, two—"

Marshall, annoyed, cut him off with a withering question: "You are talking about your client's rights. Don't these underprivileged people have some rights?"

COLVIN: "They certainly have the right to compete—"

MARSHALL, INTERRUPTING: "To eat cake."

COLVIN: "They have the right to compete. They have the right to equal competition."

MARSHALL: "So numbers are just unimportant?"

COLVIN: "The numbers are unimportant. It is the principle of keeping a man out because of his race that is important."

MARSHALL: "You're arguing about keeping someone out, and the other side is arguing about getting somebody in."

COLVIN: "That's right."

MARSHALL: "So it depends on which way you look at it, doesn't it?"

COLVIN: "It depends on which way you look at it—"

MARSHALL, INCREDULOUS: "It does?"

STEVENS: "Do you dispute that all [the minority students admitted] were qualified?"

BYRON WHITE CHIMED IN: "Do you agree that [racial] goals are compelling?"

Colvin, surprising the justices and the audience, answered in a way that seemed to conflict with his primary argument: They were permissible "to the extent that it gave some clue to the admissions committee, meaning that it ought to consider an applicant's prior history of economic, educational, or whatever deprivation, persecution, or what ever it may be. However, there must be limits [placed] on the race-conscious remedy to compensate for the disadvantage of the individual applicant."

As if to save Colvin, Rehnquist quickly asked him: "Is it a permissible goal to want to increase black doctors in California?"

Colvin responded in a manner that contradicted his last answer: "Taking account of race is per se unconstitutional."

Then Powell asked Colvin: "In a single admission program, could race and sex be factors in the evaluation process for a class of medical students?"

COLVIN RESPONDED: "No, any use of race is per se unconstitutional and in violation of Title VI."

With that, Rehnquist and Burger asked, simultaneously: "Are you asking us to decide the Title VI question?"

COLVIN: "Yes."

REHNQUIST AGAIN: "Where race is taken into account but is not a crucial factor, is that OK?"

COLVIN: "No, [UCD] may not take race into account except to identify disadvantage."

Colvin was categorical in his criticism of racial quotas, even a quota of one. He was trying to persuade the Court to do something the justices rarely do: "Take an absolute position on the question of affirmative action, regardless of the damage to important social values," wrote the *New York Times'* Anthony Lewis.

At the end of a very turbulent two hours (Lewis wrote that it was an "extraordinarily exciting two hours"), the chief justice intoned: "Thank you gentlemen, the case is submitted." The next stage was the justices' discussion of *Bakke*, and other cases argued that week, in their conference session on Friday, October 14, 1977.

The Conference Session after Oral Argument

There is not a great deal of lengthy conversation in the Court's conference session. It is the natural place for the justices to retire to in order to convey to each other their initial response to the constitutional and statutory questions presented in the briefs and oral argument. There is simply no time for the justices to "study a case between the time it was heard and the conference," said Justice Powell after his retirement. He recalled Potter Stewart's comments to him on that matter: "You'd better know as much about a case before you hear it as you will [not review it again] until you write the opinion."

Justice Antonin Scalia once remarked of the conference session: "To call our discussion of a case a conference is really something of a misnomer. It's much more a statement of the views of each of the nine justices." It is the locale where the justices initially discover how they all feel about the legal issue before them. Chief Justice Rehnquist said that the conference "now serves only to discover consensus." Rarely does one justice try to persuade another on the issue. It is, wrote Rehnquist, to a great extent, a very civil process, with little or no controversy between the brethren. "The conference," Rehnquist noted, moves "the Court to a final decision of a case by means of a written opinion."

In 1978 the Court discussed approximately ten to twelve cases heard earlier in the week. In addition, at every conference session the justices also voted on the hundreds of petitions for certiorari received since the last conference session. Given the dramatic increase in the receipt of petitions (in 1977, the Court was receiving more than 5,000 petitions annually) and in the plenary case load of the Court (in 1977, there were more than 140 decisions on the merits handed down by the Court), there was never enough time to do anything but briefly record one's comments and vote on the question.

The chief justice (often referred to as "the Chief") always begins the discussion of a case. He presents his comments and conclusions on the questions of law presented, albeit in summary fashion, thus indicating how he "votes" on the case. After the Chief speaks, the eight associate justices comment, seriatim, starting with the senior associate justice and ending with the Court's freshman justice. By that point, with eight commentaries preceding the junior jurist, there is generally little to be added, and that jurist's comments are very brief. Typically, that jurist simply says, for example: "I join the Chief's position."

Justice Brennan's conference notes provide a glimpse into the *Bakke* conference sessions. Burger said that he "could affirm on Title VI. I have considered what UCD could do constitutionally. Diversity is a consideration but it ought to be sought at lower levels than graduate school. UCD could have make-up courses, etc."

Brennan, the note taker, quickly followed and argued that the UCD use of race was consistent with the Fourteenth Amendment and that the California Supreme Court should be reversed by the Court.

Potter Stewart, an Eisenhower appointee, spoke next. For him, there was "nothing in the Equal Protection clause [that allows] a state [to] bar admissions to whites." He would decide the case on Fourteenth Amendment grounds since that was the basis on which the California Supreme Court decision rested. "If the Equal Protection clause does nothing else, it forbids discrimination based alone on a person's race. That's precisely what the Davis program does and injurious action based on race is unconstitutional." He concluded quickly: "No state agency can take race into account."

Byron White, appointed by President Kennedy in 1962, spoke next. For him, Title VI was inapposite because Congress did not provide for a cause of action for private parties like Bakke. "We must reach the Fourteenth Amendment," he said, concluding that, on that issue, "Davis may set this quota and fill it with qualified Negroes. I'll rely on the legislative and executive view of what's permissible under the Fourteenth Amendment."

Thurgood Marshall said: "I agree substantially with Byron and Bill, although I'm not sure there wasn't a private cause of action present under Title VI. On the quota question, this is not a quota to keep people out—it is a quota to get someone in."

It was Lewis Powell's turn (because Justice Harry Blackmun was ill and back in Minnesota). He said: "I can't join Thurgood, Byron, and Bill in thinking that sixteen or eighty-four or any quota was OK. [If I believed that, then] the symbolic effect of the Fourteenth Amendment is completely lost." Powell said that "the colossal blunder here was [when UCD] picked a number. Diversity is a necessary goal to allow a broad spectrum of Americans an opportunity for graduate school. Each applicant should be able to compete with others and taking race into account [such as done in the Harvard admissions process] is proper—but never setting aside a fixed number of places. I agree that the California Supreme Court judgment must be reversed insofar as it enjoins Davis from taking race into account."

The next to speak was Associate Justice Rehnquist. He said: "Basically, I agree with Potter Stewart. I don't agree with Lewis that race can be taken into account. Title VI is more difficult for me—I'm not sure that there isn't a private cause of action and I'm not sure that Title VI and the Fourteenth Amendment are congruent."

The last to comment on *Bakke* was the Court's junior associate justice, John Paul Stevens. He told his colleagues that he "would decide *Bakke* on Title VI. If Bill, Thurgood, and Byron prevailed, we'd have a permanent conclusion that blacks can never reach the point where they'd not be discriminated against. Affirmative action programs have performed a fine service but they ought to be temporary—[However] I can't ever believe the day would come when the two track admission system would be unnecessary. If we can duck the constitutional holding, we should."

After Stevens concluded, the tally of the eight justices showed that there were three men, Brennan, Marshall, and White, who would reverse the California Supreme Court decision in its entirety. A quartet of justices—the Chief, Stewart, Stevens, and Rehnquist—would affirm the California Supreme Court judgment in its entirety.

One, Lewis Powell, believed that race could be used as a factor in the admissions process but that the UCD process was an unconstitutional racial quota; therefore the California Supreme

Court should be affirmed in part and reversed in part. While the ill Justice Blackmun would participate because he could listen to tapes of the oral arguments and had all the briefs filed by the parties and the amici, it would be some time before the brethren heard from him.

Immediately after the conference, when each of the justices is back in chambers and after they all have had "debriefing" discussions with their law clerks, the fur begins to fly. Within hours, at times, the first memos, sometimes heated ones, are written. Tempers flare, voices are raised, and passionate debate through the written word takes place. *Bakke* was no exception. Four of the justices were convinced that, at some point, they would have to answer the constitutional question. As Powell wrote to his colleagues: If they decided *Bakke* on statutory grounds without dealing with the constitutional question, "again we will have resolved finally nothing." He warned his brethren that "any action by us that may be perceived as ducking this issue for the second time in three years would be viewed by many as a 'self-inflicted wound' on the Court."

Brennan, White, and Marshall agreed with Powell's contention, although not with the standard (strict scrutiny) he proposed the Court use to decide the matter. Brennan believed that standard should be used in cases where race was used to stigmatize and demean. In the UCD case, where race was used for remedial purposes, the standard should not be strict scrutiny but "nonetheless . . . scrutiny more exacting than minimal rationality."

Marshall insisted on using his more flexible standard, one that he had discussed and used on a number of occasions before *Bakke*. It took into account the importance of the governmental purpose as well as the severity of the discrimination. He also argued, as he did in all "equality" cases, that the Court could not deal with the issue of affirmative action in the purely rational legalistic fashion appropriate for an ideal world. Furthermore, for Marshall, the "legality of affirmative action simply could not be resolved without consideration of the historical, legal, and sociological context of past racial policies and practices."

William Rehnquist also believed that the Court had to deal

with the *Bakke* case on the merits. Rehnquist wrote to his colleagues: "I take it as a postulate that difference in treatment of individuals based on their race or ethnic origin is at the bulls-eye of the target at which the Fourteenth Amendment's Equal Protection Clause was aimed."

He rejected Marshall's law clerk's contention that the Fourteenth Amendment and Title VI "protects only minorities." For Rehnquist, "the thing prohibited [in the Constitution and in the statute] is discrimination on the basis of race, any race." For Rehnquist, the standard the Court had to use was the strict scrutiny one—one that accepted the notion that the Constitution was color-blind.

Chief Justice Burger and the recently appointed Justice Stevens were the only ones who urged avoidance of the constitutional issue from the beginning. They did not want the Court to decide the case by interpreting the Fourteenth Amendment's Equal Protection Clause.

The Chief hoped that the brethren would not imprudently move toward the constitutional issue simply because the "mildly hysterical media" urged them to do so. Burger urged a prompt resolution, using the strict scrutiny standard when the Court was prepared to address it. And if it were to take years "to work out a rational solution of the current problem, so be it. That is what we are paid for," he wrote his colleagues.

At the end of each conference session, Court majorities emerge on each case discussed. Either the Chief or, if he is not in the majority, the senior associate justice, assigns the writing of the opinion to one of them. Because of the multiplicity of views that did not command a majority along one line of argument, and because the *Bakke* discussion was relisted for conference discussion with Blackmun participating, Burger deferred the assignment in *Bakke* until the entire group spent more time discussing these questions—through "Memos to the Conference"—and until Blackmun gave his colleagues, on May 1, 1978, his long-overdue view of the issue.

In addition, the decision to assign the opinion writer was put off for another important reason: Less than one week after oral arguments, the Court asked the two parties and the U.S. government to file supplemental briefs with the Court.

On October 17, 1977, only five days after the oral arguments in *Bakke*, the Court met to take a vote on whether to ask for supplemental briefs from both parties and the U.S. government. In a 5 to 4 vote (with Blackmun participating via telephone), the justices voted to instruct the parties to prepare supplemental briefs on the question of Title VI "as it applies to this case" and Allan Bakke's standing to sue under Title VI of the 1964 Civil Rights Act.

The chief justice and Justices Byron White, Harry Blackmun, William Rehnquist, and John P. Stevens voted "yes" on the question. Justices Brennan, Marshall, Stewart, and Powell voted not to ask for supplemental briefs on the appropriateness of a private person using Title VI. Justice Powell made a vain effort to stop the Court from calling for a special briefing on the statutory issue. There were "no compelling reasons" for such an order because the Howard University amicus brief in particular (along with a number of others) "about covers the field" on the Title VI question.

Typically, a Title VI action by a federal agency, such as the EEOC or the Department of Labor, is triggered when it receives a complaint from a person—for example, stating that he was discriminated against on account of his color by an institution receiving federal dollars. The agency then seeks to ascertain the validity of the claim of discrimination. If it turns out to be a valid complaint, then the federal agency, not the individual complainant, begins administrative proceedings that could conceivably end all federal funds received by that state agency.

The Court's unusual order for supplemental briefs in *Bakke* was issued because there were at least four justices who believed that the Court should consider basing its judgment on Title VI. The parties and the U.S. as amicus curiae had really not addressed the Title VI issue as substantively as they had the meaning and the scope of the Fourteenth Amendment. It was a segment of the affirmative action controversy that was, in the words of a *Washington Post* reporter, "submerged for about a year."

For the Chief, who was chafing at the media's demand for a quick major constitutional decision on the question, it was appropriate that the justices substantively explore the possibility of resting the *Bakke* decision on statutory grounds. After all, there were four justices leaning in that direction; if one more justice moved to their side, then Burger would have a "court."

On November 16, 1977, Reidhaar's supplemental brief for the petitioner arrived at the Court. His brief noted that "Title VI allows state universities receiving federal funds free to provide more nearly equal educational opportunities to minorities for purposes and in a manner consistent with the 'Equal Protection' clause of the Fourteenth Amendment."

Reidhaar maintained that when one examines the congressional debates surrounding Title VI, the record clearly shows that Congress did not intend to authorize private persons such as Bakke to file private lawsuits and wanted to "tie federal funding to compliance with [Fourteenth Amendment] equal protection standards and not create new standards or new causes of action." Finally, Bakke did not have standing to sue under Title VI.

Title VI, in Reidhaar's view, mirrored the Equal Protection Clause; it was no more or no less than a statutory version of the Fourteenth Amendment. As such, Reidhaar maintained, Title VI "permits voluntary race-conscious affirmative action consistent with the equal protection clause." His conclusion: Do not remand for further examination of this issue; Bakke "is barred from pressing an independent claim under Title VI by his previous conduct of this action."

A day later, November 17, 1977, Colvin's supplemental brief arrived. In it, he argued that Allan Bakke did have a private right of action under Title VI. The legislative record, to him, was clear: private actions were permitted. First of all, Bakke was not required to resort to administrative appeals with the Department of Health, Education, and Welfare before commencing the legal actions in California. The bottom line for Colvin, once again, was that the UCD special program violated the plain language of Title VI.

Contrary to Cox's view of the legislative record on this issue, Colvin maintained that the legislative record prohibited such programs based on racial quotas. Colvin surprised the readers with his final observation: The remedy under Title VI was an inappropriate one for his client. Colvin did not want federal funds to the University of California system to be shut off. The remedy he wanted was admission for Bakke to the UCD medical school!

On November 28, 1977, McCree filed his supplemental brief with the Court. While a private person such as Allan Bakke "may sue" under Title VI, the U.S. government's position was that a minority-sensitive, narrowly tailored program to counter the effects of past discrimination did not violate Title VI.

The UCD program was "designed to assist minority persons in obtaining the benefits of federally assisted programs." Furthermore, he concluded, federal regulations that had interpreted Title VI "endorse minority-conscious programs." The brief ended with a plea to the justices to reverse and remand: to send *Bakke* back because of its defective record.

The Court had sought "help" from the parties and the U.S. government, and the three advocates provided the justices with their views on the appropriateness of using Title VI as a remedy for alleged racial discrimination. There was no oral argument scheduled on this issue. The justices added these supplemental briefs to the thousands of pages of briefs and other materials they had amassed since granting certiorari in *Bakke*.

———

The next, longest, period of time was the eight months between oral argument and the announcement of the Court's decision. It was a time when the brethren wrote and circulated lengthy memo after lengthy memo on the *Bakke* case, trying to persuade just one more member of the Court to change his position on affirmative action. The dynamics of decision making, however, had failed to move any of the brethren when the final judgments were announced in late spring 1978.

CHAPTER 6

Bakke and the Dynamics of Supreme Court Decision Making

It was now decision time for the justices. Although the Chief had decided that there would not be a decisive vote in conference on the case until later in 1978, the flood of memos, circulated by all the brethren except Blackmun (who was still at the Mayo Clinic recovering from prostate surgery), had given the justices a lot to digest as well as a clear sense of how eight of them lined up. In one such extended multipage memo, written in January 1978, Powell wrote that "my first impulse is to 'cringe' when I see another [memo]."

The Process of Reaching a Decision in the Supreme Court

No majority opinion of the U.S. Supreme Court is the work of one jurist. The opinion of the Court must have at least five of the nine men and women agreeing on the decision—to reverse, to affirm, to reverse and remand, and so on—as well as agreeing on the justifications for that decision. If there are fewer than five, then there is only a judgment of the Court. Judgments of the Court occur occasionally in controversial cases, and *Bakke* was no exception. At no time were there five jurists who agreed with each other on the decision and the reasoning.

Ordinarily, after the discussion of a case ends in conference, the discovered consensus leads, no later than the beginning of the next week, to the assignment of the majority opinion writer. This power is generally considered one of the Chief's most important ones. A Chief who knows colleagues, who selects carefully and in a balanced manner so that all justices receive an equal amount of majority opinions to write, is acknowledged as a good "task" leader.

The primary task of the majority opinion writer is the same in every case: hold the majority! The justice assigned the opinion has to draft the order of the Court, and the justifications for that decision, clearly and correctly. The opinion must be written in such a manner that everyone who voted together in the initial conference is with the majority when the opinion is finally announced in open Court. The justice must, as is marvelously shown when observing Justice Brennan's wizardry in *Bakke*, be able to take colleagues' reactions to the draft and somehow massage some of these suggestions into the opinion.

Justice Felix Frankfurter once wrote of the opinion-writing task: "The writer of the Court's opinion is not singing a solo, but leads the orchestra, to wit, the Court." The majority opinion really is a group project with the author the first among equals. As Rehnquist said: "What is significant about opinions for this Court is that they are not statements of a particular Justice's jurisprudence. Rather, they are negotiated documents forged from ideological differences within the Court." There are times when, because of the constant need to negotiate with others in the majority, the writer feels as Justice Oliver Wendell Holmes felt after he received harsh responses to his draft opinion: "The boys generally cut one of the genitals [out of it]."

Once draft opinions and memos are circulated, once the justices seriously focus on the substantive issues in a controversial case such as *Bakke*, there are times when justices change their minds and vote the other way. Even a justice assigned to write the majority opinion has occasionally changed his mind, saying, as Brennan said, "this opinion won't write." All the brethren have had the joy of seeing their dissent turn into a majority opinion or, conversely, the sadness of their majority opinion turning into a dissent because another justice changed his mind.

This gets to one of the central points about the dynamics of Supreme Court decision making: there is a "fluidity" of judicial choice that can lead to shifts in voting blocs—occurring even days before an opinion is announced. As Justice John M. Harlan

II once said: "The books on voting are never closed until the decision actually comes down. Until then any member of the Court is perfectly free to change his vote, and it is not an unheard of occurrence for a persuasive minority opinion to eventuate as the prevailing opinion."

In the *Bakke* era, the Court was led by Chief Justice Warren Earl Burger. He was appointed by Republican President Richard M. Nixon in 1969 to replace the "Super Chief," Earl Warren. Within months of his appointment, Burger showed that he did not have the "people" skills and social and task leadership qualities of his immensely popular predecessor. More problematic for the new Chief was the fact, put bluntly, that Burger was not highly regarded by most of his brethren in two ways. First, he clearly was not a legal scholar, and that dismayed a few of the brethren. More than that, many of his colleagues saw him as a manipulative person who had little difficulty passing in the conference and then voting with the majority cohort in order to assign the opinion, or write it himself, even though his views were not those of the majority.

Until his retirement in 1975, William O. Douglas was the senior associate justice. (With Douglas's retirement, Brennan became senior associate justice.) Douglas, an acerbic loner on the Court, always spoke his mind. For Douglas, Burger's manipulative behavior was intolerable, and there were many memos from Douglas chastising Burger for his boorish behavior in the conference.

One such missive, circulated on May 1, 1972, concerned Burger's assigning an important case even though he was in the minority and Douglas had already assigned the writing to Thurgood Marshall. It was sent after Douglas had received a memo from Burger telling Douglas that he had the vote count wrong in the *Lloyd* case, an important First Amendment case concerning a private shopping center.

An angry Douglas wrote back to the Chief: "The vote was not 5:4 as I had reserved and not voted at all." Angrily, Douglas pointed out basic history: "Historically, the senior in the majority assigns the opinion if the Chief is in the minority. You led the Conference battle against affirmance and that is your privilege. But it is also the privilege of the majority, absent the Chief Justice, to make the assignment. Hence, *Lloyd* was assigned and is assigned."

After Douglas's retirement, Brennan did not circulate such memos, because he was a quite different person. Although Burger continued to try to maximize his assignment role, Brennan continued to frustrate him by criticizing such proposed actions privately. And in the *Bakke* dynamics, given the fragmentation of the Court, there was no way that Burger could substantively control its outcome.

Justice Powell regularly described the U.S. Supreme Court as nine independent law firms. Each has a senior partner—the justice; a number of associates—in 1977, three law clerks selected by the justice to work for a term; and a small staff of three to assist in the management of the office and in the final production of the office's work. Each office does business and battles with the other eight offices. As one law clerk said about this concept: "Justices . . . spend little time with [other justices] and rarely see each other. They often come in and sit by themselves day after day without really talking to any of the other justices."

In such a setting, the law clerk is indispensable. The men and women picked by the justices are the cream of the crop of the nation's top law school graduates. All clerks have two central, demanding jobs: (1) to screen all the petitions for certiorari and to recommend which of the petitions should be granted—and why, and (2) to assist the justice in the writing of all his or her opinions, majority, concurring, or in dissent. As one of Justice Stevens's outgoing law clerks told the new arrivals: "You never really get ahead of the work—you just stay on top of it but that's all you can do. It's a delicately balanced year and you're always on the edge of the precipice." In the end, the justices come to rely heavily on their law clerks. Indeed, their work routine would change radically if the bosses lost their associates.

Chief Justice Rehnquist recently explained his relationship with his law clerks with respect to opinion-writing:

> If I've assigned myself a case coming out of conference, . . . I
> will sit down with the law clerk [who prepared the cert brief

for Rehnquist], and tell him that, you know, I've assigned this to us to write, and [then] go over the conference discussion with the law clerk, tell him what each justice said, and what seems to be the majority of the view [*sic*]. Perhaps, you know, A, B, C, one, two, three, and then tell the law clerk to put together a draft embodying that line of reasoning.

Then the law clerk will . . . give me a rough draft of the line of reasoning that I've talked to him about. And then I will take that and revise it, often substantially shorten it. . . . So then I'll give it back to the law clerk. . . . And then we'll circulate it to the conference. So, some opinions, I would say, that my original contributions to them are definitely a minor part of them, other opinions, my original contributions are a major part of them.

When Lewis Powell arrived at the Court in early 1972, the reality that surprised him the most was the almost total lack of a traditional form of collegiality. He told an interviewer: "I had thought of the Court as a collegial body in which the most characteristic activities would be consultation and co-operative deliberation. . . . I was in for more than a little surprise. . . . A justice may go through an entire term without being once in the chambers of all the other members of the Court."

Most Court decisions are made in the chambers of the justices, with very little personal conversation between the members. Justice Clarence Thomas, who was Marshall's successor, once told a group of visiting law students that he never went into another justice's chambers, "plopped his feet on his colleague's desk," and began to talk about a particular case. Rehnquist repeatedly admonished his colleagues, if they wanted to talk to him about a case, to write their thoughts out in detail and circulate the paper.

The primary group-communications device available to the justices was the memorandum to the conference (MTTC). It worked this way: If Justice Brennan wanted to communicate with the chief justice, generally he would send a memo to Burger—with the notation that "copies to the Conference" were also sent to the other seven members of the Court. (Obviously, if Brennan wanted to send a confidential note to Powell, he would send it only to him.)

In 1978 the memo was a critical factor in the dynamics of U.S. Supreme Court decision making. (At the turn of the twenty-first century, it still remains the major mechanism for transmitting ideas between the nine men and women who sit on the Court.) The memo conveys the ideas, concerns, criticisms, importunisms, and agreements from one justice to all the others.

Harry Blackmun once told the author that the memo has "an impact on the decisional process . . . for it sets forth in specific language the concerns entertained by the author. In some respect, this is better than general observations made orally at conference. And they tend to fill in the gap occasioned by the lack of time for extended conferences or one-on-one conversations. By a Memo, all nine are brought into the discussion."

In *Bakke*, as in all Court cases, the law clerks are the human conveyer belts of information to—and from—their bosses. The memo does the same task—conveying information, views, and attitudes to the justices.

The Supreme Court Tackles *Bakke*, 1977–1978

In *Bakke*, the justices were faced with a few thorny substantive questions, and for two-thirds of a year, they scrambled, jostled, lost their temper with each other, occasionally in very surprising ways, to find the answers and then to try to create a "Court," that is, five votes, behind one set of answers. These perplexing issues were the following:

1. Should *Bakke* be decided on statutory grounds, that is, that Bakke has standing to bring a private cause of action against UCD because the medical school's special admissions policy violated Title VI of the 1964 Civil Rights Act?
2. Should *Bakke* be decided on constitutional grounds, that is, was the UCD special admissions program in violation of the Fourteenth Amendment's Equal Protection Clause?

3. If such a "reverse discrimination" case was to be decided on constitutional grounds, as Justices Douglas's and Brennan's *DeFunis* dissents had urged in 1973, what was the appropriate standard of measurement of constitutionality to be used by the Court? Strict scrutiny, rational relationship, or some other, intermediate, standard?
4. What was the relationship between the protection afforded an individual in Title VI and the Fourteenth Amendment's equal-protection guarantee? Were they saying the same thing? Was one dominant over the other?

Burger, joined by Rehnquist, Stewart, and especially Stevens (Brennan noted in his diary that Burger and Rehnquist "would have decided the case on constitutional grounds but for JPS's insistence"), believed that, as a matter of judicial prudence, the constitutional issue should not be addressed and that the Court should affirm—in its entirety—the California Supreme Court decision on Title VI grounds alone.

Three other jurists, Marshall, Brennan, and White, believed that the decision had to be overturned on both Title VI and constitutional grounds: The special admissions plan was permissible under Title VI because race was used in a benign manner in an affirmative action program. As a matter of constitutional law, and for the same reason, the UCD special admissions plan did not violate the Fourteenth Amendment's Equal Protection Clause. Two men had not yet taken hard and fast positions in *Bakke* at this time (the end of October 1977): Justices Powell and Blackmun.

Burger, to the surprise of all his brethren, actually helped matters a great deal in two ways: First, he deferred assigning the *Bakke* opinion-writing task until there was "a definitive Conference vote." He also encouraged his brethren to "circulate memoranda" on the perplexing and complex issues they faced in *Bakke*.

One result of the Chief's suggestions, as Powell wrote, was "an unprecedented volume of circulations in this case." According to Powell's records in *Bakke*, from the end of October 1977 to mid-January 1978, there were no less than one dozen lengthy MTTCs sent by all the brethren, except for the absent Harry

Blackmun and Potter Stewart. (The Chief circulated one; Brennan, two; White, two; Marshall, one; Powell, four; Rehnquist, one; and Stevens, one.)

It was Byron White's memo, the day before the Court's October 14, 1977, initial conference after *Bakke* was argued, that led the Chief to suggest circulating memos. White's memo was unusual because it came before the discussion and vote. As he wrote: "Although not in accord with practice, I thought I would spare you listening to what I would initially say about the *Bakke* case in conference tomorrow in the event I was not dissuaded by the views of those who precede me."

All the justices, appreciating the complexity and the "politics" surrounding a decision of this importance, readily accepted the Chief's two suggestions. As Justice Rehnquist wrote to the brethren on November 11, 1977, "While [circulating memoranda] is not the 'usual' practice, . . . I have derived some benefit from [White's] and others' subsequent written circulations. I also think that some written comments before Conference on a case this complicated and multifaceted could save a lot of time in what is bound to be a long Conference discussion anyway."

After the first conference session, Burger knew he needed one more vote to cobble together a majority to affirm the California Supreme Court decision. Looking around, there seemed to be some hope. First of all, his best friend Harry Blackmun (who had been best man at his wedding, as he had at Harry's), was a possibility for a "join"—but Burger also knew that he could not push Blackmun into announcing his position until Blackmun was ready. The other possibility, very slim, was Powell. From the beginning of these discussions on higher-education affirmative action, he had repeatedly mentioned the merits of the Harvard College admissions program, which used race, among other factors, in the decision to admit an applicant to Harvard.

The Chief's optimism, from the outset of the debates, the memos, and the notes surrounding *Bakke*, was muted. Nevertheless, as Chief he had to forcefully express his views, hoping that the ideas and the words would lead to fluidity when the final tally was made.

Chief Justice Burger's views on *Bakke*, sent in a memo on October 21, 1977, set the tone for the succeeding eight months of circulating memoranda and hearing arguments in the conferences on *Bakke*. The Court must find a way, he wrote, "to affirm the California Supreme Court without putting the states, their universities, or any educational institutions in a straitjacket on the matter of broader based admissions programs." Courts do not belong in the business of "establishing fixed ground rules for educators. . . . We have far more competence to say what cannot be done than what ought to be done."

The UCD special admissions program, said the Chief, "as presently structured, is one of the more extreme methods of securing [commendable] objectives. The program excluded Bakke from the medical school on the basis of race and this is not disputed."

Next, Burger raised what was for him "the tactical consideration of how best to structure and shape a result so as to confine its impact and yet make it clear that the Court intends to leave the states free to serve as 'laboratories' for experimenting with less rigidly exclusionary methods of pursuing social goals." To begin with, the Court must apply the strict scrutiny test in *Bakke*. Applying the test, Burger concluded that UCD's "sound and desirable objectives" did not provide sufficient justification for the rigid, plainly racial bias of the Regents' Program. "I simply cannot believe the Regents' frankly race-based program is the least offensive or least intrusive method of promoting an admittedly important state interest."

The Chief then presented what he (and his law clerks, who did all of the research for him—as did the law clerks for the other eight brethren) felt were "many ways" UCD could pursue these goals "short of completely excluding whites from competing for a certain number of places in its entering class." (These included a variety of remedial programs used by many colleges, but Burger "would leave open whether and to what extent indirect consideration of race is compatible with constitutional or statutory proscriptions.")

As for the disposition of *Bakke*, Burger wrote: "The Regents' program surely appears to be in plain conflict with the explicit language of Title VI. It seems to me, as of now, that our long practice and policy has been to base our decision on the statutory ground." The other three justices in this "gang of four," to use Brennan's descriptor, favored affirming the state supreme court's decision and agreed with Burger on the need to base their decision on statutory rather than constitutional grounds.

Justice Rehnquist's lengthy memo came on November 10, 1977, less than a month after the oral arguments. In its nineteen pages he rejected UCD's justifications for the special admissions plan. "In this case," wrote Rehnquist, the UCD admissions policy "seems to me to make its 'affirmative action' program as difficult to sustain constitutionally as one conceivably could be. I take it as a postulate that difference in treatment of individuals based on their race or ethnic origin is at the bulls-eye of the target at which the Fourteenth Amendment's Equal Protection Clause was aimed."

He also rejected out of hand the argument made by some amici that the justification for the UCD program was "that the Fourteenth Amendment protects only minorities." His reading of the history of the amendment "suggests that the thing prohibited is discrimination based on race, any race. . . . The reason for the prohibition is that classification of individuals on the basis of race is, except in the rarest of cases, not a permissible basis of governmental action."

Rehnquist then argued that the "strict scrutiny" test had to be used in *Bakke* and that, in his estimate, there were no compelling state interests, with the accompanying narrowly tailored procedures, to validate the UCD special admissions process. He agreed with the Chief "that it would be very difficult to view as constitutionally sufficient most of the proffered non-race goals. . . . All are based on notions of administrative convenience and I think . . . it takes something more to justify a classification based on race."

Ending, he said that "since we are awaiting briefs on Title VI, and the sort of research that has been done in Thurgood's and John's Chambers has not been done in mine, I withhold judgment on that question."

The junior justice, appointed less than three years earlier, was John Paul Stevens. From the beginning, Stevens was clearly interested in seeing *Bakke* resolved on statutory grounds. In an important October 9, 1977, memo from one of his law clerks, Marc Richman, Stevens was told that "the Court may first wish to direct the parties, and the United States, to brief the question [which did occur]. Of course, the Court could decide the statutory question without a remand."

Although the statutory issue had been raised in the superior court, the California Supreme Court, wrote the clerk to Stevens, "completely ignored this potentially dispositive ground, and rushed directly to the federal constitution. This Court should not do the same thing." Furthermore, he wrote, very few amici "confront the statutory questions," and "the parties, and the SG, are woefully deficient on this matter." Clearly, for Stevens's law clerk, the statutory issue was paramount over the constitutional issue. Justice Stevens wholeheartedly agreed with Richman.

From the first, Stevens saw *Bakke* not as a class action but as litigation "between two specific litigants." The controversy, he argued, must be resolved by the justices' statutory construction of Title VI of the 1964 Civil Rights Act. There was no need to raise the constitutional issues if, through interpretation of a statute, a remedy was found.

Unlike Powell and the Brennan group, Stevens and his allies believed that Title VI was not merely a statutory restatement of the Fourteenth Amendment. Title VI had "independent force, with language and emphasis in addition to that found in the Constitution."

Finally, Stevens held adamant views about the scope of a *Bakke* decision. For the quartet, as Stevens wrote in his final draft, "it is perfectly clear that the question whether race can ever be used as a factor in the admissions decision is not an issue in this case, and that discussion of that issue is inappropriate." In the end, his opinion for the quartet did not reach the constitutional question. As a consequence, in *Bakke* only five of the nine brethren spoke to the meaning and the scope of the Fourteenth Amendment's Equal Protection Clause: Lewis Powell and the Brennan quartet.

By November 1977, a trio of justices, White, Marshall, and Brennan, had expressed themselves on the constitutionality of the UCD special admissions program. For them it was a legitimate effort to address the consequences of centuries of discrimination against African Americans and other minorities. All believed, as Brennan wrote in November, that "Title VI affords no escape from deciding the constitutional issue." For them, as well as for Powell, Title VI "essentially incorporates Fourteenth Amendment standards and treats affirmative action as does the Amendment."

They agreed with Brennan's belief that the Fourteenth Amendment "stat[ed] an abstract principle of color-blind equality without reference to the national will to eradicate the legacy of slavery and racism which gave it birth is to be blind to history." The trio also maintained that a particular kind of state action "triggers the Fourteenth Amendment protection": Did the state agency "in fact use race with ill will toward anyone. [Did UCD] on account of race, insult or demean a human being by stereotyping his or her capacities, integrity, or worth as an individual?" For them, the answer was no. "The Fourteenth Amendment does not tolerate government action that causes any to suffer from the prejudice or contempt of others on account of race."

For Brennan and the others, "under any standard of Fourteenth Amendment review other than one requiring absolute colorblindness, the Davis program clearly passes muster. . . . [It] used race in furtherance of educational and social objectives that are proper and even compelling." For them, in the words of Byron White: "the [appropriate and limited] principle [was that] preferences may be extended to racial minorities as a means of compensating for or eliminating the effects of past racial discrimination, whether private or public."

Justice Marshall sent his sharply worded memo on April 13, 1978. He opened it with his oft-repeated view of the problem: "I repeat, for next to the last time: the decision in this case depends on whether you consider the action of the Regents as admitting certain students or as excluding certain other students." The former group would see the UCD program as "affirmative action to remove the vestiges of slavery and state imposed segregation by 'root and branch.' If you view the program as excluding students, it is a program of 'quotas' which violates the principle that the 'Constitution is color-blind.'" (After this sentence, Marshall penned: "Take your choice." However, that phrase and others like it were removed by Marshall before the memo was circulated.)

Then, in his inimitable style, Marshall wrote: "As to this country being a melting pot—either the Negro did not get into the pot or he did not get melted down. . . . If only the principle of color-blindness had been accepted by the majority in *Plessy* in 1896, we would not be faced with this problem in 1978. . . . For us to now say that the principle of color-blindness prevents the University from giving 'special' consideration to race when this Court, in 1896, licensed the states to continue to consider race, is to make a mockery of the principle of 'equal justice under law.'"

Marshall concluded with an emphatic statement: "We are stuck with this case. We must decide it. We are not yet all equals, in large part because of the refusal of the *Plessy* Court to adopt the principle of color-blindness. It would be the cruelest irony for this Court to adopt the dissent in *Plessy* now and hold that the University must use color-blind admissions."

All who study the contemporary goings-on of the U.S. Supreme Court know that Justice Harry A. Blackmun painfully agonized over many cases, a pattern that led to inevitable delays before he announced his decision. By the beginning of February 1978, the votes were split: 4 (Burger, et al.) to 1 (Powell) to 3 (Brennan, et al.). All were eagerly awaiting Harry Blackmun's input after he recovered from prostate surgery. He had returned in January 1978, and months later there was still silence from him.

Blackmun's failure to express his view literally held up the decision in *Bakke* for months. Brennan failed to move Blackmun. Brennan wrote in his diary that "in April, the only wish shared by all the brethren regarding *Bakke* was that Harry cast his vote." It led his friend the chief justice to visit Blackmun in chambers in April to try to find out when Blackmun's input could be expected. Blackmun told him firmly that he was not yet ready to vote. They would simply have to wait!

Although there were four justices (Powell, Marshall, Brennan, and White) who agreed that admissions decisions using race as a factor were not per se unconstitutional, they were divided on what standard should be used to determine the validity of various affirmative action programs. All of the brethren, even the four who wanted to rule on statutory grounds only, had something to say about what standard should be used in reaching a constitutional judgment.

A few weeks after the Marshall memo was read by Blackmun and the others, on May 1, 1978, Blackmun finally spoke. Brennan, White, and Marshall got their wish—Harry Blackmun came down foursquare on their side. "Thank you," Blackmun wrote in the cover letter, "for the patience of each and all of you. *Bakke* is of such importance that I refused to be drawn into a precipitate conclusion. I wanted the time to think about it and to study the pertinent material. . . . I do not apologize; I merely explain."

After reading the tons of paper on *Bakke* written by his brethren, especially Marshall's tough mid-April draft opinion, "and having given the matter earnest and, as some of my clerical friends would say, 'prayerful' consideration," Blackmun joined Brennan, Marshall, and White. What he said pleased Marshall more than anything any of his other colleagues said in the *Bakke* discussions.

Blackmun maintained that Title VI did not prohibit UCD's type of race-conscious special admissions program. Affirmative actions were necessary, and they were not inconsistent with the Fourteenth Amendment. Addressing Rehnquist's abstract, rigid, color-blind world, Blackmun stated, simply, that "this is not an ideal world. . . . We live in a real world."

Blackmun understood what Marshall was trying to get the brethren to comprehend. For him, "Title VI, as with the Fourteenth Amendment, was concerned with the unconstitutional use of race criteria, not with the use of race as an appropriate remedial feature." Addressing the abstract notions of equality that Rehnquist relied on, Blackmun wrote:

The original aims [of the Fourteenth Amendment] persist. And that, in a distinct sense, is what affirmative action, in the light of proper facts, is all about. To be sure, it conflicts with idealistic equality in the sense that Bill Rehnquist proposes, but if there is tension here it is original Fourteenth Amendment tension and a part of the Amendment's very nature until equality is achieved. . . . It is the unconstitutional use of race that is prohibited, not the constitutional use.

As was noted afterwards, "it appears to have been Marshall's opinion that most affected Blackmun." Blackmun himself, in his May 1, 1978, memo, acknowledged his indebtedness to Marshall: "There is much to be said for Marshall's 'cruelest irony' approach as set forth in his memorandum of April 13."

Outside the Court, the delay in announcing the Court's judgment led to interest-group activity. Some groups planned marches on the Court in support of or in opposition to Allan Bakke. For example, on April 6, 1978, the captain of the Supreme Court police sent a memo to the justices advising them that "a permit has been granted to the National Committee to Overturn the Bakke Decision [and others, the National Lawyers Guild, the Black American Law Students Association, and the Peoples Alliance] to conduct a mass march, with signs, placards, and bullhorns on Saturday, April 15, 1978 from 1:00 P.M. . . . There are indications that about 10,000 persons are expected to participate in the march."

Although he had written a number of MTTCs since his first one in November 1977, it wasn't until mid-May 1978 that Justice Brennan reluctantly concluded that he would have to write a separate opinion for himself and the three others who believed that the California Supreme Court should be reversed in its entirety. What led him to that conclusion was the fact that Powell's views on race and what standard to use when examining the question were so far apart from his own that a unified, that is, a five-justice, partial reversal was out of the question. At best, to maintain the existence of affirmative action programs across the nation, there was the need for a Brennan-written opinion that dissented in part from but also concurred in part with the Powell opinion.

This strategy meant that Brennan had to work hard with Powell on those parts of Powell's judgment that reversed the California Supreme Court ruling, while at the same time (and while he was writing and reading on three other cases) drafting an opinion that "held" the votes of Blackmun, White, and Marshall. It was to be an incredibly herculean task for the wizard of compromise, probably the most daunting of his more than three decades of efforts at "cobbling" together Court opinions.

Powell, by mid-May 1978, however, had circulated six memos. He said in all of them that UCD violated the Fourteenth Amendment's Equal Protection Clause because that clause prohibited all programs where race was the only factor in the admissions process.

Early on, Brennan began talking with Powell about his position. If Powell stood firm, it made no difference how Blackmun might vote. Powell would become the fifth vote against affirmative action. After a number of one-on-one visits where the Harvard College admissions process was discussed, Brennan finally exhorted Powell to distinguish between the UCD "quota" and other affirmative action programs where race was one of a number of factors taken into consideration by admissions committees. Subsequent memos displayed Powell's new, critically important, position on race and affirmative action.

By May 1978 Powell noted that if the Court merely affirmed the state court judgment without giving further guidance about when and under what circumstances race might be used in affirmative action programs, it would be shirking its responsibility. He believed that it was erroneous to hold, as the state court did, "that race may never be considered to any extent in admitting students to a university."

Powell would remain firmly in the middle—and in the driver's seat. Unlike Burger's quartet, Powell believed that race could be a factor—one of many—taken into account by a college's or graduate school's admissions committee. However, unlike Brennan's "gang," he rejected the view that the challenged UCD program was constitutional. As he wrote in January 1978: "I consider it both necessary to a reasoned opinion, as well as prudential, to negate petitioner's basic position by demonstrating that valid and less restrictive means are available to further the asserted states interest."

Powell also disagreed with the Brennan cohort over which standard to use when determining constitutionality: Powell defended the use of the strict scrutiny standard. Brennan disagreed, writing that "my position [is] that racial classifications established for remedial purposes, which do not demean or stigmatize, are not subject to 'strict scrutiny.'"

For the Virginian, the UCD scheme was too extreme a remedy. As he said in his January 5, 1978, memo: "The need for resolution of the issue certainly has not lessened. If the Court now were to affirm this case on Title VI without reaching the Fourteenth Amendment, again we will have resolved finally exactly nothing."

With Blackmun's thoughts now on the table, the Court was clearly split 4 to 1 to 4. Burger, as chief justice, would make the assignment. Brennan, the senior associate justice, knowing of Burger's "use [of the] assignment power in an unorthodox manner in other important cases," went to the Chief and suggested that Powell write the opinion. Powell was suggested because he was the only one of the nine justices "not in partial dissent." It was an unbelievably difficult task; Powell had to "find a common ground on which five could join with respect to both parts of the judgment." Burger's initial response, according to Brennan, was to reject the proposal, but he changed his mind very quickly.

On May 2, 1978, the day after the brethren received and read Blackmun's letter, they received a memo from the Chief. Burger wrote: "Given the posture of this case, Bill Brennan and I conferred with a view to considering what may fairly be called a 'joint' assignment. There being four definitive decisions tending one way, four another, Lewis' position can be joined in part by some or all of each 'four group.' Accordingly, the case is assigned to Lewis who assures a first circulation within one week from today."

Brennan then had a personal meeting with Powell. Powell told Brennan "that he expected the process of reaching a consensus among five [Powell plus the Brennan quartet] to reverse that part of the [California Supreme Court] judgment prohibiting the use of race would be long and difficult but that he was ready to try."

Clearly, at this point and thereafter, the key justice in *Bakke* was Lewis Powell. He was to say, at the time of his retirement in 1987, that *Bakke* "was his most important opinion." According to his biographer, Powell had resolved the affirmative action questions very early on in the *Bakke* discussions. He believed that it would be disastrous for the nation if the Court invalidated affirmative action programs. "On the other hand," said Powell, it would be equally disastrous to give carte blanche for racial preferences (such as the UCD plan).

His support for some type of affirmative action came as a surprise to his colleagues. As a former Virginia school board administrator involved with desegregation of the public schools, Powell "did no more than was required to hasten desegregation. On the great question of busing, he resolutely opposed minority aspirations. . . . For this unresisting heir to the traditions of white supremacy to have endorsed reverse discrimination would have been . . . inconceivable. Yet on the Court he did just that." As a "pragmatic conservative," Powell accepted affirmative action, as he had accepted *Brown* in 1954, because it was necessary to do so. By May 9, 1978, Powell circulated the first of eight *Bakke* draft opinions (the last circulated on June 23, 1978, just five days before the *Bakke* case was announced in open court). Immediately Brennan and Marshall told Powell they could not accept any of it because he had used the strict scrutiny standard to strike down the UC Davis program.

Powell's use of the strict scrutiny standard in *Bakke*, even though the university's discrimination was the central element in a remedial effort to improve professional opportunities for minorities, was at the very least insensitive, thought Justice Marshall. Furthermore, the expression of his views seemed patently racist to Marshall. Powell had written (and was to leave the sentences in his final version), for example, that

it is far too late to argue that the guarantee of equal protection to all persons permits the recognition of special wards entitled to a degree of protection greater than that accorded others. The Fourteenth Amendment is not directed solely against discrimination due to a "two-class theory"—that is, based upon differences between white and Negro.

Marshall had fought legal battles for decades against gentrified education board lawyers like Powell in Virginia, Mississippi, Alabama, and Georgia, precisely because of "racial discrimination due to a 'two-class theory.'" Powell, in Marshall's view, retained "remnants of old [Southern ways and] attitudes." He earned Marshall's disdain because Powell, according to his biographer, "still had a gentleman's sense of responsibility for the less fortunate and a southerner's instinct for paternalism toward blacks."

These southern traits of Powell's enraged Marshall. Marshall wrote him that "I will dissent 'in toto.' I doubt that I can join any part of your opinion." Brennan recorded in his diary that his friend Thurgood "was livid over LFP's opinion which he regarded as racist."

The irony in this horribly strained relationship was that Marshall knew that without Powell's vote in *Bakke* (and in the almost one dozen affirmative action cases that followed), all affirmative action programs would have been killed. Clearly, as *Bakke* illustrates, Powell's was "the key vote." What galled Marshall was the fact that "he owed his victory to the Court's lone southerner, a former segregationist and consistent foe of forced busing, the Justice whose background seemed least likely to produce the decisive vote for affirmative action." But without Powell's opinion on the use of racial preferences, strongly held from beginning to end, "*Bakke* would probably have been the death-knoll of all voluntary affirmative action programs. . . . It would have dealt as serious a blow to integration as *Plessy v. Ferguson*."

Justice Brennan was the jurist on the Court who was able to move the tribunal to judgment. Bill Brennan was very different from Chief Justice Burger in appearance and in intellect, as well as jurisprudentially. Burger was the living portrait of what a chief justice should look like: ruggedly handsome, over six feet tall, with pure white flowing hair, and with a very magisterial voice. Brennan, on the other hand, the possessor of a "keen intelligence," was described as "small and feisty, almost leprechaun-like in appearance, yet he has a hearty bluffness and an ability to put people at ease."

Bill Brennan, acknowledged by all his colleagues as the Court's grand wizard of compromise, negotiation, and cobbling majorities in the twentieth century, knew that he had to work very hard to keep his trio together. The difficult person, thought Brennan, was Marshall. (He was, it turned out, wrong on that score.) Brennan, Marshall's only real friend on the Court, knew of Marshall's disdain for Powell. Somehow he had to convince Marshall to join the others and concur in the appropriate segments of the Powell opinion.

If Brennan failed, the affirmative action remedy, one practiced across the nation in education, would be in jeopardy. As he wrote in his diary in July 1978, "it was immediately apparent to me that HAB's vote, if it could be counted upon, meant at least a partial victory for the view [about benign race discrimination] I had championed." To get even a partial victory, Marshall had to be a part of the Brennan quartet!

As Brennan soon found out, his problem was not with Marshall, but with the other two brethren: the laconic, at times unreasonable and petty Justice Byron R. White and the sensitive, stoic, and very plodding jurist, Harry A. Blackmun.

Bakke was one of dozens of opinions being prepared at the same time. Brennan, as the senior justice in the group, made the writing assignments when the Chief was not part of that cohort. Because Brennan's office had "four other Court opinions in progress and each of the clerks was occupied assisting on these," Brennan asked White to prepare a draft opinion for the quartet if it became necessary.

Brennan felt it was important for them to agree on a joint signed opinion because it "was a course which I hoped would amplify the message that a majority had held that most affirmative action programs are permissible under both Title VI and the Constitution."

However, White demurred, claiming other writing chores, and also noting that his views of Title VI would be dominant in any draft he wrote. Besides, he felt comfortable in joining Powell's equal-protection language. Brennan knew that such a draft opinion would never get Marshall to sign on because of the African-American jurist's feelings about Powell. "I became convinced," wrote Brennan confidentially, "that only I might be in a position to obtain the votes of the remaining three."

Brennan grudgingly took on the task of framing an opinion for the four jurists, one that tied in with some of Powell's ideas in his judgment of the Court. Brennan wrote to the other three that "I repeat I am determined to do what I possibly can to have Harry, [Byron] and I and, if possible at all, to have Marshall agree on a joint opinion."

His initial effort was with Marshall. The two men had adjoining chambers, and one of Marshall's clerks recalled that the tile floors were worn out because of the constant movement from one office to the other by the pair's law clerks. After repeated visits to Marshall's chambers, by mid-May Marshall did finally join Brennan's opinion and he did accept, although not without considerable resistance, a portion of Powell's opinion. Of Marshall's joining the gang at the end, Brennan, who must have had a twinkle in his eye, had only this to say: "Why he changed his initial adamant view that he would not join is still a puzzle to me."

After a most encouraging conversation with Powell on May 2, Brennan "returned to Chambers somewhat hopeful that a unified position for the Court could be reached. These hopes were shortlived, however," as Brennan recorded in his diary after reading Powell's first proposed *Bakke* judgment decision, dated May 9, 1978. In his cover letter, Powell said:

In light of the views previously expressed, there are four votes to affirm the judgment of the Supreme Court of California in its entirety, and four votes to reverse it. I will join the four votes to affirm as to Bakke himself and the invalidity of petitioner's program, but I will take a different view—and therefore will reverse—as to that portion of the judgment enjoining petitioner from any consideration of race in its admission program. Accordingly, the judgment of this Court would be: "Affirmed in part and reversed in part."

The "attached roadmap," that is, the outline Powell planned to use in writing the judgment, was so conservative on the constitutionality of benign racial processes and on the judicial standard that was used by the Court that Brennan immediately wrote Powell: "My views differ so substantially from your own that no common ground seems possible" and "I would therefore work out my views separately." Privately, in his diary, Brennan wrote that "at this point I was, of course, dismayed that common ground could not be reached for a partial reversal."

Marshall wrote, telling Powell that he would "dissent in toto." Blackmun, however, on May 16, gave Powell "a tentative vote of joinder on one of the five parts," adding that "I shall defer commitment on the balance of your circulation of May 9." Finally, White wrote a memo to Powell that committed him to "joining certain parts of your circulation, but not others." He concluded: "Of course, I would reverse the judgment entirely."

Always cobbling, Brennan now became increasingly concerned that if the rationale for a partial reversal was fragmented, the legality of all affirmative action programs might appear questionable, giving the upper hand to opponents of affirmative action in the political arena. This concern led to renewed and ultimately successful chats with Powell. By May 16, the two were exchanging memos to each other. And Brennan noted the parts of Powell's draft judgment that he could "join," while pointing out other parts that needed, the wizard remarked, additional modifications.

By this time Powell was receiving comments and suggestions for "improving" the draft judgment from most of the other justices. "In view of the 'paper chase' that goes on here at this time of the year," he wrote, "I will await circulations from other Chambers before recirculating my opinion."

By mid-May 1978, Brennan knew he had infinitely greater problems with the other two men who had tentatively joined

Brennan and Marshall: White and Blackmun. Brennan's law clerk told his boss that White had told his law clerk that he was supporting Powell's use of the strict scrutiny standard "for political reasons and it was essential to label the standard of review as strict scrutiny."

With the end of term "so close at hand," Brennan realized that "the objective of producing a jointly signed opinion would founder if a circulation were not quickly made."

> We worked at a furious pace to accomplish a first typewritten circulation by the first week of June. That effort was . . . impeded by HAB, however. Blackmun "was furious" [with a Brennan oversight in another case.] Given HAB's sensitivity, . . . I feared losing his vote for the proposed joint opinion in *Bakke*. I apologized obsequiously and promised to have [the oversight cleared up] the following opinion day.

Before writing and circulating his draft, Brennan talked, via the memo, with the other three men on a daily basis, and with the "gang of four" when their circulations were received. He wrote to White on May 30: "I am shooting for the beginning of next week to get a copy of the constitutional treatment to you. Other things are also in the works and I may be too optimistic but I am going to try."

Brennan's first draft was circulated to four other brethren—White, Marshall, Blackmun, and Powell—on June 8, 1978. Brennan wrote: "my hope, of course, is that we can end up with a joint opinion."

It contained language that separated Brennan from Powell. For Brennan, when racial classifications "stigmatized or demeaned racial groups as inferior," strict scrutiny was the appropriate standard. However, in the *Bakke* fact situation, that kind of discrimination was not present. There was, instead, the use of race "for purposes of remediating past discrimination. That use of race should not be subject to the traditional strict scrutiny which has been 'strict in theory but fatal in fact.'"

In his diary, Brennan wrote that he was also "concerned that, because of the potential for abuse of racial classifications and latent race hatred," the rational relationship test was "inappropriate." Nevertheless, the draft "clearly rejected LFP's conclusion that any racial classification must satisfy the traditional strict scrutiny involving less restrictive alternatives and closely tailored means-ends analysis and therefore LFP's response on June 10th, declining to join, was not surprising." Marshall quickly joined Brennan. White, noted Brennan, "was cool. . . . On June 13, while withholding assent, BRW nevertheless communicated several areas of disagreement."

Powell immediately suggested that one of his law clerks work with one of Brennan's to iron out some editing changes. Powell noted that he was "entirely in accord" with the quartet's views of Title VI and "I plan to join your Part I. Thus, we will have 'cross joins' on this issue" (Title VI). He closed cordially: "I congratulate you on producing a major draft with such celerity." Brennan immediately began to make some changes in the June 8 draft, based on Powell's response that the two men differed over "semantics."

However, as Brennan noted, "BRW's suggestions were more difficult to consider and resolve." In a three-page memo sent only to Brennan on June 13, White offered no less than fourteen suggestions for Brennan to consider and then place in the new draft—"and I hope you will forgive me if they appear curt." Brennan immediately accepted three of them and then had to work with White on the other eleven. These "comments" ranged from removing "unnecessary" language in the draft to substantive discussions about the strict scrutiny standard.

For example, in "comment" three, White wrote: "I am frank to say that I don't see much help in the gender discrimination cases." That was in direct opposition to Blackmun's position in *Bakke*. Blackmun, the author of the controversial *Roe v. Wade* abortion decision handed down a few years before, wrote of the gender discrimination cases in his *Bakke* memo. (Blackmun "thought they were important and consistent with his position.") If Brennan acquiesced to White on this point, he would lose Blackmun. Brennan didn't.

White also pleaded with Brennan, in his sixth comment, to "keep the decibel level as low as possible. We won't accomplish much by *beating a white majority over past ills* or by describing what has gone on as a system of *apartheid*." Brennan agreed with White on that score, and his clerks edited the earlier draft to remove the offensive terms.

"Worse yet," wrote Brennan in his diary, "BRW's resolve to say 'strict scrutiny' at any cost [agreeing with Powell], would lose Marshall." Brennan's immediate response was "to work with his clerks to change the standard of review set out in the first draft opinion."

His June 8 draft showed Brennan at his masterful best. Instead of strict scrutiny, Brennan offered a new standard for reviewing such remedial affirmative action programs. His first sentence announced the proposed standard: The justices must search for an "important and articulated" purpose for a racially discriminatory act, rather than looking for a state "compelling interest."

The second sentence of the test "would bring it in line with the gender cases [thereby keeping Blackmun]." The proposed standard also had the merit, he hoped, of holding White's vote by using a "politically correct" phrase in the suggested standard—while at the same time keeping Marshall in the cohort because it was not the same phrase used by his nemesis, Powell!

> An *important and articulated purpose* for use of racial classifications must be shown. *In addition, any statute must be stricken that stigmatizes any group* or that singles out those least well represented in the political process to bear the brunt of a benign program. Thus our review under the Fourteenth Amendment should be *strict* and *searching* nonetheless.

Brennan's June 8 draft "test" led to responses from his colleagues and to

> much debate in Chambers during the week of June 6–June 16 as to whether that test, in fact, had been satisfied by Davis, such a requirement is necessary to prevent abuses which the Fourteenth Amendment aimed to prevent, whether such a requirement, as a practical matter, could ever be achieved, and whether a requirement of screening for "disadvantaged" would not unavoidably identify economic disadvantage and

whether such identification would not be inconsistent with the premise of the constitutional discussion that the program is not subject to strict scrutiny because it seeks to remedy past racial discrimination. These were new questions upon which no one up until this point had focused.

Although "troubled," Brennan stayed with the test he had devised to get himself out of the dangerous box constructed by the other four. By the time of Brennan's next draft, circulated on June 16, some controversial sentences in the earlier draft had been "jettisoned" in order to finally get the quartet to agree on one opinion. As Brennan noted, the draft was, very directly, "my attempt to remove ideas BRW did not like."

It also meant greater clarity in other segments of the Brennan draft. Justice White "questioned the accuracy of my assertion [in the opinion] that the 'central meaning' of the *Bakke* decision was: 'Government may take race into account when it acts not to demean or insult any racial group, but to remedy disadvantages cast on minorities by past racial prejudice.'"

> This assertion was intended to give some guidance and assurance to those who wanted to keep affirmative action alive. I was dismayed to find that BRW thought it inaccurate. I immediately called LFP, who assured me that he had no trouble with the form of the assertion—a position he later retracted somewhat. I quickly relayed LFP's position to BRW and this seemed to mollify him.

Brennan was in a race against time. Powell's opinion was nearly ready, as was Stevens's opinion affirming both prongs of the California Supreme Court decision. The target day for the public announcement of *Bakke* was less than two weeks away, and there was no unanimity among Brennan's "gang." Then came another example of "Murphy's Law": White and Powell "got into a tiff over Title VI, which caused Byron to insist that none of the four of us should join LFP's Title VI discussion. BRW's reasoning was that a join on Title VI implied an agreement with LFP's constitutional analysis."

Fortunately, that tiff petered out, and by June 16, Brennan and his clerks had hammered out another draft. They sent it this time to only three others: White, Marshall, and Blackmun. The responses were positive. Blackmun "quickly joined the draft, which it turned out was the first he had had time to read. . . . BRW also quickly acquiesced. TM also agreed to join this opinion."

"It was with great joy that I sent the following memo on June 20," recalled Brennan.

> Byron, Thurgood, Harry and I will file a single joint opinion in this case, which I now send to all of you. . . . Byron will file a separate opinion based on his Title VI Memo, which will discuss his view that there is no private right of action under Title VI. Harry circulated yesterday a statement of his further views on this case. Thurgood will shortly circulate a draft opinion which sets forth his further views. I have to catch a ferry [to Brennan's annual summer place on Nantucket Island], and therefore I will break ranks and remain uncharacteristically silent!

However, once again Brennan's "joy was short-lived." First, Powell circulated changes to his opinion "which attacked ours as unprincipled." Brennan immediately spoke with Powell on the phone and "quickly resolved the compromise language found in the final draft on the 'central meaning' point." Brennan wrote in his diary on this issue: "I should stress that LFP finally agreed that the ultimate language chosen accurately reflected his view of what his opinion and mine jointly stood for."

Meanwhile, White was sending more suggested changes to Brennan, and Brennan and his law clerks "set to work trying to accommodate BRW and answer LFP." The first was a nuisance, but it "proved reasonably easy." The Powell clash "was to prove almost my undoing," Brennan later confessed. Powell now asserted that Brennan's new standard meant in reality "one test for whites and one for blacks." Brennan immediately retorted that the standard applied equally, and moreover, "it reconciled all the important equal protection cases that LFP and I discussed in our opinions."

By 5 P.M. on Friday, June 23, barely three days later, Brennan circulated yet another draft, which tried to respond to the criticisms. "The very next day," he wrote in his diary, "all hell broke loose."

> First, BRW called me at home to say he could not live with the changes relating to the standard of review. He was absolutely insistent that we say "strict scrutiny" and further, that our analysis remain superficially traditional. I went to the office to discuss this with BRW. On arriving there, my clerks told me that HAB had called. I called HAB and he, too, indicated that he was pulling out of the opinion. HAB was simply very mad that we had made a lot of changes [without clearing them with him]. He stated that he had not read any of them, and that he was just in no position to even consider *Bakke* any further.

Brennan found a compromise with White. At the same time, Powell circulated a response to the June 23 draft "which said quite bluntly that my opinion condoned Jewish quotas. This was too much. BRW quickly called LFP and told him to retract this material. My clerks and I were particularly mad about this [assertion]. . . . In any case, LFP yielded to BRW's insistence and this was resolved." With White joined and with Powell's ruffled feathers stroked, Brennan had to deal with the last member of his cohort: Harry A. Blackmun.

Brennan had Blackmun's law clerk come over and pick up the draft, read it, and then suggest to his boss, Blackmun, that he join the Brennan opinion. "Later that [Saturday] afternoon HAB called me at home to say that there were no substantive problems, that the consent draft was fine, and that he was back with us if I would promise to make no more changes. I promised[!]"

Compared to the Brennan marathon, the other gang of four had a walk in the park. Burger joined the last of the Stevens circulations on June 13, 1978, noting in a scribbled "p.s." that "some suggestions may evolve when all the 'returns' are in." Very quickly thereafter, Stewart and Rehnquist sent their "joins" to Stevens. The quartet's position had not changed since the oral argument and the initial conference session: The California

Supreme Court was correct (1) in invalidating the UCD program; (2) in saying that race may never be taken into consideration when reviewing applications for admission to medical school; and (3) in ordering Bakke admitted to UCD immediately.

Four days later, the justices, in open Court, announced the judgment of the Court in Number 76-811, *Regents of University of California v. Bakke.*

At the End: The Six Opinions in *Bakke*

From the October 12, 1977, oral argument to the June 28, 1978, announcement of *Bakke*, the justices relentlessly debated the issue of affirmative action. For more than eight months, while attending to the regular business of the Court, they and their clerks plowed through the fifty-eight amicus curiae briefs and the huge amount of paper the justices themselves generated in the form of MTTCs and draft opinions.

Finally, *Bakke* was ready to come down. It was without a doubt a brokered judgment of the Court. There were six separate opinions written, totaling 154 pages (and more than 40,000 words) in the *U.S. Supreme Court Reports.* It was announced in Court on June 28, 1978. In the end, there was no opinion of the Court, that is, a pronouncement that had the full support of five or more of the nine justices. Instead, there was a bifurcated judgment of the Court announced by Powell, with each of the "gangs" of four concurring and dissenting in different segments of the Powell "judgment."

In a memo sent the day before the public announcement, Powell reflected on the many ironies that *Bakke* produced: "It is a bit difficult to refer—with brevity—to the various authors and 'joiners' of the several opinions. . . . As I am a 'chief' with no 'Indians,' I should be in the rear rank, not up front!"

Brennan wrote an opinion for his group of four, concluding that the UCD plan was valid in every respect, whether from the Title VI perspective or from the Fourteenth Amendment's Equal Protection Clause. The California Supreme Court opinion should have been reversed in its entirety. (Justices Blackmun and

White wrote brief separate opinions. Marshall wrote a much longer and emotionally stirring opinion.)

Justice Stevens wrote the opinion for his quartet of Burger, Rehnquist, himself, and Stewart. He argued that the UCD plan was invalid in every respect and that the California Supreme Court opinion should have been affirmed in its entirety. Stevens concluded that Bakke was excluded from UCD in violation of Title VI. Differing dramatically from the other five justices, the Stevens cohort rejected any use of race as a factor in admissions processes at colleges and universities. For Stevens (who was to change his position on affirmative action shortly after *Bakke*), "it is perfectly clear that the question whether race can ever be used as a factor in an admissions decision is not an issue in this case, and that discussion of that issue is inappropriate."

Regarding the avoidance of a decision in *Bakke* based on the Court's interpretation of the Constitution's Fourteenth Amendment, the quartet maintained that, as a matter of judicial parsimony and self-restraint, there was no need for the Court to reach the constitutional question if the case could be resolved through statutory construction.

Since Title VI's "plain meaning of the words" forbids the use of racial quotas and the use of race even as one among many factors examined in the admissions process, there was absolutely no need to open the Constitution at all. By this action, Stevens and the three who joined in his opinion, wrote Archibald Cox, "escaped the necessity of discussing the underlying philosophical and social issues as questions of constitutional law." However, five justices did examine the constitutional and philosophic questions associated with *Bakke:* Justices Powell, Brennan, Marshall, Blackmun, and White.

The Brennan opinion, joined by White, Marshall, and Blackmun, was a milestone opinion of sorts. For the very first time, four justices jointly created or subscribed to a transformational constitutional interpretation of the Fourteenth Amendment. Like Powell, Brennan prepared a summary version of the opinion he authored. Four justices, he said in his opening comments, "have filed a jointly signed opinion supporting [the] view that the judgment of the California Supreme Court should be reversed in all respects—not only insofar as it prohibits the University from establishing race-conscious programs in the future, but also insofar as the judgment orders that respondent Bakke be admitted to the Davis Medical School."

Brennan's opinion reflected his group's views on the matter of affirmative action and received Powell's tempered approval.

> The central meaning of today's opinions is this: Government may take race into account when it acts not to demean or insult any racial group, but to remedy disadvantages cast on minorities by past racial prejudice, at least when appropriate findings have been made by judicial, legislative, or administrative bodies with competence to act in this area.

Brennan's introductory paragraph was narrowly correct, for his faction plus Powell added up to five, a Court majority on the issue of treating the race of a candidate affirmatively. Since Brennan's group disagreed with Powell's view that the UCD admission plan was unconstitutional, there was no "majority" opinion committed to that "central meaning" statement of Brennan's. Moreover, the placement and the language used by Brennan to describe the "central meaning" of *Bakke* angered the other four-person faction. Justice Stevens noted that "it is hardly necessary to state that only a majority can speak for the Court or determine what is the 'central meaning' of any judgment of the Court."

In *Bakke*, Powell stood alone. In a prepared statement read from the bench (which had received the prior approval of the other eight justices), Powell said:

> I am authorized to announce the judgment of the Court. There is no opinion joined in its entirety by five members of the Court. The facts in this case are too well known to require restatement. Perhaps no case in modern memory has received as much media coverage and scholarly commentary. Beginning with more than 60 briefs filed with the Court, we have received the unsolicited advice—through the media and the commentaries—of countless extra-judicial advocates.

The case was argued some eight months ago, and as we will speak today with a notable lack of unanimity, it may be fair to say that we needed all of this advice.

His written opinion began with a summary of the disposition of *Bakke* and the voting patterns of the Court:

I believe that so much of the judgment of the California court as holds petitioner's special admissions program unlawful and directs that respondent be admitted to the Medical School must be affirmed. For the reasons expressed in a separate opinion, my Brothers THE CHIEF JUSTICE, MR. JUSTICE STEWART, MR. JUSTICE REHNQUIST, and MR. JUSTICE STEVENS concur in this judgment.

I also conclude that the portion of the court's judgment enjoining petitioner from according any consideration to race in its admissions processes must be reversed. For reasons expressed in separate opinions, my Brothers MR. JUSTICE BRENNAN, MR. JUSTICE WHITE, MR. JUSTICE MARSHALL, and MR. JUSTICE BLACKMUN concur in this judgment. Affirmed in part and reversed in part.

Powell then presented his "rationale" for the judgment. For Powell, there were two central questions raised in *Bakke:*

1. Did the UCD special admissions process "discriminate unlawfully against Bakke, either under the Constitution or Title VI of the Civil Rights Act of 1964?"
2. "Is it ever permissible to consider race as a factor relevant to the admission of applicants to a university?"

Powell concluded that the UCD special admissions program unconstitutionally denied Bakke equal protection and that therefore the California Supreme Court order admitting Bakke to the medical school was valid. He did note that the use of numbers or quotas or set-asides may be justified in a fact situation where there was proof in the record that the institution receiving federal funds had indeed discriminated against applicants on the basis of race or color. However, it was not necessary to explore that matter since UCD had no record of intentionally discriminating against minorities.

But Powell also wrote that universities and colleges could develop an admissions formula that took the race of an applicant into account, and in an Appendix he offered Harvard College's admissions program as an example. However, as Powell said in Court: "The process of constitutional analysis by which I reach this result differs significantly from that of the four Justices who have filed a joint opinion."

Furthermore, Powell stated that Title VI does not "control" in this case. "Justices Brennan, White, Marshall, Blackmun, and I have a different view as to Title VI. We believe, despite its more detailed provisions, that it goes no further in prohibiting the use of race than the Equal Protection Clause."

However, the five-person majority held, as expressed in Powell's opinion, that "in enjoining petitioner from ever considering the race of any applicant, however, the courts below failed to recognize that the State has a substantial interest that legitimately may or may not be served by a properly devised admission program involving the competitive consideration of race and ethnic origin."

Marshall's separate opinion, described by many as one that was "passionate and tinged with bitterness over the lot of the Negro minority in America," publicly revealed the thoughts he had shared privately with the brethren in his April 13 draft opinion. It was a lengthy one that recapitulated the shameful history of three centuries of "denial of human rights" to African Americans.

It described the "enforced segregation of the races" from post–Civil War times "well into the middle of the twentieth century." Recent history, Marshall wrote, demonstrated that "the position of the Negro today in America is the tragic but inevitable consequence of centuries of unequal treatment. Measured by any benchmark of comfort or achievement, meaningful equality remains a distant dream for the Negro." Finally, it was time to criticize the Court for their actions in *Bakke*. "The racism of our society has been so pervasive that none, regardless of wealth or position, has managed to escape its impact." In the end, he summed up what he had tried, unsuccessfully, to demonstrate to others on the Court:

If we are ever to become a fully integrated society, one in which the color of a person's skin will not determine the opportunities available to him or her, we must be willing to take steps to open these doors. I do not believe that anyone can truly look into America's past and still find that a remedy for the effects of that past is impermissible.

Blackmun's brief concurring and dissenting opinion in the case gratified Marshall immensely. He defended his judgment that the Davis two-track admissions system was "within constitutional bounds, though perhaps barely so [because] it is surely free of stigma."

Blackmun noted the impossibility of a university's trying to create a race-neutral affirmative action program (a proposal that Justice Douglas had suggested in his *DeFunis* dissent). "To ask that this be so is to demand the impossible." He spoke about the time—in the future—when affirmative action programs would be "unnecessary and a relic only of the past." However, in 1978 "we must first take account of race. . . . And in order to treat some persons equally, we must treat them differently. We cannot—we dare not—let the Equal Protection Clause perpetuate racial supremacy."

White's position in *Bakke* had not changed in the eight months since he circulated his first memo on October 13, 1977. His entire opinion focused on the question he had raised then: Does a private person have a cause of action under Title VI? He was the only justice to address this seemingly technical and somewhat anachronistic issue.

The Reactions

Following the Court's *Bakke* announcement came the press headlines. Conservative newspapers trumpeted the fact that the UCD affirmative action plan was invalidated by the Court. "White Student Wins Reverse Bias Case; Justices OK Some Racial Preferences," shouted the *Chicago Sun-Times* headline. The *Wall Street*

Journal stated correctly, in its fashion, that *Bakke* was "The Decision Everyone Won."

Liberal newspapers focused on the other side of the *Bakke* opinion. "High Court Backs Some Affirmative Action by Colleges, But Orders Bakke Admitted," headlined the *New York Times*. The *Washington Post* stated in bold letters: "Affirmative Action Upheld: Court Orders School to Admit Bakke, Curbs Racial Quotas." One *Los Angeles Times* headline read: "Historic Ruling Strikes Down Davis Quotas," while another, adjacent to the first, blared: "School Ruling Seen a Victory for Civil Rights." And *Time* Magazine put it simply and accurately: "Quotas, No; Race, Yes."

Editorialists and commentators, and political cartoonists, had a field day with the *Bakke* decision. The *Los Angeles Times* observed, in an editorial entitled "A Calm, Reasoned Opinion," that the decision "does not require any drastic shifts in the direction of national policies to assure civil rights." That same day, the *New York Times* editorial "Who Won?" appeared: "Americans determined to repair a history of discrimination gained the blessing of the Supreme Court to let race and ethnicity count in programs of 'affirmative action.' If the will to remedy historic injustice is still widely felt, the Court has left us the means to work on toward the American dream."

Anthony Lewis, the *New York Times'* liberal columnist who has won many awards for his "Abroad, At Home," and "At Home, Abroad" essays, praised the Court's action in an essay entitled "A Solomonic Decision."

To analyze the *Bakke* decision in cold terms does not do justice to what actually happened in the court room. I have seen great moments there, but nothing to match the drama as five members explained their positions in homely terms. . . . [Their explanations] underline the unique quality of what the American Supreme Court does often and did in this case: grapple with the fundamentals of a society.

All the major pressure groups who participated in the case could claim victory in the case because of what the Court said.

The ADL called *Bakke* "a significant victory in the effort to end racial quotas in college admissions," while the ACLU, though concerned about the decision "sapping the will of officials responsible for achieving racially integrated enrollment," breathed a sigh of relief because "it is not the disaster we might have had." John Mack, co-chair of the California Black Leadership Coalition, said, simply: "It's a mixed bag."

In 1978, Robert H. Bork was a very well known and respected conservative law professor and lawyer. He had been Nixon's solicitor general at the time of the infamous 1973 "Saturday Night Massacre." In 1981, Bork would be appointed to the U.S. Court of Appeals, D.C. Circuit. His views on affirmative action were a significant part of his developed jurisprudence, and they were shared by a majority of Americans—including a future president of the United States, Ronald Reagan, and Reagan's political staffers in the White House and the DOJ.

Bork's response to the *Bakke* judgment, published in the *Wall Street Journal*, was sharp and to the point: All those who supported the UCD plan, including those sitting on the Court, were "the hard-core racists of reverse discrimination." The Fourteenth Amendment, he argued, was a color-blind clarion call for an equality of merit. His criticism of *Bakke* was very potent, for he expressed the views and attitudes of a vast number of persons in America. Bork articulated the meritocratic vision of the Fourteenth Amendment in a direct, no-nonsense manner that was used by the opponents of affirmative action.

Over at the White House, however, U.S. Attorney General Griffin Bell took a much different position. After speaking with President Carter, he said: "My general view is that affirmative action has been enhanced" and that there would be no immediate changes in the 110 federal programs that granted some form of preference to persons on the basis of membership in a disadvantaged racial or ethnic group. Eleanor Holmes Norton, the chair of the EEOC, said that "*Bakke* doesn't dismantle affirmative action and it doesn't take employers off the hook. As a law-enforcement official, I have to say that the *Bakke* case has not left me with any duty to instruct the EEOC staff to do anything different or to recommend a change of policy to the Commission."

AT UCD, the vice chancellor said that the special admissions program would be overhauled when UCD received "definitive guidelines from the university's general counsel." Minority students at UCD and other California universities staged protests the day after the decision came down, concerned that *Bakke* would adversely impact future minority enrollments. "It's going to hurt," was the refrain of the small number of minority medical school students at UCD: "A lot of minorities are not going to apply." And Paul Mishkin, who, along with Cox, was the primary author of the petitioner's brief, said that "at the very least, the Court repudiates the California Supreme Court's simplistic position that race cannot be taken into account."

A happy Reynold Colvin said that *Bakke* had set reasonable parameters for affirmative action programs: "The decision is not the end of the road for affirmative action. [It] sets an outer limit and the case stands on its own facts. A quota is not the same thing as affirmative action." Colvin also read a message from his now thirty-eight-year-old reclusive client, Allan Bakke: "I am pleased and, after five years of waiting, I look forward to entering medical school in the fall."

After his win in the U.S. Supreme Court, Allan Bakke asked the University of California for funds to cover his legal expenses. Colvin, on June 6, 1979, submitted a request for $437,295 from the University of California for his legal fees. When the University rebuffed him, the matter went into California Superior Court. On January 15, 1980, Colvin (and his three law associates) were awarded $183,089 by a California Superior Court judge. In addition, Colvin had his "fifteen minutes" of fame: He began to give lectures in California and elsewhere about the *Bakke* case.

Implicit in all the responses was the unanswered question: What would be the impact of *Bakke* on a university's ability to diversify its student population to overcome three centuries of racial segregation? Across California (and in other states as well) less than a week after *Bakke* came down, educators were assembling, with their legal counsel, to determine what, if anything, they had to do to be in accord with the guidelines established in that case.

Drew Days III, the assistant attorney general, Civil Rights Division, doubted that *Bakke* would have major impact on federal affirmative action policies and regulations. "To the extent that the Federal agencies have not been doing their homework, they will have to do it now." They will have to be "focused" on the real causes and remedies for discrimination. Clearly, he advised employers and admissions officials alike to "avoid rigid quotas" and to "press forward with other forms of affirmative action."

Alan M. Dershowitz, the noted Harvard Law School professor and criminal trial advocate, said that *Bakke* would "go down in history not for what it did but for what it didn't do. It neither legitimized racial quotas nor put down affirmative action programs. The decision will make the job of admissions officers a lot harder. It will make them look at people as persons, not as members of a group and not as computerized ciphers."

———

These post-*Bakke* comments and reflections raise questions about the short-term and long-term impact of the *Bakke* case on minority enrollments in institutions of higher learning. The next chapter examines that and other issues and events since the case came down in June 1978.

CHAPTER 7

Affirmative Action Public Policy in the Politically Turbulent 1990s

Who sits on the Court determines what cases the Court will hear and, to a large extent, how they will be decided. A president who has the opportunity to nominate one or more justices, if he and his key staffers do careful screening of potential candidates, has an impact on public policy long after he leaves the White House.

After *Bakke*, the moderate Democratic president, Jimmy Carter, 1977–1981, did not have a single Supreme Court vacancy to fill. A vacancy occurs in the Court by a justice's strategic retirement (giving the seat to a president of the jurist's party) or by a justice being impeached, resigning, retiring, or dying while sitting. None of these possibilities became reality for Carter. President Reagan, 1981–1989, on the other hand, had four vacancies to fill during his tenure in office. Had there been one or two vacancies for Carter to fill, the makeup of the Court, and its outputs, would probably have been very different than the sitting Court and its decisions have been since the 1980s.

All but two of the 108 men and women who have served or are presently (2000) serving on the Court were politically active before their elevation to the high bench. Because of this reality, they often choose to retire at a strategic time. For example, Republican Justice Potter Stewart, who voted against affirmative action in *Bakke*, would have been unlikely to choose to retire during the pro–affirmative action administration of President Jimmy Carter. As soon as Reagan defeated Carter in 1980, however, Justice Stewart informed the incoming conservative Republican administration that he was retiring at the end of the 1980–1981 term of the Court. Reagan's four appointees were all conservative Republicans he believed were opposed to affirmative action.

President George Bush had two openings to fill during his term in the White House, 1989–1993, and President Clinton has filled two vacancies during his years in the White House.

The Politics of Supreme Court Appointments in the Reagan, Bush, and Clinton Administrations

The most powerful critic of affirmative action was President Ronald Reagan (R), 1981–1989. Again and again, as governor of California, as spokesperson for the conservative wing of the Republican Party, as presidential candidate in 1980, and finally as president, Reagan spoke out forcefully against the notion of affirmative action. For Reagan, the 1980 election reflected the "warring concepts of racial balance and race neutrality." He said that affirmative action was "a perversion that violates the great proposition, at the heart of Western civilization, that every person is a *res sacra*, a sacred reality, and as such is entitled to the opportunity of fulfilling those great human potentials with which God has endowed man."

Ronald Reagan's successful 1980 presidential campaign seized upon the general public's overwhelming dislike of affirmative action and made opposition to that emotionally charged public policy one of the central features of the 1980 Republican platform as well as a staple issue for attacking Carter during the campaign itself. In his 1980 election victory, Reagan received the lowest percentage of African-American votes for any Republican presidential candidate in American history.

Opposition to affirmative action was a part of his moralistic social agenda, one that opposed social policies such as welfare and abortion, while fully supporting other policies such as prayer in the schools and "family values." In the party's 1980 platform, the DOJ was given a number of tasks, including "the elimination of quotas in employment and housing" as well as playing a key advisory role for the president in the "judicial appointment of those who respect traditional family values."

Reagan's election, with 51 percent of the popular vote (to 41 percent for Carter and 7 percent for the independent candidate, John Anderson), as someone noted, "ushered in the conservative revolution in American politics and changed the cast of national politics for over a decade." Speaking to the large silent majority of working-class Americans, Reagan called for tax cuts, the reduction of federal spending for social services, the reduction of federal regulations that tightly controlled business and industry in America, the end to all affirmative action programs, and a religious commitment to the idea of "family values" and the "sanctity of life."

Reagan, as candidate and as chief executive, sought to dramatically reduce the role of the federal government in civil rights legislation writing and in the enforcement of civil rights regulations by his agencies and departments. During the campaign, he said that "guaranteeing equality of treatment is the government's proper function. We will not retreat on the Nation's commitment to equal treatment of all citizens." Regarding affirmative action, Reagan pulled no punches: "To deny access to higher education when it has been won on the basis of merit is a repudiation of everything America stands for. . . . [It] is morally wrong, and will not be tolerated."

Whenever a new administration takes over the running of the executive branch, there are significant changes in both personnel and policy perspectives. These changes are very significant when the old administration supported policies such as affirmative action that the incoming policy makers considered "insidious" programs that had to be terminated as quickly as possible.

To accomplish this policy redirection, the Reagan administration had to bring on board new personnel who shared the White House views about these public policies. In the area of civil rights and affirmative action, that meant a number of changes with respect to staffing the political leadership of the federal agencies dealing with civil rights issues (the EEOC, the Commission on Civil Rights [CCR], etc.), the DOJ's Civil Rights Division, and the U.S. solicitor general. More important yet were Reagan's judicial nominations to fill vacancies throughout the federal judicial system: the ninety-four federal U.S. District Courts (the trial courts of the federal judicial system), the thirteen U.S. Courts of Appeals (intermediate appellate courts in the federal judicial system), and, naturally, the U.S. Supreme Court.

During the Carter administration, the CCR enthusiastically supported governmental and private efforts to develop and implement affirmative action programs. Its six commissioners had no fixed term of office. They were replaced when they left the commission. In October 1977, at the time of the oral arguments in *Bakke*, a Republican member, Arthur S. Fleming, CCR chairperson, openly defended the use of "numerically based remedies" in a university's efforts to overcome centuries of racial discrimination in America. And on July 2, 1978, Fleming strongly supported the Court's judgment in *Bakke* that allowed race to be used by admissions committees as one factor in their decision to admit applicants.

On May 26, 1983, after failing to persuade Fleming and three other leading members of the commission to resign, President Reagan fired the four, including his most vocal critic on the commission, Mary Frances Berry. He replaced them with four conservative members: African American Clarence Pendleton, the new chairperson; Morris B. Abram, a civil rights lawyer; John H. Bunzel, of the conservative Hoover Institution; and Robert A. Destro, a Catholic University law professor and unrelenting critic of the U.S. Supreme Court's abortion decisions. At his press conference after being fired by Reagan, Fleming said sadly: "[The CCR] has consistently been taking positions contrary to the position of the Reagan Administration. The cumulative impact of the civil rights decisions made by the Administration are very disturbing."

This Reagan action led to a firestorm of protest from liberal congresspersons and almost two hundred civil rights organizations. Berry initiated a lawsuit to enjoin the president from firing her. As a consequence of the vocal opposition to the action, Reagan and the liberals worked out a compromise: the CCR was increased to eight members; the president and the Congress were each given four positions to fill. Finally, the commissioners would serve six-year terms, and their appointments would be staggered to minimize partisanship. One of the first congressional appointees was Mary Frances Berry.

The EEOC, the federal government's major watchdog protecting equal employment opportunities for all persons, was another prime target of the Reagan administration. The liberal, outspoken chairperson of the EEOC, Eleanor Holmes Jordan, was quickly replaced by much more conservative appointees: Reagan's initial chair, Clarence Pendleton, and after Pendleton moved over to the CRC in 1983, Clarence Thomas.

In addition to significantly changing the makeup of these executive branch commissions, Reagan added conservative lawyers to independent liberal legal agencies that provided civil rights assistance to poor defendants facing criminal trials. For example, the Legal Services Corporation found itself with a new set of political leaders, including three lawyers from the conservative Pacific Legal Foundation.

At the DOJ, Reagan appointed a conservative Republican, Rex Lee, who had been the dean of the Brigham Young University Law School, to serve as his first solicitor general. Lee replaced Wade McCree, and it was a very significant difference.

Reagan's first attorney general, William French Smith, was the political appointee responsible for implementing these views of affirmative action. He, too, shared the president's condemnation of the concept: "We fully recognize and support the fundamental ideals of race and sex neutrality in the constitutional and statutory guarantee of civil rights. . . . We will not insist on quotas or goals that give non-victims preferential treatment."

The man responsible for putting into practice the anti–affirmative action policy of the Reagan administration was the assistant attorney general, Civil Rights Division (CRD), William Bradford Reynolds. Reagan immediately replaced Drew Days III with Reynolds, who was a graduate of Yale and Vanderbilt Universities. He, too, was a strong critic of affirmative action, and said, when nominated: "There's a growing awareness that the [federal] agencies that enforce civil rights have been overly intrusive." Further, the Reagan DOJ will "not support the use of quotas or any statistical formula designed to protect non-victims of discrimination or give them preferential treatment based on race, sex, national origin, or religion."

An outspoken critic of affirmative action after he was appointed, Reynolds believed that affirmative action for African Americans was "using racism to fight racism and is inexcusable." Toward the end of the first Reagan administration, Reynolds was asked to list the White House's major success in civil rights matters. Without hesitating, Reynolds answered that "we have made a lot of progress in . . . reawakening the public debate on the whole question of affirmative action. It is, I think, a monumental step forward that the majority of the people in this country are now willing to question responsibly whether preferential treatment on account of race, or sex, is a legitimate course for government to follow. As that public debate continues, I am confident it will ultimately influence a change in that policy."

In the Heritage Foundation's 1985 report, *Mandate for Leadership II: Continuing the Conservative Revolution*, the DOJ and other federal agencies were once again criticized. While the authors praised Reynolds for his "outstanding job to achieve the Reagan goal of pursuing 'color-blind justice' policies in enforcing civil rights laws," Solicitor General Rex Lee was another case. They harshly criticized Lee for his less than enthusiastic support of the Reagan administration's "family values" principles in abortion, affirmative action, and church-state litigation.

Notably, after Reagan took his oath of office in January 1985, Rex Lee resigned due to ill health and was replaced by a more committed Reagan supporter, Charles Fried. The new SG, who had clerked for Justice John M. Harlan II and had been a Harvard Law School professor, had an infinitely better relationship than did Lee with other DOJ officials, especially with Reynolds and with Edwin Meese, Reagan's new AG. Ultimately (at the end of the Reagan administration), Fried's victory percentage before the Court was lower than Lee's, but he was a much more forceful pursuer of the administration's moral-rights agenda before the high bench.

The major task for President Reagan was to redirect, through the appointment of "his kind" of federal judges, the actions of the federal judiciary, including the Supreme Court. For Reagan and his key White House staffers, this meant appointing men and women who clearly shared the administration's views on a range of issues, from "original intent" constitutional interpretation, federal-state relations, and church-state separation, to the "sanctity of life," to the constitutionality of affirmative action programs that functioned in the federal and state bureaucracies, in the private sector, and in colleges and university admissions and scholarship processes.

———

Reagan's first appointment to the U.S. Supreme Court was a historic one. When Justice Potter Stewart told the White House of his retirement plans, Reagan nominated a woman to the U.S. Supreme Court: Sandra Day O'Connor. She would be the first of her sex to serve on the Supreme Court. O'Connor was an Arizonan who grew up on a ranch and went to Stanford Law School, finishing third in her graduating class (with fellow Arizonan Bill Rehnquist the top graduate that year, 1952).

In 1964, she entered partisan politics as a volunteer precinct captain for the Republican presidential contender, Barry Goldwater (R-Ariz). In 1970 she was elected to the Arizona legislature, and two years later she became the first female majority leader in a state legislature. In 1974, she became a state trial court judge, and in 1979 O'Connor was appointed to the Arizona Court of Appeals. She served on the state court until, in 1981, she received a phone call from Reagan's AG, William French Smith, inviting her to the White House to talk about filling the vacancy created by Justice Stewart's retirement. The Senate confirmed her appointment by a vote of 99 to 0.

In 1986, Chief Justice Burger informed the White House that he would retire at the end of the term to spend full time as chair of the American Constitution's bicentennial celebrations. Reagan elevated conservative Justice Rehnquist to the Court's "center seat," and nominated another highly regarded and very outspoken conservative jurist, Antonin (Nino) Scalia, to take Rehnquist's associate justice seat. Like the O'Connor appointment,

Scalia's was also historic: Scalia is the first justice of Italian-American heritage to sit on the high bench.

After Reagan's victory, in 1982 Scalia was appointed to the U.S. Court of Appeals, D.C. Circuit. In 1986, he was confirmed to fill the vacancy created when Rehnquist moved to the center seat on the Court. Although O'Connor had not spoken publicly about the constitutionality of affirmative action policy, Scalia did, and he was categorically and unabashedly against that policy. One newsman stated that Scalia "absolutely despised affirmative action—legally, morally, and personally." A friend of Scalia's once commented: "Scalia grew up with the merit system in the New York City schools and the 'melting pot' ethic."

Scalia, as a scholar and as a member of the D.C. federal Court of Appeals, repeatedly condemned affirmative action as practiced in America because of *Bakke*. He condemned it bluntly: "It is based upon concepts of racial indebtedness and racial entitlement, rather than individual worth and individual need, and that is to say, because it is racist."

A few years before his nomination, Scalia delivered a scathing attack on the Court for its *Bakke* decision. He hated the concept used by some "Aryan" judges in affirmative action cases: "restorative justice."

> [That phrase] may explain why I feel a bit differently about these issues than, for example, Judge Wisdom, or Justice Powell, or Justice White. [I am angered] when John Minor Wisdom talks of the "evils" we must now make restoration for. My father came to this country when he was a teenager. Not only had he never profited from the sweat of any black man's brow, I don't think he had ever seen a black man. . . . Yet curiously enough, we find that in the system of restorative justice established by the Wisdoms, the Powells and the Whites, it is precisely these [white ethnic] groups that do most of the restoring.

Scalia said that he was "entirely in favor of according the poor inner-city child, who happens to be black, advantages and preferences not given to my own children because they don't need them. But I am not willing to prefer the black son [of a rich doctor or lawyer]—solely because of his race—to the son of a recent refugee from Eastern Europe who is working as a manual laborer to get his family ahead." When he took his seat on the Court in 1986, he became a colleague of the "racists" he had been condemning for almost a decade, Justices Powell and White.

The only ugly, "bloody," knock-down nomination battle during Reagan's two terms as president came in 1987. In late June, an extremely saddened Justice Lewis F. Powell, the swing justice in all the Court's affirmative action decisions, announced his retirement for health reasons. His vote made five-person majorities in every one of the many affirmative action cases heard between 1978 and 1987. He never dissented in those cases. The Reagan White House quickly announced their nominee: Robert H. Bork, then sitting on the U.S. Court of Appeals, D.C. Circuit.

Robert Bork was one of the most outstanding conservative legal scholars in America. Most considered him to be the titular leader of the conservative legal movement. On the very day Powell talked about his retirement at a press conference, Reagan told his two key staffers, Meese and Reynolds, that he wanted Bork to replace Powell.

Reagan's chief of staff, former U.S. senator (R-Tenn) Howard Baker, was greatly concerned about the nomination because he knew that the announcement would trigger aggressive efforts by the Democratic majority in the Senate and by civil rights organizations to defeat such a conservative ideologue as Bork. He suggested a Californian, sitting on the U.S. Court of Appeals, Ninth Circuit, to fill the vacancy. His advice was not taken at that time. However, after the bloody defeat of Bork in the Senate and the withdrawal of another conservative Reagan nominee, Douglas Ginsburg, Baker's man was finally nominated. He was Anthony Kennedy, who was overwhelmingly confirmed in the early Spring 1988.

For Democrats and Republicans, the Powell vacancy was the crucial battle for control of the Court on controversial issues such as affirmative action programs. The earlier Reagan appointees, O'Connor, Rehnquist, and Scalia, had all replaced persons who had voted against the use of race as a factor in affirmative action admissions programs. Their appointments, therefore, did not damage the *Bakke* precedent.

Given the Reagan administration's ardent opposition to affirmative action, the Democrats in the Senate and civil rights and education groups across America were greatly concerned about the future of affirmative action. On July 1, 1987, when Robert Bork's name was presented to the Senate for their "advice and consent," the confirmation conflict began.

Like his friend and former colleague on the court of appeals, Antonin Scalia, Bork was committed to the concept of "original intent," that is, the principle that Supreme Court justices must interpret the Constitution in light of the intent of those who wrote it and in light of the plain meaning of the words when written by them. (A third very close friend of these two judicial conservatives, since the early 1970s, was the sitting chief justice of the United States, William H. Rehnquist.)

Bork was extremely critical of the Warren Court's expansive—revolutionary—reading of the Bill of Rights protections as well as that Court's liberal interpretation of the Fourteenth Amendment's clauses. He labeled Warren's Court an "unprincipled, illegitimate" one because the opinions reflected the liberal bias of the sitting justices rather than the original meaning of the Constitution's words.

For Bork, for example, both *Brown*, 1954, which overturned *Plessy* in the area of public secondary education, and *Griswold v. Connecticut*, 1965, which set aside a Connecticut statute that prohibited the distribution of contraceptives, were sad examples of the Warren Court's creating new rights because of the majority's propensity for such policies. Recall also Bork's labeling, in 1978, of *Bakke* opinion writers Brennan, White, Blackmun, Marshall, and Powell, as "the hard-core racists of reverse discrimination."

There was, he argued publicly in his writings and lectures, precious little "judicial restraint" practiced by these liberal justices. Given his commitment to the "intent of the framers" and his avowed dedication to judicial restraint, Bork would be a very different kind of justice on the Court. And everyone knew that!

These views, expressed in the many articles he wrote, in speeches, and in his five days of testimony before the Senate Judiciary Committee, led to his defeat, 58 to 42, in the U.S. Senate on October 23, 1987. It was, as the media pointed out, the greatest margin of defeat ever for a Supreme Court nominee.

In the end, in mid-February 1988, Reagan's confirmed replacement for Powell was Anthony Kennedy. After growing up in Sacramento, California, Kennedy was an excellent, disciplined student at Stanford University. Like many others who sat on the Supreme Court—or who clerked at the Court—Kennedy went on to Harvard Law School, where he graduated cum laude.

After graduation, he took over his father's legal practice in Sacramento, the state capital, acting as a lobbyist for a number of industry clients until Ed Meese III, then Governor Ronald Reagan's chief of staff, met and liked Kennedy and brought him into the fold to draft a state tax resolution. In 1975, when an opening occurred in the U.S. Court of Appeals, Ninth Circuit, Meese recommended the very young (thirty-nine years of age) Anthony Kennedy to staffers in the Ford White House. Until he was nominated by Reagan in 1987, Kennedy's behavior as a federal appeals judge was, in the words of one reporter, "favoring the status quo," unmistakably conservative. When the Bork and Ginsburg nominations ended ignominiously, Reagan turned to the Californian sitting on the Ninth Circuit. Kennedy sailed through the hearings and easily won Senate confirmation.

Although he was described as a moderate, conservative jurist, "another Lewis Powell," he was, the Democrats in the Senate pronounced, much, much better than the orthodox conservative idealogue they had soundly thrashed in October. The Democrats claimed that Kennedy was "open-minded, fair and independent [and he] will assure continuity on the Supreme Court at this moment of historical transition." In the area of affirmative action, however, these views of the newest justice were soon to be proven incorrect. Kennedy quickly joined four other conservative jurists in affirmative action cases that seemed to turn the tide against the more moderate Burger Court decisions.

Although Republican President George Bush did not provide Americans with rhetoric critical of affirmative action such as Reagan's White House put out, he was an ardent opponent of affirmative action and a strong advocate for "family values." His campaign against the Democratic candidate, Massachusetts Governor Michael Dukakis, focused on three core themes: "family values," patriotism, and support for law enforcement, not affirmative action. In early September 1988, campaigner Bush said:

> We need a president who believes in family values, like saying the pledge of allegiance to the flag of the U.S.A. We need a president who is not going to offer some kind of program to furlough a murderer so he can go out and rape and pillage again. We need a president who will support our law enforcement community in going after drug traffickers. . . . I am that man.

Bush won the 1988 election handily. David H. Souter (1990) and Clarence Thomas (1991) were President George Bush's two appointments to the Supreme Court.

David Souter sailed through the confirmation process. Born in Boston, from the age of eleven Souter was raised in Weare, New Hampshire. In 1990, he was living with his aged mother in their old home in Weare when he was invited to meet President Bush about filling the vacancy on the Court created by Justice Brennan's retirement due to ill health. Souter had attended Harvard College and then Harvard Law School, where his outstanding work led to a Rhodes Scholarship to study law at Oxford University for two years. He then returned to New Hampshire, where he practiced law and served as a state judge.

In 1968, he was hired by Warren Rudman, then New Hampshire's AG (and in 1990 a U.S. Senator [R-NH]), to be his assistant in the office. Rudman later told a news reporter that Souter had "the single most brilliant intellectual mind I have ever met." After succeeding Rudman as AG, in 1978 Souter was appointed as a state trial court judge and then to the New Hampshire Supreme Court.

Rudman worked both the Reagan and Bush White House

staffers in a successful effort to get Souter on the short list of possible nominees to fill vacancies on the Supreme Court. Souter, understandably, did not make the short list to replace Powell in 1987. However, three years later, on July 20, 1990, he heard of Brennan's retirement, and a day later Rudman called to tell his friend that he was on a short list to replace the brilliant cobbler of majorities. A few days later, C. Boyden Grey, Bush's White House counsel, called and invited Souter to visit the White House. After almost an hour's conversation with the President, Souter was selected as the person to replace Brennan. He won overwhelming approval of the U.S. Senate and took his seat in time for the October 1990 term of the Supreme Court.

Clarence Thomas's confirmation by the U.S. Senate was quite another story. His nomination triggered yet another bloody conflict between liberals and conservatives, between Democrats and Republicans, and, after Professor Anita Hill's allegations were revealed to a shocked America, between men and women. For a week in October 1991, the entire nation sat riveted to their radios and television sets listening to and watching the unfolding of the Thomas-Hill allegations.

Souter had been called the "Stealth" nominee because there were no writings of his that could be examined by concerned senators and opposition pressure groups, especially women's groups who were worried about Souter's views on the liberty of a woman to elect to have an abortion. In that regard, his file was the complete opposite of Robert Bork's and Clarence Thomas's. Like Bork, Thomas was a popular speaker with conservative organizations across the nation, and in the 1980s he gave hundreds of partisan speeches extolling the virtues of Reagan's vision of the "city on the hill." He continued to give these talks during Bush's administration, while he was EEOC director.

Thomas was part of a small cohort of African-American conservatives who were unreservedly opposed to affirmative action programs in employment and education (even though he was a beneficiary of Yale Law School's affirmative action policy when he applied for admission to that law school after receiving an undergraduate degree from Holy Cross College). As he told a *New*

York Times reporter in 1982: "I am unalteringly opposed to programs that force or even cajole people to hire a certain percentage of minorities. I watched the operation of such affirmative action policies when I was in college, and I watched the destruction of many kids as a result."

He was born in segregated Pin Point, Georgia. When he was three, his mother sent Clarence and his younger brother to live with her father, Myers Anderson, and his wife. Clarence was sent to Catholic schools and then went off to Holy Cross College in Massachusetts, where he was promptly seen as a radical black campus activist, complete with an Afro haircut and a huge poster of Malcolm X in his dorm room. After graduation, he went to Yale Law School. He next took a job with John Danforth, an alumnus of Yale and Missouri's AG. At law school Thomas took no civil rights law classes, and at his first job he requested that he not be given assignments in the civil rights area.

After working for a large chemical firm in St. Louis, in 1979 Thomas was invited to join U.S. Senator Danforth's (R-Mo) staff in Washington, D.C. By this time, Thomas had accepted the conservative views of economists such as Thomas Sowell and fully supported the views of the 1980 Republican candidate for president, Ronald Reagan. Thomas was one of President Reagan's first political appointments: in 1981, he was made assistant secretary for civil rights in the U.S. Department of Education. Less than one year later, he was appointed chair of the EEOC, where he spent almost nine years running that important federal agency. In 1990, Bush appointed Thomas to the U.S. Court of Appeals, D.C. Circuit.

A day after Thurgood Marshall announced his retirement, C. Boyden Grey called Clarence Thomas to tell him that he was being considered by Bush as the person to fill that vacancy. On July 1, 1991, Bush announced that he was nominating Clarence Thomas to fill the Marshall vacancy, saying that Thomas was the "best man in the country for this job." The candidate went before the Senate Judiciary Committee two months later—a committee then controlled by the Democrats, with Senator Joseph Biden (D-Del) its chairman. The lengthy proceedings (five days of questioning Thomas about his jurisprudence) ended in a tie vote in committee, and his nomination was sent to the full Senate without a recommendation from the judiciary committee.

However, the Thomas confirmation took a bizarre turn with a report that blitzed the media: a woman claimed she had been sexually harassed by Thomas when he was in the Department of Education, continuing when both moved over to EEOC. On Monday, October 7, 1991, Professor Anita Hill, then teaching at the University of Oklahoma's law school, made her claim public.

By Thursday, she was before the Senate Judiciary Committee, telling the fourteen men of her "ugly" experiences with Thomas. The following day, Thomas categorically denied all her claims: "I have never, in all my life, felt such hurt, such pain, such agony. My family and I have been done a grave and irreparable injustice. This is not America. This is Kafkaesque. It has to stop. It must stop for the benefit of future nominees and our country. Enough is enough."

With such a unequivocal rejection of Hill's assertions, it became a "he said–she said" tragic farce. Ultimately, Thomas was confirmed by a vote of 52 to 48, the narrowest confirmation margin in the entire history of the Supreme Court. He took his seat on the high bench a few weeks after the 1991 term of the U.S. Supreme Court began its work.

When Democratic challenger Bill Clinton defeated the incumbent, George Bush, in 1992, the civil rights community sighed with relief. When he announced his first cabinet, there were four African Americans, three women, and two Hispanic-American men. Political appointees throughout the federal executive branch reflected a similar upsurge in the number of minorities and women selected by the Clinton transition team.

However, almost immediately he ran into difficulty with the Republicans in the U.S. Senate over his nomination of Lani Guinier for the position of assistant attorney general, civil rights. Because of hardball pressure from Republicans—who called Guinier a "quota queen" and a supporter of "proportional representation"—Clinton withdrew his nomination of his wife's good friend.

As a consequence of this embarrassing defeat, he moved very cautiously to fill civil rights positions. A civil rights watchdog pressure group, the Citizens Commission on Civil Rights, wrote in 1994 that "the President's slow pace of appointments in key civil rights posts would prove damaging to hopes that momentum in civil rights enforcement would be established." It took Clinton over two years to fill all the key civil rights positions in the DOJ, the EEOC, and the Departments of Labor and Health and Human Services.

Clinton's two Supreme Court nominees, both U.S. Court of Appeals judges when nominated, sailed through the confirmation process without any difficulty. Ruth Bader Ginsburg (who was a co-author of the ACLU amicus brief in *Bakke*) was confirmed in late July 1993. She was the first Supreme Court nominee of a Democratic president since 1967, when President Lyndon B. Johnson nominated Thurgood Marshall.

Ginsburg, a native "Brooklyner," went to the city's public schools. She received her law degree from Columbia Law School, took a job teaching law at Rutgers University, and became a key advocate for women's civil rights while working for the ACLU in New York City. Ginsburg was also the chief architect of a women's rights strategy and project that successfully challenged gender discrimination in employment, in the military, and in government agencies. On behalf of women's equality, she argued—successfully—a number of important Fourteenth Amendment equal protection cases before the U.S. Supreme Court in the 1970s.

In 1980, President Carter nominated her to serve on the U.S. Court of Appeals, D.C. Circuit, where she became a colleague of Scalia and, in 1990, of Thomas. Clinton, after many months of indecision while he searched for a politically active nominee who was, as Clinton said, a "home run" hitter (Democratic New York Governor Mario Cuomo was an early name floated by the Clinton staffers), finally selected a good "singles hitter" when he announced Ginsburg's nomination in the White House Rose

Garden in July 1993. She, like Kennedy, sailed through the nomination process and received 99 votes for confirmation in the U.S. Senate.

Stephen Breyer was an honors graduate of Harvard Law School who had clerked for U.S. Supreme Court Justice Arthur Goldberg after graduation from law school. Importantly, he had served a year as chief counsel for the Democrats on the Senate Judiciary Committee and in this role had befriended a number of Republicans on the committee, including the Republican senator from Utah, Orrin Hatch.

He was another "singles hitter" selected by Clinton. At the time of his nomination in July 1994 to replace retired Justice Harry Blackmun, he had been a federal appeals judge on the U.S. Court of Appeals, First Circuit, since his appointment by President Carter in 1980.

Because of his highly praised work as a federal appeals judge, his humor, and his intellect, as well as his friendship with a number of senators on the judiciary committee, Breyer received overwhelming approval from the U.S. Senate the year following Ginsburg's confirmation. Since his confirmation in 1994, the Court's personnel picture has remained stable.

The Politics of Affirmative Action at Century's End

As America moved closer to the twenty-first century, the turmoil over the constitutionality of affirmative action continued in the courts and in other political arenas. By 1990, African-American enrollment in colleges and in graduate and professional programs reached an all-time high (and then continued to increase in subsequent years): African-American students constituted 11.9 percent of the students attending institutions of higher education. Simultaneous with this development, an organized white backlash against preferential treatment for minority-group applicants began, culminating in decisions against affirmative action in the last decade of the twentieth century. In federal and state courts, from Texas to Michigan, to Maryland, to California, and other states, new challenges to these preferential programs began.

Politically, affirmative action during the presidential elections of 1992 and 1996 saw Republican nominees speak of affirmative action as the "Willie Horton" issue of the 1990s. (Willie Horton was a felon who received a weekend furlough from a Massachusetts prison and then killed two people. Candidate George Bush during the 1988 campaign condemned his opponent, Michael Dukakis, who was governor at the time Horton was released, for being soft on crime.) After the Republicans gained control of the two houses of Congress in 1994, the more radical House of Representatives introduced in 1996 the Civil Rights Act of 1997, which would have prohibited, if passed (it never left the House), any preferential treatment based on sex, race, or ethnicity in the awarding of federal contracts or employment.

The 1990s decade has been witness to ever more ideological stridency in the American political arena. During the presidential campaigns of 1992 and 1996, both George Bush and Bob Dole, the Republican candidates, spoke out strongly against affirmative action and in support of a number of statewide anti–affirmative action ballot initiatives. On February 5, 1995, Dole (until then a longtime supporter of affirmative action programs in education and employment) asked: "Why did 62 percent of white males vote Republican in 1994? I think because of things like this [the affirmative action controversy], where sometimes the best-qualified person does not get the job because he or she may be of one color—and I'm beginning to believe that may not be the way it should be in America."

Democratic President Bill Clinton, on the other hand, while committed to preferential affirmative action programs in order to eliminate the consequences of hundreds of years of racial and ethnic discrimination, acted cautiously because of the growing cries from Republicans in Congress to end all federal affirmative action programs. His slogan for changes in federally supported affirmative action programs was "Mend it, don't end it."

After the 1994 midterm congressional elections saw Republicans win majorities in both houses of Congress, to forestall the new majority's efforts to pass anti–affirmative action legislation, President Clinton announced, on March 7, 1995, the creation of a task force that would conduct an "urgent review" of all federal affirmative action programs. He asked the group to enumerate all federal programs, to determine if they worked, and to ascertain whether all these federal affirmative action programs were fair.

Little more than four months later, in late July 1995, the completed "Review of Federal Affirmative Action Programs" was presented to Clinton by the task force leaders, George Stephanopoulos, senior advisor to the president for policy and strategy, and Christopher Edley Jr., special counsel to the president.

The report recommended a number of changes, but essentially concluded that most federal affirmative action programs were in compliance with both federal statutes and the federal Constitution. By remedying past educational and employment discrimination and by promoting inclusion of all groups in education and in employment, they worked to lead the nation toward the goal of equal opportunity.

Most of the programs examined were also deemed fair because there was not a rigid quota or set-aside program in place. They recommended that Clinton instruct each of his federal agency and department heads as follows:

> In all programs for which you are responsible that use race, ethnicity, or gender as considerations in order to expand opportunity or provide benefits to members of groups that have suffered discrimination, I ask you to take steps to ensure adherence to the following policy principles. Any program must be eliminated or reformed if it: creates a quota; creates preferences for unqualified individuals; creates reverse discrimination; or continues even after its purposes have been achieved.

In a July 19, 1995, "Memorandum for Heads of Executive Departments and Agencies," Clinton used the above language, word for word, to instruct his subordinates across the federal government to begin a careful review of all affirmative action programs that existed in their departments and bureaus. For the *New York Times* editorial board, the speech was "the defining moment of Clinton's presidency in the civil rights era, and it knocked the pins out from under his opponents." Outflanked by Clinton, the Republicans, especially Republican presidential candidate Bob Dole, backed away from pushing the affirmative action issue hard during the 1996 presidential campaign—which was won by the Democratic incumbent.

The day after Clinton gave his archives speech on affirmative action, California's Republican governor, Pete Wilson (like U.S. Senator Robert Dole, a former supporter of affirmative action), publicly called for the end of affirmative action in the University of California system and reaffirmed his support for a proposition on the ballot (Proposition 209) that, if passed, would end preferential affirmative action programs in all state agencies.

However, the board of regents of the University of California system did not await the outcome of the ballot initiative prepared by anti–affirmative action groups in California. The regents, especially in the 1990s, have been key opponents of affirmative action in higher education. Led by trustee Ward Connerly, a conservative African-American businessman who abhorred "reverse discrimination," the regents voted to end all racial preferences in admissions, employment, and other activities of the university system, effective, for professional and graduate programs, in the fall of 1997. (The following year, the University of California, Berkeley, law school had a drop of 81 percent in the number of African-American students admitted to its first-year law school class—fourteen rather than seventy-five students.)

Under the regents' new plan, now in effect, between 50 and 75 percent of all students admitted to the system must be selected on the basis of their academic grades in high school and their scores on the standardized tests (ACT and SAT).

———

With a 54 percent majority, Californians approved Proposition 209 on November 5, 1996. Called the California Civil Rights Initiative, its formal title is "A Prohibition against Discrimination or Preferential Treatment by State and other Public Entities, Initiative Constitutional Amendment." Proposition 209 provides in part that

> the state shall not discriminate against, or grant preferential treatment to, any individual or group or the basis of race, sex, color, ethnicity, or national origin in the operation of public employment, education, or public contracting.

With its passage, it became article I, section 31, of the California constitution.

Leading the battle against preferential affirmative action programs was Ward Connerly. He believed that affirmative action violated the Constitution's notion of color-blindness found in the Equal Protection Clause of the Fourteenth Amendment. He was the chairperson of the California Civil Rights Initiative (CCRI) and, along with Republican Governor Pete Wilson and Pamela A. Lewis, the cochair of the CCRI, traveled across the state to urge support of Proposition 209. In addition, Californians against Discrimination and Preferences (CADAP), was created in August 1994 to orchestrate the actions of the CCRI.

Proposition 209 directly affected admissions to the state's public college and university systems. The California State University (CSU) campuses used race and ethnicity as factors in some admissions decisions. The University of California board of regents had already in 1995 changed its admission policies to eliminate all considerations of race or ethnicity in admission decisions (the prohibition was to begin with the 1997–1998 academic year). Proposition 209 went beyond proscribing preferential admissions. It also ended all assistance programs (outreach, counseling, tutoring, financial aid programs) for students, faculty, and staff who were members of disadvantaged racial, ethnic, or gender groups.

The day after California voters passed Proposition 209, the Black Leadership Conference and the ACLU filed suit in federal district court to block enforcement of the anti–affirmative action policy. Their argument: 209 denied racial minorities and women the equal protection of the laws and was void under the Constitution's Supremacy Clause because it conflicted with Titles VI and VII of the 1964 Civil Rights Act and Title IX of the Educational Amendments of 1972. They sought a declaratory judgment that 209 was unconstitutional and a permanent injunction enjoining the state from implementing and enforcing 209.

The U.S. District Court judge, Thelton E. Henderson, issued a temporary restraining order and a preliminary injunction, ruling that the civil rights groups were likely to prevail on the merits. However, the Ninth Circuit U.S. Court of Appeals, in *Coalition for Economic Equity, et al. v. Pete Wilson, Governor*, reversed Henderson's actions, concluding that Proposition 209 was constitutional. After the appeals court sat en banc and reached the same conclusion, there was an appeal to the U.S. Supreme Court. However, on November 3, 1997, the Court denied certiorari.

Just a year after Proposition 209 was implemented, minority enrollment in the University of California system dropped precipitously. At law schools in the system, African-American admissions dropped by a whopping 72 percent, while Hispanic-American admissions dropped 35 percent. At the UC Berkeley campus, overall admission of African-American, Hispanic-American, and Native-American applicants was cut in half.

The two premier campuses of the University of California system, UC Berkeley and UCLA, experienced the most severe decline in the enrollment of minority students when article I, section 31, took effect for the 1998–1999 academic year. At Berkeley, only 98 of the 3,600 students who entered in fall 1998 were African-American. A year earlier, the last year preferential affirmative action programs were employed, 224 African-American students had entered the university. There were 185 Hispanic Americans who entered Berkeley in fall 1998, compared with 411 Hispanic first-year students who entered a year earlier.

UCLA had similar patterns of decline: 131 African Americans entered in 1998, a drop from the previous year's first-year class of 219 African Americans. There were 329 Hispanic Americans admitted in 1998, a drop from the previous year's total of 452 Hispanic-American students admitted. However, the UC's three least-selective campuses, Irvine, Riverside, and Santa Cruz, showed double-digit increases in the number of African Americans and Hispanic Americans who were admitted.

Some officials expressed grave concerns over this development. Dr. Theodore Mitchell, vice chancellor for external affairs at UCLA, said that "the most devastating possible outcome is that the University of California becomes a segregated system in which students of color are clustered in a few campuses, and Asian students and whites cluster in other campuses."

In March 1999, the UC board of regents, partly in response to the concerns of educators such as Mitchell and partly in response to complaints that higher education in the state would remain lily-white unless alternatives were taken to bring minority students into the system, changed its admission policy. Under a plan similar to those in a few other states, beginning in 1999, the top 4 percent of California high-school graduates were guaranteed admission to any of the campuses in the UC system.

———

On November 3, 1998, voters in the state of Washington approved Initiative 200, a mirror-image version of California's Proposition 209, passed two years earlier. Using the identical language found in Proposition 209, it banned "preferences" based on race or sex in state contracting, hiring, and admissions to public colleges and universities. The ballot title presented to the voters asked: "Shall government be prohibited from discriminating or granting preferential treatment based on race, sex, color, ethnicity, or national origin in public employment, education, and contracting?"

The state, known for rain, Starbucks coffee, and its political independence, became "ground zero in the nation's ongoing war over affirmative action," the *New York Times* reported in May 1998. For more than a year, the anti–affirmative action forces, led by Ward Connerly's organization and state conservatives, worked across the state to sell the initiative to the voters of Washington state (who were overwhelmingly white, with a minority population of almost 12 percent, mostly Asian Americans).

The petition needed 180,000 signatures to qualify I-200 for

placement on the ballot in November 1998. At the end of 1997, only about 90,000 signatures had been collected. Connerly and his organization entered with experience and with funds, donating almost $200,000 to the effort. The state's Republican Party leadership, by a vote of 62 to 3, supported the initiative and worked to get it on the November 1998 ballot. Also working for its passage were the Libertarian Party and the Log Cabin (gay and lesbian) Republican groups.

In opposition to the initiative were over fifty organizations (including the AAUW, the King County Bar Association, the Washington Association of Churches, the Japanese-American Citizens League, and Hands Off Washington) who participated in the unsuccessful "No! 200" campaign. Although they spent more than double the amount spent by the supporters of I-200, the opposition (even with major financial support from Starbucks Coffee, Boeing, and Microsoft) did not have much impact on the voters.

Supporters' efforts paid off. By the winter of 1997–98, 70 percent of persons polled favored the ban on preferences, while only 16 percent favored affirmative action. Marco DeFunis, practicing law in Seattle, came out in support of the initiative. He told a *Seattle Times* reporter that it was time "for public scrutiny of the admissions process at all state-supported schools. The public has a right to know what's going on."

With the "overwhelming" success of I-200 in November 1998, December 3, 1998, became a watershed date. On that day, all preferential programs ended in the state of Washington. State hiring agencies were no longer able to use race or sex in making personnel decisions. Contractors bidding for state or local subdivision contracts were no longer required to have minority subcontractors, and at the University of Washington and the other public colleges and universities, preferential admissions programs were terminated.

By 1998, there were ballot initiatives ending affirmative action in state agencies in almost a dozen states, including Arizona, Colorado, Florida, Georgia, Missouri, Nebraska, New Jersey, New York, Ohio, South Carolina, and Texas. They all called for an end to all preferences based on race, ethnicity, and gender in state and local government employment, contracting, and education. If passed, these proposals would end all state affirmative action policies that have been in effect since the 1978 *Bakke* decision. However, other than Washington state's passage of I-200 in 1998, no other state to date (2000) has placed the anti–affirmative action initiative on the ballot.

Georgia's strategy for ending affirmative action called for the passage of legislation that would amend an existing state statute "so as to provide that neither the State of Georgia, its agents, nor any of its political subdivisions shall use race, color, creed, gender, or national origin as a criterion for either discriminating against or granting preferential treatment to any individual or group."

Passage has not yet occurred. Rather, there is the decision—in the face of a federal district court judge's warnings—by the University of Georgia to continue to use race as a factor in admitting up to 20 percent minorities in its undergraduate first-year class.

The September 30, 1999, announcement by the president of the University of Georgia, Michael F. Adams, that the institution would continue to use race as one of the admissions factors put the university on a collision course with Judge B. Avant Edenfield of federal district court. A few months earlier, in a decision not binding on the university, Edenfield had written that the university "cannot constitutionally justify" the use of race in admissions. Said the president of the university: "I believe that all of us have a responsibility to deal with the legacy of segregation as an issue in both academics and in government. My commitment to providing opportunity to all is fundamental, and under my leadership the University of Georgia will remain committed to this basic right."

Florida had a preferential higher education affirmative action policy since *Bakke*, and there had been significant diversification of its formerly all-white public universities since the 1970s. At the University of Florida, the state's flagship institution of higher learning, in 1999 the student population included almost 10 percent Hispanic-American and 6 percent African-American students.

(Overall, in 1999, there were more than 200,000 students in the university system: 64 percent white; 14 percent African-American; and 14 percent Hispanic-American.)

The state, however, was literally invaded in 1999 by the opponents of affirmative action, especially Ward Connerly and his organization, now called the American Civil Rights Coalition (ACRC). Connerly arrived in the state in the spring of 1999. He and his organization were planning on spending almost $2 million in the effort to acquire the signatures of 430,000 Florida registered voters to support a statewide petition drive to eliminate the state's affirmative action programs (by amending Florida's constitution with language identical to the words approved by California voters a few years earlier). Pollsters had indicated that 84 percent of voters polled were in favor of a ban on preferential affirmative action programs.

He was, however, a pariah to Florida's African-American and Hispanic-American political leaders, as well as to the state's two political parties. Both Democratic and Republican Party leaders wanted nothing to do with his campaign to get the anti–affirmative action initiative on the 2000 ballot. (Governor Jeb Bush's brother, Texas Governor George W. Bush, was a leading candidate for the Republican Party presidential nomination in 2000 and had been eagerly seeking the votes of Hispanic Americans and African Americans. It was felt that Connerly's actions in Florida might adversely affect the Bush presidential campaign. Both Bush brothers, however, were against "rigid quotas and set-asides," as Jeb Bush informed Connerly in a letter.)

Before a statewide vote could take place, in mid-November 1999, Governor Bush signed two executive orders ending the use of race and ethnicity as factors in Florida university admissions policies and barring racial/ethnic set-asides in state contracting decisions. The first order ended the use of race- and gender-specific classifications in Florida's public college and university admissions procedures. (Race, gender, artistic talent, and athletic ability had been factors specifically mentioned by Florida's board of trustees for public higher education.)

His executive order guarantees state university admission to the top 20 percent of each high school graduating class. It is similar to California's new higher education program, which guarantees admission to the California university system for the top 4 percent of that state's high school seniors, and to Texas's new "Top Ten" program, which assures the top 10 percent of high school seniors admission to a Texas public university of their choice.

His proposal also adds $20 million to the state's university financial aid budget and, finally, makes it easier for minority businesses to be certified to work across the state. (The education executive order must be approved by Florida's board of regents, while the contracting executive order must be approved by the Florida legislature. The chancellor of the University of Florida system, African-American Adam Herbert, has already endorsed it and expects the Bush plan to fly through the board of regents.)

At a news conference held November 9, 1999, Bush said: "We can increase opportunity and diversity in the state's universities and in state contracting without using policies that discriminate or that pit one racial group against another."

Educators at Florida's law school and other professional schools generally praised the governor's effort as a common-sense alternative to threatened affirmative action programs. Although University of Miami political science professor James Corey asked: "How many generations do we have to go through with quotas?" Professor Kenneth Nunn, associate dean of the University of Florida's law school said that it was possible that "it could turn out to be a positive plan, especially since we're in an environment where there is opposition to affirmative action as it's presently structured. The [Bush] program has promise. Whether it lives up to that promise remains to be seen."

Some African-American Florida legislators opposed the Bush plan, while others responded with cautious optimism. Representative Lee Miller, of Tampa, said that "the Governor is taking a positive step toward protecting racial and gender inclusiveness in Florida's universities and contracting practices." At a later press conference, however, he disagreed with himself, saying: "I don't like it [Bush's executive order] at all."

Ward Connerly, leading the anti–affirmative action force

Florida, said that his organization, ACRC, would review the governor's executive order to determine whether or not to end the petition drive. Shortly thereafter, Connerly's organization rejected the Bush plan and vowed to continue to collect signatures so that a ballot initiative could take place in that state.

On November 13, 1999, the *New York Times* editorialized that Bush's "executive orders have provided a reasoned basis for the coming debate over affirmative action. . . . Unbending to the last, Mr. Connerly has rejected the Bush proposals and pledged to continue his campaign for a referendum. But even in the distance, one can feel Mr. Connerly's sails collapsing for lack of wind."

By the spring of 2000, Governor Bush's program, called the One Florida Initiative, faced challenges from both the right and the left. Ward Connerly on the right (who was leading the call for a statewide referendum to end all affirmative action programs) and black and Hispanic legislators and civil rights advocates on the left (who wanted to retain the affirmative action plans) were equally critical of the plan. Bush insisted that his plan, approved by his cabinet in late March 2000, "walked a middle ground" between these two warring groups. The Florida legislature was expected to approve the final parts of the program during its spring 2000 session.

One must look, finally, at the question of *Bakke*'s impact and its fate as legal precedent in America. The next chapter raises these and other questions about the future of preferential affirmative action programs in higher education.

CHAPTER 8

The *Bakke* Legacy: Hanging by a Thread?

When *Bakke* was announced in late June 1978, UCD medical school students had different takes on Bakke's campus reception. Saul Schaefer, a white second-year student, said that Bakke "will be treated by most students as a first-year medical student. People aren't going to throw pies in his face. They're going to ignore him."

A minority student, Llorens Penbrook, said that he "was not going out of my way to make him uncomfortable. There's nothing wrong with him as an individual but he just represents a reversal trend of the gains minorities made in the 1960s." Another third-year minority med student, Jay Starks, said: "I think I will be polite to him. But I am sure we do not have the same ideas and views on medicine." But Sharon Jackson, a second-year med student, was saddened and angry at the decision and the man who represented what to her was a backward move in civil rights: "If it took 200 years to build a house and someone comes along with a match and tries to burn it down, how would you feel? We don't want the house to be burned down!"

Allan Bakke entered UCD medical school in late September 1978. The opening day of classes saw more than one hundred anti-*Bakke* demonstrators chanting "Smash the *Bakke* decision now!" He passed the protesters completely unnoticed by them. For the most part, Bakke was ignored during his tenure in medical school, and four years later, at the age of forty-two, he graduated from the UCD medical school.

During an informal ceremony on March 18, 1972, the graduating medical students met to see where they would be doing their internships. According to a reporter covering the event,

Bakke received "the loudest applause among the medical graduates" after he read his letter telling him that he received an internship at the prestigious Mayo Clinic in Rochester, Minnesota.

Rita Clancy was admitted to UCD medical school because of Allan Bakke's victory. Clancy, a twenty-three-year-old Russian-born immigrant, daughter of survivors of Nazi concentration camps, arrived in America when she was fourteen years old, speaking only Hungarian and Russian. The family went on welfare months after they arrived in America, because of a sudden, disabling injury to her father. Like Marco DeFunis and Allan Bakke, Rita worked while she attended UCLA, where she majored in psychobiology and graduated with an A– grade point average.

In 1976 she applied for admission to the UCD medical school but was denied admission, although minority students with grades and scores inferior to hers were admitted under the UCD special minority admissions process. She sought counsel, and the lawyer immediately brought suit in federal court, arguing, as Bakke did, that Rita was a victim of discrimination by UCD and that she should be admitted. While *Bakke* was being argued in the fall of 1977, she was admitted to UCD's medical school under a federal court order.

A week after the *Bakke* decision was announced, July 8, 1978, Donald Reidhaar, the University of California's chief counsel, dropped the university's effort to bar the white woman from staying in medical school. And so Rita Clancy and Allan Bakke became first-year medical school classmates in September 1978.

Was the Clancy story to be repeated multiple times in light of the judgment of the U.S. Supreme Court? After *Bakke* came down, everyone began to gauge its impact on higher education. The NAACP view, in January 1979, was that *Bakke* already had "a chilling impact" on minority education in America. The president of the University of Pennsylvania, speaking for some educational administrators, said that after *Bakke*, all special minority admissions committees are "potential litigation breeders."

As we look back after almost a quarter century, the questions are still there: What has been the effect of *Bakke?* Is *Bakke* still viable precedent? Has the U.S. Supreme Court majority sub

{ *The* Bakke *Case* }

silento overturned *Bakke?* Has *Bakke* been transcended by alternative political remedies that accomplish the same end?

From 1981 through the end of the century, there were significant personnel changes on the Court—changes that were, in a few instances, classic examples of raucous hardball Washington confirmation politics. The eight personnel changes between 1981 and 1994 were:

1981	Stewart replaced by Sandra Day O'Connor	(R)
1986	Chief Justice Burger replaced by Associate Justice Rehnquist	
1986	Rehnquist replaced by Antonin Scalia	(R)
1987	Powell replaced by Anthony Kennedy	(R)
1990	Brennan replaced by David Souter	(R)
1991	Marshall replaced by Clarence Thomas	(R)
1993	White replaced by Ruth B. Ginsburg	(D)
1994	Blackmun replaced by Stephen Breyer	(D)

However, at the end of the twentieth century, the Court's voting breakout on affirmative action is about where it was in 1978! Three justices, Rehnquist (Reagan), Scalia (Reagan), and Thomas (Bush), are categorically ideologically opposed to all preferential programs that benefit minority group members. Four justices, Souter (Bush), Stevens (Ford), Ginsburg (Clinton), and Breyer (Clinton), have voted to support affirmative action programs. Justice Kennedy generally sides with the Rehnquist trio but occasionally has joined in the concurring opinions of Justice Sandra Day O'Connor.

The person in the middle—on cases involving racial and gender discrimination—is the first female appointed to the Court, conservative pragmatist Sandra Day O'Connor. Like Powell, she has cast the key vote in affirmative action cases since 1987. Unlike her conservative brethren, O'Connor believes that affirmative action programs "should be used as a modest, temporary response against discrimination." And unlike her more liberal colleagues, she insists that the strict scrutiny standard must be used to evaluate the constitutionality of all challenged affirmative action programs.

During the 1980s O'Connor voted in favor of some affirmative action programs, saying that: "The unhappy persistence of both the practice and the lingering effects of racial discrimination against minority groups in this country is an unfortunate reality, and the government is not disqualified from acting in response to it." While she disagreed with her four more liberal brethren, she was more flexible than the Rehnquist trio, who would strike down *Bakke* and all other decisions of earlier Courts that validated preferential affirmative action programs.

Joan Biskupic, the *Washington Post*'s Supreme Court reporter, wrote, in 1997, that O'Connor "is an intriguing justice to be at the center of an emotionally charged discrimination [issue]. Although she has a conservative approach, . . . O'Connor has felt the sting of bias."

———

Many events, political and legal, have occurred since Allan Bakke initially challenged the constitutionality of UCD's medical school's preferential admissions program in 1974. Questions now posed in the legal anatomy lesson focus on both *Bakke*'s impact and its legacy. Has *Bakke* had an effect on realizing the goal of greater diversity in higher education—both undergraduate and graduate and professional programs? While it has not happened except for the Fifth Circuit U.S. Court of Appeals *Hopwood* decision, what would happen if *Bakke* was overturned by the U.S. Supreme Court? What is *Bakke*'s legacy in higher education? Are there alternatives to the *Bakke* remedy for unequal educational opportunities?

———

The Supreme Court's Leading Affirmative Action Jurisprudence after *Bakke*

In addition to the new appointments, there was the fluid movement of sitting justices on the issue of affirmative action. Justice White flipped his stance on the issue and was in the 1980s part of the Rehnquist cohort. However, Justice Stevens moved over to the Brennan camp after *Bakke,* and by 1981 he was an integral part of that pro–affirmative action cohort. These moves led to some significant changes in the way in which the Court dealt with preferential affirmative action programs after Powell's retirement in 1987 and the 1988 confirmation of his successor, Anthony Kennedy. Although there have been a number of affirmative action cases decided by the Court, three cases in particular—*Wygant, Croson,* and *Adarand*—reflect the present Court's perspectives on affirmative action programs in education, employment, and housing.

In a 1986 case from Michigan, *Wygant v. Board of Education,* the Court divided 5 to 4 regarding the constitutionality of a lay-off plan, part of a collective bargaining agreement between a school board and the teachers union, that gave preferential protection to minorities. Due to budgetary problems, the Jackson school board laid off white teachers with greater seniority than minority teachers who were retained. The non-minority teachers brought suit in federal district court, claiming that they had been laid off due to their race in violation of the Fourteenth Amendment's Equal Protection Clause. The federal trial judge dismissed their claims, stating that the presence in the classroom of minority teachers provided "role models for minority school children." The Sixth Circuit validated the trial court's action, agreeing with the "role model" assessment. The white teachers then took their case to the Supreme Court.

At the conference session after oral argument, the Court seemed evenly divided. Four jurists voted to reverse (Burger, Powell, White, and Rehnquist), another four voted to affirm (Brennan, Blackmun, Stevens, and Marshall) the lower court judgment in favor of the plan, and O'Connor voted to remand.

However, in late November 1985, the tide turned as O'Connor voted to reverse. The Court majority struck down the Michigan school board's voluntary plan for laying off teachers that gave preference to minority faculty over more senior white faculty. Societal discrimination alone was an insufficient justification for the use of racial classifications. "Without more," wrote Powell, it is "too amorphous a basis for imposing a racially classified remedy."

The Jackson plan was in violation of the Fourteenth Amendment's Equal Protection Clause, Powell argued. Employing the strict scrutiny standard in the case, Powell believed that the school board had not presented "compelling" reasons for the plan nor had they "narrowly tailored" its use of the racial criterion to remedy past discriminatory hiring practices.

Like *Bakke*, *Wygant* produced deep division among the jurists and led to the production of six opinions. Justice O'Connor wrote the critical concurring opinion. In opposition to justices who viewed statutory relief in narrow terms, she noted that affirmative action programs could be devised "that need not be limited to the remedying of specific instances of identified discrimination." Justice White, also concurring, thought that none of the Court's affirmative action precedents supported "the discharge of white teachers to make room for blacks, none of whom has been shown to be a victim of racial discrimination."

Marshall's dissent in *Wygant*, joined by Brennan and Blackmun, employed his "sliding scale" Fourteenth Amendment standard to reach the conclusion that the school board plan's layoffs were "substantially related to important governmental objectives." The "goal of easing racial tension was an acceptable governmental objective whether or not the elimination of societal discrimination was a permissible governmental interest."

The fourth dissenter, John Paul Stevens, argued that the plan was constitutional because it advanced educational goals by having African-American school teachers as role models for minority students in the school system.

Three years later another challenge to a preferential affirmative action plan—this time one implemented by a local government—came to the Court from Richmond, Virginia. Half the city's population was African-American, but only 1 percent of the over $25 million awarded in city contracts went to minority businesses. Richmond, the capital of the Confederacy during the Civil War, was making a good-faith attempt to remedy past and present racial discrimination in municipal construction contracts. The city created a set-aside construction funds program that awarded a portion of its municipal contracts (30 percent) to minority business enterprises. By definition, these were construction companies owned by "citizens of the United States who are Blacks, Spanish-speaking, Orientals, Indians, Eskimos, or Aleuts." Both the federal trial court and the Fourth Circuit U.S. Court of Appeals upheld the Richmond ordinance. The lower federal court agreed with the city's findings that there was a history of past racial discrimination that was remedied by the city's program.

In *Richmond, Va. v. J. A. Croson Co.*, the majority struck down the ordinance. The six-person majority, including the three justices appointed after 1981, invalidated the affirmative action program that set aside city funds for minority-owned contractors. Six separate opinions were written, reflecting the continued disagreements between the justices over the constitutionality of affirmative action. Justice O'Connor wrote the opinion for the Court, joined only by Rehnquist, White, and Kennedy. Justices Stevens, Kennedy, and Scalia wrote separate concurring opinions. Marshall wrote a dissent, joined by Brennan and Blackmun. Justice Blackmun wrote a separate dissent, joined by Brennan.

O'Connor's opinion striking down the Richmond set-aside effort focused in part on the differences between the sources of federal authority and state authority. The city of Richmond could not do what Congress did in its affirmative action programs because the state was bound by the "constraints" of the Fourteenth Amendment, while Congress "has a specific constitutional mandate to enforce the dictates of the Fourteenth Amendment. The power to 'enforce' may at times also include the power to define situations which Congress determines threaten principles of equality and to adopt prophylactic rules to deal with those situations."

Furthermore, Richmond's effort to remedy past racial discrimination was rigid and overinclusive at the same time, leading to "stigmatic harm," and for those reasons was unconstitutional. Past history, "standing alone, cannot justify a rigid quota in the awarding of public contracts in Richmond, Virginia." Using the strict scrutiny mechanism, she said: "we think it obvious that such a program is not narrowly tailored to remedy the effects of prior discrimination." Because Richmond "failed to identify the need for remedial action in the awarding of its public construction contracts, its treatment of its citizens on a racial basis violates the dictates of the Equal Protection Clause." Under the Fourteenth Amendment, she concluded, the analysis requirement is strict scrutiny "of all race based action by state or local governments."

Kennedy's concurrence, like Scalia's, addressed the "moral imperative of racial neutrality" as "the driving force of the Equal Protection Clause." The Fourteenth Amendment's color-blindness center was transformed, through their interpretation, into a core concept of "race neutrality." Neither concept, for Kennedy and Scalia, allowed a state or a city "to act affirmatively to ameliorate the effects of past discrimination"—unless there was an identifiable victim of state racial discrimination.

Harry Blackmun's dissent was short and unusually acerbic. "I never thought that I would live to see the day when the city of Richmond, Virginia, the cradle of the Old Confederacy, sought on its own, within a narrow confine, to lessen the stark impact of persistent discrimination. But Richmond, to its great credit, acted. Yet this Court, the supposed bastion of equality, strikes down Richmond's efforts as though discrimination had never existed or was not demonstrated in this particular litigation."

Marshall dissented from the majority's "shallowness," and again he was joined by Brennan and Blackmun. *Croson* was "a deliberate and giant step backward in this Court's affirmative action jurisprudence." Race-conscious remedies that "serve important governmental objectives" and that are "substantively related to the achievement of these objectives" are constitutional, he maintained. He condemned the "majority's perfunctory dismissal" of the testimony of Richmond's appointed and elected leaders. The "armchair cynicism" of his colleagues in the majority was "deeply disturbing" to Marshall. Their failure to comprehend what was really going on in Richmond led them to minimize the effects of past segregation and racial discrimination.

This case, wrote one of Marshall's clerks, "scarred" Marshall's heart. As he said in his dissent, the majority "sounds a full-scale retreat from the Court's long-standing solicitude for race conscious remedial efforts." It was the "civil rights massacre of

{ *The* Bakke *Case* }

1989." The majority still continued to maintain, Marshall wrote, that "racial discrimination [was] largely a phenomenon of the past, and that government bodies need no longer to preoccupy themselves with rectifying racial injustice."

In the second part of the 1990s, there have been two important affirmative action cases that may affect the future of the *Bakke* precedent. One of them is *Adarand Constructors v. Pena*, 1995; the other was a non-decision of the Court a year later, *Texas v. Hopwood.*

Adarand was only the third case to come to the Court that challenged federal affirmative action practices used by federal agencies. The two earlier cases, which would be overturned in major part by *Adarand*, were *Fullilove v. Klutznick*, 1980, and *Metro Broadcasting v. Federal Communications Commission*, 1990.

Although not a case involving affirmative action in higher education, the *Adarand* decision provides observers with a clearer portrait of the Court's approach to evaluating all affirmative action cases coming to the Court after 1995. In *Bakke* there was no majority that supported the use of the strict scrutiny standard in affirmative action; Powell was the only justice to employ it in *Bakke*. In both *Fullilove* and *Metro*, the Court majorities used Brennan's intermediate scrutiny standard to validate federal affirmative action programs.

In *Adarand* the justices divided 5 to 4 (with six opinions again written, including three dissents, by Ginsburg, Souter, and Stevens, and two concurring opinions, by Thomas and Scalia). The majority agreed that strict scrutiny was the appropriate judicial standard to employ to determine whether equal-protection language [in both the Fifth and the Fourteenth Amendments] was violated by the challenged federal agency's affirmative action program. (There were over forty major federal affirmative action programs in existence at the time of *Adarand*.)

Since the late 1960s most federal agency contracts must contain a "subcontractor compensation" clause, which gives the prime contractor financial incentives to hire subcontractors that have been certified as a "small business controlled by socially and economically disadvantaged individuals," defined by the federal

Small Business Administration to "include Black Americans, Hispanic Americans, Native Americans, Asian Pacific Americans, and other minorities."

In 1989, the Central Federal Lands Highway Division of the U.S. Department of Transportation awarded a prime contract to Mountain Gravel and Construction Company. The company then sought bids for the guardrail portion of the contract. The Gonzales Construction Company was awarded the subcontract although the petitioner, Adarand Constructors, Inc., had submitted the low bid for that subcontracting work. Adarand filed a lawsuit against the respondent, the U.S. Secretary of Transportation. Their claim: race-based presumptions used in subcontractor compensation clauses violate the equal-protection component of the Fifth Amendment's Due Process Clause. The U.S. District Court summarily ruled in favor of the federal incentives program. The Tenth Circuit U.S. Court of Appeals affirmed, using Brennan's *Bakke* intermediate scrutiny standard.

Adarand appealed, and the Supreme Court, rejecting any standard less than strict scrutiny, reversed the lower federal courts' judgments and remanded the case for a new hearing. Justice O'Connor wrote the judgment of the Court. Broadening the impact of the *Croson* decision, she concluded that all racial classifications, "imposed by whatever federal, state, or local governmental actor," must be analyzed by a reviewing court under "strict scrutiny."

There are, she wrote, three general propositions with respect to the constitutionality of all affirmative action programs:

1. Skepticism: "Any preference based on racial or ethnic criteria must necessarily receive a most searching examination [using the strict scrutiny analysis]."
2. Consistency: "The standard of review under the Equal Protection Clause is not dependent upon the race of those burdened or benefitted by a particular classification."
3. Congruence: "Equal protection analysis in the Fifth Amendment is the same as that under the Fourteenth Amendment."

From these, the conclusion followed: "Any person, of whatever race, has the right to demand that any governmental actor subject to the Constitution justify any racial classification subjecting that person to unequal treatment under the strictest judicial scrutiny."

All federal classifications, O'Connor concluded, "like those of a state," must serve a "compelling governmental interest" and "must be narrowly tailored to further that interest." Requiring strict scrutiny, she wrote, was the "best way to ensure that courts will consistently give racial classifications a detailed examination, as to both ends and means. It is not true that strict scrutiny is strict in theory, but fatal in fact. Government is not disqualified from acting in response to the unhappy persistence of both the practice and the lingering effects of racial discrimination against minority groups in this country. When race based action is necessary to further a compelling interest, such action is within constitutional constraints if it satisfies the 'narrow tailoring' test."

The case was remanded because *Adarand* "alters the playing field in some important aspects." The court of appeals was directed to employ strict scrutiny, that is, to determine whether the subcontractor compensation clause served a "compelling state interest" and whether the means taken by the federal agency was the most "narrowly tailored" one to reach the compelling governmental ends and interests. Chief Justice Rehnquist joined O'Connor, as did Justices Kennedy, Thomas, and, in some segments, Scalia.

Justice Scalia concurred in most of O'Connor's judgment. However, his conclusion was much harsher with respect to affirmative action programs based on race or color. Scalia said that government *never* has a "compelling interest" in discriminating on the basis of race in order to "make up" for past racial discrimination in the opposite direction. Under the "color-blind" Constitution, "individuals who have been wronged by unlawful racial discrimination should be made whole; but under our Constitution there can be no such thing as either a creditor or debtor race. That concept is alien to the Constitution's focus on the individual . . . and its rejection of dispositions based on race . . . or based on blood."

Justice Thomas concurred in order to re-emphasize his concern about the psychological effects of an affirmative action program on individuals who received the programmatic benefits. For the African-American jurist, the psychological damage, the "adverse stigmatic effect on its intended beneficiaries," that resulted from such race-preferential programs was too high a cost to allow such programs to exist. There was no difference between benign and negative governmental discrimination: "In my mind, government-sponsored racial discrimination based on benign prejudice is just as noxious as discrimination inspired by malicious practice. In each instance, it is racial discrimination, plain and simple."

In addition he was concerned because all governmental affirmative action programs "not only raise grave constitutional questions, they also undermine the moral basis of the equal protection principle. Purchased at the price of immeasurable human suffering, the equal protection principle reflects our Nation's understanding that such classifications ultimately have a destructive impact on the individual and our society."

Justice Stevens filed a dissent, joined by Justice Ginsburg. He objected to the use of the strict scrutiny analysis in all affirmative action cases. "The majority's conception of 'consistency' ignores a difference, fundamental to the idea of equal protection, between oppression and assistance. The majority's concept of 'congruence' ignores a difference, fundamental to our constitutional system, between the Federal Government and the States. And the majority's concept of stare decisis ignores the force of binding precedent. I would affirm the judgment of the Court of Appeals."

Justice Souter also dissented, joined by Justices Ginsburg and Breyer. He believed that the Brennan intermediate scrutiny standard was the appropriate one courts should use when examining affirmative action programs. He thought, however, that many governmental programs would pass constitutional muster even when the strict scrutiny standard was applied by the Court.

Justice Ginsburg also filed a dissent, joined by Justice Breyer. Like the other dissenters, she believed that Congress must be treated differently than state and local governments. The judiciary should defer to congressional power to use the enforcement section of the Fourteenth Amendment to redress vestiges of racial discrimination in America. Racial discrimination and inequality are still prominent characteristics of the American landscape at the end of the twentieth century:

> Job applicants with identical resumes, qualifications, and interview styles still experience different deals. People of color looking for housing still face discriminatory treatment by landlords, real estate agents, and mortgage lenders. Minority entrepreneurs sometimes fail to gain contracts though they are the low bidders, and they are sometimes refused work even after winning contracts. Bias both conscious and unconscious, reflecting traditional and unexamined habits of thought, keep up barriers that must come down if equal opportunity and nondiscrimination are ever genuinely to become this country's law and practice.

In the end, however, Ginsburg tried to find a common ground between the O'Connor majority opinion and the opinions of the four dissenters. The major section of her dissent, in effect, was to put a "good spin" on the O'Connor opinion. Ginsburg wrote "separately to underscore not the differences the several opinions in this case display, but the considerable field of agreement—the common understandings and concerns—revealed in opinions that speak together for a majority of the Court." The common threads were the Court's

> recognition of the persistence of racial inequality and a majority's acknowledgement of Congress' authority to act affirmatively, not only to end discrimination, but also to counteract racism's lingering effects. Those effects, reflective of a system of racial caste only recently ended, are evident in our workplaces, markets, and neighborhoods. . . . Properly, a majority of this Court calls for [strict scrutiny] review that is searching in order to ferret out classifications in reality malign, but masquerading as benign. . . . Today's decision thus usefully reiterates that the purpose of strict scrutiny is precisely to distinguish legitimate from illegitimate uses of race in governmental decision making.

In the last sentence of her opinion, Ginsburg expressed hope for the future of affirmative action: "I see today's decision as one that allows our [affirmative action] precedent to evolve, still to be informed by and responsive to changing conditions."

Over in the Clinton administration's DOJ, Walter Dellinger, an assistant attorney general in the Office of Legal Counsel, on the day *Adarand* came down, sent a "Memorandum To General Counsels, Re: Adarand." It was sent "to provide a general overview of the Court's decision and the new standard for assessing the constitutionality of federal affirmative action programs." Strict scrutiny, wrote Dellinger, is now applicable to federal as well as state and local affirmative action measures. He did, however, point out that seven of the justices acknowledged "the unhappy persistence of both the practice and the lingering effects of racial discrimination against minority groups in this country." Concluding, he reminded the lawyers that *Adarand* "makes it necessary to evaluate federal programs that use race or ethnicity as a basis for decisionmaking to determine if they comport with the strict scrutiny standard. No affirmative action program should be suspended prior to such an evaluation."

Affirmative Action Litigation That the U.S. Supreme Court Did Not Review in the 1990s

After *Adarand*, the U.S. Supreme Court did not hear any major litigation involving affirmative action for the remainder of the decade. However, in a number of cases, either the justices did not grant certiorari or the case became moot or was remanded by a federal appeals court.

Podberesky v. Kirwin, 1996, was one such affirmative action case that was reversed and remanded by a lower federal appeals court and has not yet reached the Supreme Court. In this case, a white student challenged the constitutionality of the University of Maryland's Benjamin Banneker Scholarship program, available only to black students. The university's counsel argued that the scholarship program was designed to address the underrepresentation of African Americans in the student body.

Podberesky's lawyers maintained that the only constitutional way to provide scholarship awards was using a reference pool of all graduating high school students—African Americans, Native Americans, Caucasians, and others—and to provide scholarships to those in this inclusive pool who did the required academic work in high school, maintained no lower than a 2.0 grade point average, and received an SAT verbal score of 270 or higher and math score of 380 or higher.

The university maintained that it did not use such rigid, quantitative data to make funding support decisions. The lawyers argued that the reference pool for the scholarships were only African Americans who graduated high school, took the SAT, and graduated with an academic diploma.

The federal district court judge did not use the plaintiff's criteria, nor did he try to create a minimum set of criteria for the university to use in granting the scholarships. The judge warned against using "objective criteria" to establish the minimum criteria because they "ignore the variables in the admissions process." He concluded: "The judge should look at the statistics as a whole to determine if they provide strong evidence of the existence of the present effects of past discrimination." The university's action in awarding the Banneker scholarships did not violate the Fourteenth Amendment's Equal Protection Clause.

On appeal to the Fourth Circuit U.S. Court of Appeals, the district court judgment was reversed and remanded to the federal trial court. The appeals court judges concluded that the trial judge erred in declining to determine the effective minimum criteria used in the disbursement of the Banneker scholarships.

In 1998, the Supreme Court lost an opportunity to hear another controversy over a preferential affirmative action program in education. *Board of Education v. Taxman*, 1998, was removed after the Court granted certiorari because the Piscataway, New Jersey, Board of Education settled out of court with the white teacher, Sharon Taxman.

In 1990, Taxman had intervened in a lawsuit brought against the board of education by the Bush administration's Department of Justice. The Bush White House, no friend of affirmative action, saw it as a very good case to bring to the U.S. Supreme

Court. The hope, quite an imaginable one, was that the conservative majority on the Court would take the case and use it to end all non-remedial affirmative action programs.

The constitutional issue arose when the board of education, in 1989, had to lay off one teacher in the high school's business department. The department consisted of ten faculty, nine white and one African American. Though the seniority system was the sole criterion for making these decisions, a white teacher, Sharon Taxman, and an African-American teacher, Debra Williams, had identical hire dates nine years earlier and somewhat equivalent teaching credentials.

Prior to the adoption of its affirmative action program in 1975, that deadlock would have literally been decided by a toss of a coin. Because of the existence of an affirmative action program, and given that Williams was the only African-American business teacher, the board laid off Taxman.

After the Bush DOJ brought suit under Title VII of the 1964 Civil Rights Act against the Board, Taxman intervened to assert claims under both Title VII and the New Jersey Law against Discrimination (NJLAD). (Title VII banned all employment discrimination based on "race, color, sex, or national origin" and created the permanent EEOC to enforce the provisions of the 1964 Civil Rights Act.) In a summary judgment, the federal district court judge found the board to be liable under both statutes and awarded damages to Taxman; a jury also awarded additional damages to her under the NJLAD for "emotional distress." (In 1993, Taxman was subsequently rehired to replace a retiring business faculty member.)

The board then appealed to the Third Circuit U.S. Court of Appeals. The court of appeals majority, 8 to 4, in its opening paragraph of its en banc opinion said that "We must decide whether Title VII permits an employer with a racially balanced work force to grant a non-remedial racial preference in order to promote 'racial diversity.'"

That court ruled in favor of Taxman because the school board's action violated Title VII of the 1964 Civil Rights Act: "Given the clear anti-discrimination mandate of Title VII, a

{ *The* Bakke *Case* }

non-remedial affirmative action program, even one with a laudable purpose, cannot pass muster." The school board's lawyers sought review in the U.S. Supreme Court.

The Clinton administration filed an amicus brief. It was a request that the Court not hear this "atypical" case because "the affirmative action issue would be better presented" by a more typical affirmative action controversy.

Against the advice of Clinton's solicitor general, on June 27, 1997, the Supreme Court granted certiorari and scheduled oral argument in the case early in its upcoming 1997 term (with a decision expected in May or June of 1998). While opponents of affirmative action were extremely pleased with the grant of certiorari, civil rights groups were mortified by the possibility of a Rehnquist majority opinion in *Taxman* that might end all non-remedial affirmative action plans.

In a highly unusual move, after certiorari had been granted, seventeen civil rights organizations, including the NAACP, the SCLC, and the National Urban League, concluded that they had to provide financial aid to the board so that it could settle with Taxman before the U.S. Supreme Court heard oral arguments. A November 21, 1997, press report in the *Newark Star-Ledger* announced the settlement:

> The Black Leadership Forum, a confederation of leading civil rights organizations, agreed to pay [70 percent] of the $433,500 settlement [$188,000 to Taxman, the balance to her lawyers]. School board members, who voted 5:3 in favor of the settlement, said that outside help persuaded them to drop their appeal to the Supreme Court.

In its own newsletter, the ACLU noted that the settlement of the New Jersey case came only two weeks after the Supreme Court refused to grant certiorari in another affirmative action case from California (the ACLU challenge of California's Proposition 209).

The major higher education case involving preferential affirmative action programs came to the Court in 1996. *Texas v. Hopwood* challenged the University of Texas School of Law's (UTSL) preferential admissions policy. This was ironic, because in the

1950 Supreme Court decision *Sweatt v. Painter,* the Supreme Court ended "Jim Crowism" in higher education when it ordered the University of Texas law school to admit the African-American petitioner, Heman Sweatt, and all other qualified black students. In the 1990s, the same law school was challenged by white applicants because, they believed, the school was practicing preferential "reverse discrimination" in violation of the Fourteenth Amendment's Equal Protection Clause.

The law school evaluated minority candidates under separate processes and employed different standards than those used to evaluate white applicants. The "goals" established by the law school were 10 percent Hispanic Americans and 5 percent African Americans. Four people who were denied admission, Cheryl Hopwood, a white, middle-aged working mother of a severely handicapped child and wife of a member of the U.S. Air Force, and three white males—Douglas Cavell, Kenneth Elliot, and David Rogers—challenged the affirmative action policy. Their claim: UTSL discriminated against them in violation of the Fourteenth Amendment's Equal Protection Clause.

The federal district court judge in *Hopwood* upheld the numerical goals used in the law school preferential admissions plan. They were, he concluded, both "compelling and constitutional." However, the university had not "narrowly tailored" the program to achieve its compelling goals. Consequently, he invalidated the procedures for separate screening of applicants. He did not award the punitive damages requested by Hopwood and the others because the judge found that the law school had acted in good faith. However, like Allan Bakke, Cheryl Hopwood and the other three were not ordered admitted to the University of Texas law school by the federal trial judge. Hopwood appealed the decision to the Fifth Circuit U.S. Court of Appeals.

A three-judge circuit panel of the Fifth Circuit U.S. Court of Appeals, all conservative jurists appointed by Republican presidents Reagan and Bush, reversed the district court judge's order and invalidated in toto the university law school's preferential admissions program. Using the strict scrutiny standard, the appeals court panel raised two questions:

1. Does the racial justification serve a compelling governmental purpose?
2. Is it narrowly tailored to the achievement of that goal?

Before answering the questions, they took the highly unusual step of invalidating Justice Powell's *Bakke* judgment for the Court.

They explicitly rejected Justice Powell's *Bakke* judgment, referring to it as a "lonely opinion," that race could be used as one of a number of personal factors to determine whether an applicant would be admitted. They held that the use of race as a factor in law school admissions was "per se proscribed . . . [for] it carries the danger of stigmatic harm." Although the ruling stated that the admissions committee could not use race as a factor in the process, it did state that

> a university may properly favor one applicant over another because of his ability to play the cello, make a downfield tackle, or understand chaos theory. . . . An admissions process may also consider an applicant's home state or relationship to school alumni. Schools may even consider factors such as whether an applicant's parents attended the college or the applicant's economic and social background, [however], the law school may not use race as a factor in law-school admissions. The use of race to achieve diversity undercuts the ultimate goal of the Fourteenth Amendment: the end of racially motivated state action.

Two of the three judges on the circuit panel maintained that "Justice Powell's view in *Bakke* is not binding precedent [because much of his opinion] was joined by no other justice." Powell's argument in *Bakke*, they concluded, did not have a majority of five to make it a meaningful precedent. The concurring judge, Wiener, disagreed with his colleagues' "overreaching": "If *Bakke* is to be declared dead, the U.S. Supreme Court, not a three judge panel of a circuit court, should make that pronouncement."

The university then requested that the entire Fifth Circuit, all sixteen federal appeals judges, sit en banc to hear the *Hopwood* case again. By a vote of 9 to 7, the judges rejected the request. All nine of the judges who declined to rehear the case were Reagan and Bush appointees; six of the seven dissenters were appointed by Democratic presidents Jimmy Carter and Bill Clinton. The dissenters wrote that the majority went out of its way "to break ground that the U.S. Supreme Court itself has been careful to avoid and purports to overrule a Supreme Court decision. . . . The radical implications of this opinion will literally change the face of public educational institutions throughout Texas, the other states of this circuit, and this nation."

In the immediate aftermath of the *Hopwood* decision, the dissenters proved to be correct in their estimate of the opinion's consequences for minority student enrollments in the University of Texas law school. In 1996, before *Hopwood* was applied to grad- uate and professional school admissions, there were sixty-five African Americans and seventy Mexican Americans attending the law school. A year later, in 1997, after *Hopwood*'s proscriptions went into effect, there were only five first-year African Americans and eighteen Mexican Americans in attendance at the law school. And, in 1998, there were only four first-year African Americans attending the University of Texas law school, along with a correspondingly smaller number of Mexican Americans.

The university's lawyers filed for a writ of certiorari from the U.S. Supreme Court. Two civil rights organizations, the Thurgood Marshall Legal Society and the University of Texas Black Pre-Law Association, filed amicus curiae briefs with the Court, urging that certiorari be granted. In addition, the Clinton administration, through a brief filed by the solicitor general, nine states (Arizona, Hawaii, Iowa, Maryland, Massachusetts, Minnesota, New Mexico, Oklahoma, and West Virginia), and the District of Columbia all supported the University of Texas by filing amicus curiae briefs.

Their actions did not persuade the Court to grant review. On the last day of its 1995 term, the U.S. Supreme Court chose to deny certiorari in *Hopwood*. In a statement that accompanied the denial of certiorari, Justice Ginsburg, joined by Justice Souter, pointed out that the university's law school had abandoned the affirmative action program that had been challenged by Cheryl

Hopwood after the federal district court judge's decision and before the court of appeals' shocking opinion.

The new law school admissions policy, which moved away from separate processes, was not the focus of the challenge, nor was it the subject of the federal appellate court's judgment. "Accordingly," Ginsburg wrote, "we must await a final judgment on a program genuinely in controversy before addressing the important question raised in this petition."

The result: the federal appellate panel's judgment became precedent in the states in the Fifth Circuit's orbit: Texas, Mississippi, and Louisiana. The case was remanded to the federal district court for a second trial in order for the judge to reconsider whether the plaintiffs were entitled to damages.

At the second trial, the judge, in March 1998, issued an injunction that banned the use of all racial preferences. However, regarding damages the plaintiffs incurred, the judge awarded them only one dollar each because he concluded that they would not have been admitted to the law school even in the absence of the preferential affirmative action admissions policy. The university again went into the Fifth Circuit to challenge the judgment of the district court judge. So too did the four white plaintiffs, because of their unhappiness over his damages assessment—and his slashing by 50 percent their request for $1.5 million for attorney fees. (This second *Hopwood* go-around is sure to be the basis for another certiorari petition to the U.S. Supreme Court, probably during its 2001 term.)

The Top Ten Plan:
Texas's Response to *Hopwood*

The Texas legislature, in the hopes of neutralizing the impact of *Hopwood* on minority undergraduate enrollments, passed legislation requiring Texas's public colleges and universities to accept applicants who graduated in the top 10 percent of their high school class. Graduating seniors in this bracket were guaranteed admission to the Texas public university of their choice.

However, the legislation did not address the question of diversifying graduate and professional school enrollment. In Texas the year after the Court denied certiorari in *Hopwood*, Latino and African-American graduate enrollments at the University of Texas—which had been at an all-time record high—plunged by 64 percent and 88 percent respectively.

Michael Sharlot, the dean of the University of Texas School of Law, spoke of one measure that might address the dilemma over recruitment of law (and medical) school minority applicants: Identify college seniors who performed better in college than their SAT or ACT scores indicated, and provide them with an $800 stipend to cover the cost of an LSAT (or an MCAT) prep course offered by commercial companies such as Kaplan. The recipients would be selected on a race-neutral basis. However, the law school dean's expectation was that there would be a disproportionate number of minority students who would be assisted because, historically, they did poorly on the ACT and SAT standardized tests.

Texas politicians, Republicans and Democrats, after *Hopwood*, attempted to create an alternative to *Bakke*. As Texas Democratic Senator Royce West, a supporter of affirmative action in education, said bluntly:

> Texas has two choices. We could just follow *Hopwood* and say, "to hell with diversity," or we could be proactive and creative in trying to zero out its effects, which is what we're doing. I don't believe affirmative action is dead in the United States. But it is broken, and we're trying to fix it [in Texas].

In America, in 2001, there is still a great deal of school segregation—due to moves to the suburbs by middle-class Americans. Given this continual resegregation of American society since the 1950s, in Texas, as in Florida and California, the other states that have created a political alternative to preferential racial and ethnic admissions programs, there are many high schools that are predominantly or wholly populated by minority students.

Under Texas's Top Ten program, many Hispanic-American and African-American students are rethinking the possibility of attending a public university in their home state. As with so many other students, while they were in the top 10 percent of their high school's graduating class, they did not do well on the standardized college entrance examinations. Without the Top Ten policy, they were not able to enter the competitive Texas system of higher education.

There are still problems with the Texas program, which are being addressed by the politicians. One is the matter of financial assistance for these disadvantaged minority students entering the university. In almost all cases, these young minority students are the first of their family to attend college. For them it is both an honor and a fright. One minority student told a reporter: "Back where we're from, we were always ranked real high, we were always in honors. You still feel a lot of pressure. That you can't fail."

Given *Hopwood*, Texas university administrators, alumni, and faculty searched for ways to support these newly enrolled students. Texas higher education recruiters are now implementing a scholarship program, called the Longhorn Opportunity Scholarships. These scholarships, funded by alumni, provide eight thousand dollars—full tuition, room, and board—for students in the Top Ten who come from over sixty identified underrepresented high schools; most of the schools are overwhelmingly African-American or Hispanic-American. As Rochelle Brown, a first-year African-American student from Houston and a recipient of one of the 115 Longhorn scholarships, who is attending UT at Austin said: "I got the money, and I was like, well, maybe they do really want me." In addition, in 1999, the Texas legislature approved $100 million for need-based academic scholarships.

For students attending excellent, predominantly white, suburban schools, there is a very different problem: Top Ten meant that many highly motivated and very bright students would fall below the 10 percent mark and would have a more difficult time trying to enter the university system.

The Top Ten program is also an undergraduate-only admissions one; graduate and professional schools still remain under the constraints of the *Hopwood* judgment. Educators, however, believe that proper advisement and some tutoring would effectively prepare minority students for graduate and professional educational experiences. For example, on the University of Texas at Austin campus there is the Partnership for Excellence in the Natural Sciences (PENS). It provides a small number of first-year students who fell 200 points or more below the average SAT scores with small classes in calculus, chemistry, and biology, as well as study-skills sessions with peer mentors. "Without [this] intervention, only one in ten will go on to get a degree and make it into the health profession," said Professor David Laude, the PENS director. However, all students could benefit from small classes, but they are very expensive to staff.

It is fairly easy to account for the differences between inner-city schools and the much more affluent suburban schools. During the Supreme Court's deliberations in the *Swann v. Board of Education*, 1971, Justice Douglas wrote to his colleague William J. Brennan about these differences:

> It is notorious, North and South, that white schools are better than black schools, not because they are white but because they have better libraries, better physical plants, better laboratory equipment, broader criteria. A neighborhood school that is all black is usually managed by whites. History has shown that it is extremely difficult, if not impossible, in these circumstances to summon the resources necessary to upgrade the school of the blacks.

Earlier, in the Court's secret conference session after the *Swann* oral arguments, Justice Thurgood Marshall had bluntly told his brethren that "under freedom of choice no white student was ever ordered to go to a Negro school. No one wants to go to an inferior school and Negro schools are inferior."

According to a *New York Times* story filed on November 23, 1999, by Jodi Wilgoren, "Texas' Top 10% Law Appears To Preserve Racial Mix," minority enrollment has increased at most of the state's premier institutions, and both the educational leaders and the politicians are working toward resolution of the remaining problems with the Texas program. With the new program in effect since 1998, the minority population has returned to where it was prior to the *Hopwood* decision that ended affirmative action in the Fifth Circuit. In 1996, the last year of affirmative action in Texas, there were 4.1 percent undergraduate African Americans and 14.5 percent Hispanic Americans attending Texas universities. In 1997, the figures fell to 2.7 percent and 12.6 percent. In 1998, the first year of the Top Ten program, enrollments increased to 3.0 and 13.2 percent. In 1999, the figures were 4.1 percent African American and 13.8 percent Hispanic American.

Finally, because of the *Hopwood* judgment, until the Top Ten program was implemented, Texas was invaded by university recruiters from other states. Dozens of midwestern colleges have increased their efforts to bring minority students from Texas back to Indiana, Missouri, Iowa, and Kansas.

In the spring of 1999, there was another education case with facts quite similar to those in *Hopwood*. White students who had been denied admission to the University of Michigan brought suit in federal district court seeking admission as well as damages and legal fees because the institution was employing a preferential affirmative action admissions policy.

Their legal counsel were lawyers who worked for a conservative D.C. public law firm, the Center for Individual Rights (CIR), who had argued on behalf of Cheryl Hopwood. The CIR had been involved in legal challenges to affirmative action programs since it filed its amicus brief in the *Bakke* case. In addition, its legal staff prepared information for potential anti–affirmative action plaintiffs to follow if they wished to successfully challenge a university affirmative action program.

At the same time, the University of Massachusetts, fearful of a legal challenge to its affirmative action admissions program, unilaterally ended it. The administration announced that it would, starting in 1999, (1) examine quantitative data (GPAs, SAT scores) and (2) assess the financial background of every applicant. There would be preferences for all students who had good quantitative scores and who were members of a disadvantaged class of applicants. Faculty critics pointed out that such an admission process would surely exclude, disproportionally,

African-American and other minority students who did not score well on the standardized tests but were disadvantaged.

These legal challenges to affirmative action educational programs continue to flow into the federal courts. It is certain that the U.S. Supreme Court must hear a *Hopwood*-type case in order to determine whether *Bakke* is still good precedent.

The Supreme Court and the *Bakke* Precedent

It has been almost a quarter of a century since *Bakke* came down in 1978. It is not hanging by a thread, but it has been battered by lower federal court judges and by political opponents of preferential affirmative action programs in American higher education. However, there are still some unresolved questions surrounding the affirmative action controversy. Does one make it in America by virtue of one's merit, character, intelligence, and virtues? Or does one make it by virtue of special treatment afforded that person because of membership in a racial or ethnic group that has been severely disadvantaged throughout American history? And how long must society compensate members of these groups? While "all persons have a fair chance to achieve success" may be one of America's most prominent societal ideals, does the *Bakke* precedent nullify that goal?

Many, especially those in academia, reject the validity of these questions because of the nation's three hundred years of racial discrimination. Over the course of the past generation, they have faithfully adhered to *Bakke*. At the same time, it has been continually condemned by interest groups, by state and national Republican Party leadership, and by Republican presidential administrations since 1981.

Bakke has been rejected by a few Reagan-appointed federal judges, at both the federal district court and the federal court of appeals levels *(Hopwood)*. Yet only three justices of the U.S. Supreme Court, Chief Justice Rehnquist and Associate Justices Thomas and Scalia, have concluded that any and all racial classifications imposed by a government agency, such as a state university, for any purpose whatsoever are absolutely forbidden and in violation of the Fourteenth Amendment's Equal Protection Clause. There are only two exceptions to their almost categorical bar against racial and ethnic preferences. As they wrote in *Adarand*: A racial classification is "tolerated" only if it is absolutely necessary to end existing racial discrimination in a particular public agency, or if, as the Scalia minority said, there is "a social emergency rising to the level of imminent danger to life and limb."

On the Court, as society entered the twenty-first century, were six justices who disagreed with the draconian pronouncements of the trio. Four justices, Stevens, Souter, Ginsburg, and Breyer, have accepted the Brennan view of affirmative action and have dissented, as a group, in affirmative action cases decided by the Court in the 1990s. As Ginsburg wrote in her *Adarand* dissent: *Bakke* as precedent must be "allowed to evolve, . . . to be responsive to changing conditions."

Justice Sandra Day O'Connor has become the latter-day Justice Powell in affirmative action and other controversial litigation before the High Bench. Many of her opinions have been joined by Associate Justice Kennedy. Like the Rehnquist trio (and Powell), she believes that the appropriate standard to use in these affirmative action cases is strict scrutiny. But her premises for use of that standard differ dramatically from those of Rehnquist's group. As she wrote in her separate concurring opinion in *Adarand*, racial classifications violate the Fourteenth Amendment "only when they have been generated by the unacceptable attitudes of prejudice or stereotype that the [Equal Protection] Clause outlawed."

For O'Connor, use of strict scrutiny places the burden on the state agency to produce evidence of a proper motive for the racial classification. It must be one that is "sufficiently compelling" to rebut any accusation that unacceptable motives were the basis for the preferential affirmative action program. Unlike the Rehnquist trio and, at the same time, much closer to the four moderate justices, O'Connor has accepted the general university argument that the search for racial diversity in the student populations of undergraduate and graduate schools is a "compelling" state goal that survives strict scrutiny. As early as her separate opinion in *Wygant*, 1986, O'Connor wrote that "a state interest in the promotion of racial diversity has been found sufficiently 'compelling' at least in the context of higher education, to support the use of racial considerations in furthering that interest."

The Supreme Court has not overturned the *Bakke* precedent. In *Adarand*, a set-aside government contracting case, the key jurists were Justices Kennedy and O'Connor. Her opinion, joined in only by Kennedy on the following point, spoke to the importance of precedent in American society. O'Connor went out of her way, to the chagrin of Justice Scalia, to point out the tough societal dilemmas that accompany judicial efforts to overrule an important case (such as *Bakke*) around which major social expectations have congealed.

Powell's opinion, echoed by O'Connor, in effect said that "democratic diversity" in higher education is so important that schools can take race and ethnicity into consideration in the university admissions process. Because American colleges and universities are naturally places where diversity must exist, "absolute color-blindness is not constitutionally required in the educational context."

Unless the Court expressly overrules *Bakke*, it remains a viable precedent for America. As Dan T. Coenen, a professor at the University of Georgia's law school, said: "Until the U.S. Supreme Court speaks again, *Bakke*'s still the law of the land." As America enters the new millennium, there are at least five, possibly six, presently sitting justices of the U.S. Supreme Court who would vote to extend *Bakke* as precedent.

However, as American history clearly evidences, Court majorities can be fleeting ones. All it takes to change the voting pattern is for one of the five to die in office or retire due to poor health. If the president who fills the vacancy is a Democratic chief executive like Clinton, the nominee will be a person who (the president believes) agrees with the president on the constitutionality of preferential affirmative action programs. If, however, the nominating president is a conservative Republican in the mold of Ronald Reagan or George Bush, then the nominee put forward (the president hopes) will agree with the Rehnquist trio that all affirmative action programs are unconstitutional. It is supremely ironic that the future of the *Bakke* precedent ultimately rests with unpredictable events such as who wins a presidential election and which of the justices dies or is forced to retire from the Court.

Bakke's Impact

What has been the actual effect of *Bakke* on efforts to diversify colleges and universities? One major impact of *Bakke* is seen in its social and academic acceptance by most university officials and faculty. As an educator said:

> An entire generation of Americans has been schooled under *Bakke*-style affirmative action, with the explicit blessing of— indeed, following a how-to-do-it manual from the U.S. Reports. Only a handful of modern Supreme Court cases are now household words in America. But *Bakke*—like *Brown* and *Roe*—is surely one of them.

Enrollment data since *Bakke* has been analyzed by a number of scholars in an effort to answer the question of impact. And the answer, as America enters the twenty-first century, is that *Bakke* has had a dramatic impact on the diversification of American undergraduate and graduate and professional schools.

Interestingly, minority enrollments crested in the mid-1970s, before *Bakke*, because higher education institutions had begun separately evaluating, based on race, color, and ethnicity, their applicant pool in the late 1960s. Ironically, the *Bakke* decision terminated the use of quotas or set-asides based on race or ethnicity and, for some time, served as a restraint on diversification. However, by the end of the last decade of the twentieth century, it has become clear that *Bakke*'s impact has been invaluable in the diversification of college and university campuses. Even though it has been challenged in a number of states, and the Fifth Circuit, in *Hopwood*, effectively nullified its impact in Texas,

Louisiana, and Mississippi, it is still the law of the land in all other American states.

Bakke's "implementing population"—that is, state and federal judges and the admissions directors of America's higher education institutions—had no problem in carrying out the perceived mandate of the Court. The Association of American Law Schools (AALS), one of *Bakke*'s "implementing populations," in its November 1999 *Newsletter* again discussed the importance of diversity in law schools and the critical importance of *Bakke:* "While I urge us not to lose sight of the fact that *Bakke* is still good law, we cannot totally rely on legal cases to support our diversity efforts." The author, President Gregory H. Williams, then said that

> we cannot ignore the fact that there is substantial public opposition to affirmative action. . . . We need to think about ways we can carry our message of the value and importance of diversity to the public. . . . Today, approximately 30% of the American population are people of color, yet over 90% of the legal profession is white.

This legitimization of affirmative action practices by *Bakke* led to the dramatic improvements in diversity in the 1990s. Between 1988 and 1995, overall African-American enrollment increased more than 30 percent. The number of degrees earned by African Americans during this same period increased 34 percent for bachelor's degrees and over 40 percent for master's degrees. Hispanic-American growth has been even higher. Between 1988 and 1995, their enrollments increased by over 50 percent.

Medical school and law school progress has also been quite spectacular. In the same 1988–1995 period, minority enrollments in first-year medical school classes increased by 40 precent; Hispanic-American enrollments (including Puerto Ricans) increased by over 43 percent. Minorities, by 1995, accounted for almost 15 percent of the total enrollment in American medical schools. These figures were replicated for minority enrollment in American law schools. (See Figures 8.1 and 8.2.)

Viewing data from the beginning of the Johnson administration's push for affirmative action to the mid-1990s (1965–1995)

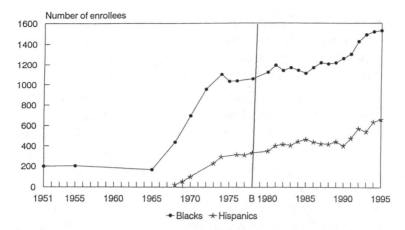

Figure 8.1 Black and Hispanic first-year medical school enrollment, 1951–95. "B" marks the date of the *Bakke* decision. (Data from Shea and Fullilove 1985; Medical School Admission Requirements, selected years.)

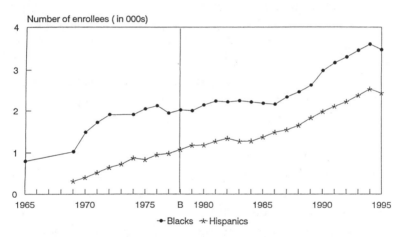

Figure 8.2 Black and Hispanic first-year law school enrollment. "B" marks the date of the *Bakke* decision. (Data from Shea and Fullilove 1985; *Lawyer's Almanac* 1986; American Bar Association Survey.)

clearly shows that the percentage of African-American and Hispanic-American graduates from college and professional schools has grown enormously. The percentage of African Americans who graduated from college rose from 5.4 to 15.4 percent. Hispanic Americans who graduated from college in this same time frame rose from 4.5 to 9.3 percent. African-American graduates from law schools rose from 1 to 7.5 percent, while African-

American medical school graduates rose from 2.2 to 8.1 percent. Between 1960 and 1990, the number of African-American doctors doubled, and the number of attorneys and engineers tripled.

Beyond doubt, the *Bakke* decision was positively received by its implementing public, and inroads were made in the effort to provide equal educational opportunities for formerly disadvantaged minorities. A recently published watershed study of the impact of *Bakke* on minority admissions to dozens of very selective colleges and universities and graduate programs in medicine and law in America, *The Shape of the River*, noted that on the authority of Powell's "decisive" *Bakke* opinion, "all selective colleges and professional schools have continued to consider race in admitting students." Further, if there was a return to the use of a race-neutral standard, then minority student enrollment would immediately drop below 2 percent.

Another study of the effects of affirmative action in law schools, compiled by University of Michigan law professor David Chambers and entitled "Doing Well and Doing Good: The Careers of Minority and White Graduates of the UMLS, 1970–1996," presented data showing the value and importance of considering race in the law school admission process. Minority graduates of UMLS have made "significant achievements" in the legal profession. The study found that LSAT and undergraduate GPA's "have no relationship to achievement after law school, whether achievement is measured by earned income, career satisfaction, or service contributions."

However, after 1995, affirmative action again came under fire from political critics across America. Although political efforts to end affirmative action failed in many states, there was the passage of anti–affirmative action ballot initiatives in California and Washington. There was also the very unusual federal court of appeals decision in *Hopwood*. As a consequence, after 1995 there were declines in minority enrollments in a small number of professional schools.

According to the data collected by the Association of American Medical Colleges (AAMC), as of January 1999, the number of underrepresented minorities (African Americans, Native

{ *The* Bakke *Case* }

Americans, Mexican Americans/Chicanos, and mainland Puerto Ricans) in medical schools dropped precipitously in California, Texas, Louisiana, and Mississippi. However, the AAMC stated that the data also shows that

> fortunately, at the national level, the number of underrepresented applying to medical schools did not suffer further appreciable reductions from last year; there were 4,516 underrepresented minority applicants in 1997 and 4,479 in 1998. Similarly, the number of minorities entering medical schools nationwide did not fall further. (1998) entrants numbered 1,865 compared with 1,754 in 1997. The peak enrollment occurred in 1994 when 2,014 [minority students] entered medical school.

Has *Bakke*'s impact as national precedent—validating the use of race as one of a number of factors in a college's admissions processes—come to an end in light of (1) the *Adarand* decision of the U.S. Supreme Court, (2) lower-court decisions in the area of affirmative action, and (3) passage of statewide initiatives in California and Washington state that prohibit preferential, race-based affirmative action policies in the educational sector?

Adarand and other contracting affirmative action cases are different from the higher education affirmative action litigation. In the contracting cases, set-asides or quotas mean that minority groups win some projects and white firms such as Adarand Constructors do not. Such a quota system "can Balkanize the races by encouraging their segregation. Education in contrast, unites people from different walks of life." Instead of insular corporations performing various discrete contracts in isolation—the minority firm adds the guardrail after the white firm lays the asphalt—universities draw diverse people—students, faculty, and staff—into spaces where they mingle with and learn from each other.

Powell's message to the implementing community was not complicated. All students benefit from affirmative action programs that give pluses to certain factors, such as race. Strict quotas or set-asides, however, cannot be implemented in order to achieve educational diversity. Use the Harvard College process for screening applicants to assure a constitutionally valid affirmative action program.

With the exception of the three-judge panel of the Fifth Circuit Court of Appeals and the successful, political anti–affirmative action initiatives in California and Washington state, *Bakke* has remained the law of the land. In some of those states affected by the opponents of affirmative action, there has been political action to try to provide minorities with access to higher education. Probably all of the men and women who have sat on the Court during these affirmative action cases would agree with Justice Douglas's overriding view of the issue. For him, as he said to Justice Brennan in 1971: "the problems of [diversity in higher education] are problems for educators and school boards, not for federal courts." *Bakke* underscored Douglas's vision, for it allows educators to take good-faith measures, without resorting to quotas, to diversify their student, faculty, and staff populations. That is a fine legacy for a society committed to democratic diversity.

1962	Allan Bakke graduates University of Minnesota with a degree in mechanical engineering.
1964	1964 Civil Rights Act becomes public law. Title VI prohibits discrimination based on race, color, sex, or national origin in all institutions receiving federal funding.
1967	Captain Allan Bakke returns from a tour of duty in Vietnam and joins NASA's Ames Research Center in California as a research engineer.
1968	University of Washington School of Law (UWSL) implements a preferential affirmative action admissions program in order to diversify its student population.
1970	University of California, Davis, Medical School (UCD) implements a preferential affirmative action admissions program, using a set-aside number for minority students, in order to diversify its student population.
May 1970	Marco DeFunis graduates magna cum laude and Phi Beta Kappa from the University of Washington.
1970, 1971	Marco DeFunis twice rejected by the UWSL admissions committee.
April 1971	Washington Superior Court rules in DeFunis's favor and orders him admitted to the UWSL in September 1971.
September 1971	UWSL admits DeFunis pending outcome of litigation.
May 1972	Washington State Supreme Court overturns lower court judgment, validating UWSL affirmative action program.

August 1972	DeFunis files petition for certiorari in the U.S. Supreme Court.
August 1972	Supreme Court Justice William O. Douglas issues a stay of action to UWSL pending a final determination of the issue by the Court; DeFunis continues his legal education.
1972	Allan Bakke, thirty-two years old, begins to apply to medical schools.
May 1973	Allan Bakke rejected for admission into UCD.
September 1973	Allan Bakke rejected for early admission into UCD.
November 1973	U.S. Supreme Court grants certiorari in *DeFunis v. Odegaard*, Docket No. 73-235.
February 26, 1974	U.S. Supreme Court hears oral argument in *DeFunis*.
April 23, 1974	U.S. Supreme Court dismisses *DeFunis* for mootness.
April 1974	Allan Bakke rejected again by UCD medical school.
May 1974	Marco DeFunis graduates UWSL, practices law in Seattle, Washington.
June 1974	Allan Bakke brings suit in Yolo County, California Superior Court.
November 1974	Judge sets aside the UCD preferential admissions program but does not admit Bakke to medical school.
May 1975	Regents of University of California appeals to California Supreme Court.
September 1976	California Supreme Court validates lower court judgment and orders Bakke admitted to the UCD medical school, 6 to 1.
December 1976	Regents of the University of California appeals state supreme court decision to the U.S. Supreme Court. Order admitting Bakke to medical school stayed pending results of the appeal.

January 1977	Bakke's response in opposition.
February 22, 1977	U.S. Supreme Court grants certiorari in *Bakke*. Oral arguments set for October 1977, Docket No. 76-811.
February–October 1977	Fifty-eight amicus curiae briefs filed in Court.
June 1977	Brief on the merits filed by University of California.
August 1977	Bakke's response brief filed in Court.
October 1977	U.S. government's amicus brief filed in Court.
October 1977	Reply briefs filed by UC and by Bakke.
October 12, 1977	Oral arguments in *Bakke*.
October 14, 1977	Initial secret conference session to discuss *Bakke*.
October 17, 1977	U.S. Supreme Court requests supplemental briefs on Title VI issue.
September 1977–May 1978	Circulation of MTTCs and other information by the justices.
May 1, 1978	Justice Harry Blackmun finally casts his vote in *Bakke*.
June 28, 1978	U.S. Supreme Court announces its judgment in *Regents of the University of California v. Bakke*.
November, 1980	Ronald Reagan defeats Jimmy Carter for the presidency.
1981	President Reagan nominates first U.S. Supreme Court female justice, Sandra Day O'Connor.
1986	Chief Justice Burger retires; President Reagan nominates William Rehnquist to fill Burger's seat and nominates Antonin Scalia to fill Rehnquist's seat.
June 1987	Justice Lewis F. Powell retires.
July 1987	President Reagan nominates Robert Bork to fill Powell's seat on Court.

October 23, 1987	Robert Bork rejected in Senate, 58 to 42.
November 1987	President Reagan's Supreme Court nominee Douglas Ginsburg withdraws after reports surface that he smoked marijuana at Harvard Law School.
February 1988	President Reagan nominates Anthony Kennedy to fill Powell's seat; confirmed by Senate.
June 1988	*Wygant v. Board of Education* handed down by the Court, 5 to 4.
November 1988	George Bush defeats Michael Dukakis for presidency.
June 1989	*Richmond, Va. v. J. A. Croson Co.* handed down by Court, 5 to 4.
June 1990	Justice William J. Brennan announces his retirement.
July 1990	President Bush nominates David H. Souter to fill Brennan vacancy; confirmed by the Senate.
June 1991	Justice Thurgood Marshall announces his retirement.
July 1991	President Bush nominates Clarence Thomas to fill Marshall vacancy; after Anita Hill allegations, confirmed by Senate, 52 to 48.
November 1992	Bill Clinton defeats George Bush for presidency.
March 1993	Justice Byron R. White announces his retirement.
July 1993	President Clinton nominates second female to fill White's seat, Ruth Bader Ginsburg; confirmed by Senate.
April 1994	Justice Harry A. Blackmun announces his retirement.
July 1994	President Clinton nominates Stephen Breyer to fill Blackmun's seat; confirmed by Senate.

{ *The* Bakke *Case* }

June 1995	*Adarand Constructors v. Pena* handed down by U.S. Supreme Court, 5 to 4.
July 1995	President Clinton institutes a review of all federal affirmative action programs.
July 1995	Regents of University of California ends all preferential affirmative action admissions programs used in the system.
1996	*Podberesky v. Kirwin*, involving the University of Maryland's preferential scholarship program, challenged in lower federal courts.
1996	*Hopwood v. Texas* handed down by Fifth Circuit U.S. Court of Appeals, invalidating all affirmative action programs in the states in the circuit (Mississippi, Louisiana, Texas).
November 1996	California voters pass Proposition 209, ending all affirmative action programs in employment, education, and public contracting.
October 1997	U.S. Supreme Court denies certiorari in *Texas v. Hopwood*.
1998	Texas passes Top Ten plan legislation to counter impact of *Hopwood* decision.
October 1998	*Board of Education v. Taxman* settled before oral arguments in the U.S. Supreme Court.
November 1998	Washington state voters pass Initiative 200, ending all affirmative action programs in employment, education, and public contracting.
September 1999	Florida governor issues executive order enabling top 20 percent of high school graduates to enter public university of their choice; forestalls statewide anti–affirmative action ballot issue.

RELEVANT CASES

Adarand Constructors v. Pena, 515 U.S. 200 (1995)

Baker v. Carr, 369 U.S. 186 (1962)

Board of Education v. Taxman, No. 94-5090 (3d Cir. 1996), cert. granted, June 25, 1997. No. 96-679. Case dropped, October 1997.

Brown v. Board of Education, 347 U.S. 483 (1954)

Coalition for Economic Equity, et al. v. Pete Wilson, Governor, No. 97-15030 (9th Cir. 1997)

Cooper v. Aaron, 358 U.S. 1 (1958)

DeFunis v. Odegaard, 416 U.S. 312 (1974)

Fullilove v. Klutznick, 448 U.S. 448 (1980)

Hopwood v. Texas, 78 F.3d 932 (5th Cir. 1996); *Texas v. Hopwood,* cert. denied, 518 U.S. 1033 (1996)

Korematsu v. United States, 323 U.S. 214 (1944)

Loving v. Virginia, 388 U.S. 1 (1967)

Metro Broadcasting v. Federal Communications Commission, 497 U.S. 547 (1990)

Plessy v. Ferguson, 163 U.S. 537 (1896)

Podberesky v. Kirwin, 838 F. Supp. 1075 (D. Md. 1993); remanded, 38 F.3d 147 (4th Cir. 1996)

Regents of the University of California v. Bakke, 438 U.S. 205 (1978)

Richmond, Va. v. J. A. Croson Co., 488 U.S. 469 (1989)

Swann v. Board of Education, 402 U.S. 1 (1970)

Sweatt v. Painter, 339 U.S. 629 (1950)

United States v. Carolene Products, 304 U.S. 144 (1938)

Webster v. Reproductive Health Services, 492 U.S. 490 (1989)

Wygant v. Board of Education, 476 U.S. 267 (1986)

BIBLIOGRAPHICAL ESSAY

Note from the Series Editors: The following bibliographical essay contains the major primary and secondary sources the author consulted for this volume. We have asked all authors in the series to omit formal citations in order to make our volumes more readable, inexpensive, and appealing for students and general readers. In adopting this format, Landmark Law Cases and American Society follows the precedent of a number of highly regarded and widely consulted series.

The primary sources for the dissection of the *Bakke* litigation led me to take extended trips to Washington, D.C.; Austin, Texas; and Boston, Massachusetts. In Washington, D.C., I was able to work in the U.S. Supreme Court's library to examine all the briefs of the major parties in the *DeFunis* and the *Bakke* litigation as well as to read the briefs of all the amici who participated in these two affirmative action in higher education cases.

A few blocks away, in the James Madison building of the Library of Congress, is located the library's Manuscript Division. I was able to examine the files of a number of U.S. Supreme Court justices who participated in discussions and debates on either *DeFunis* or *Bakke* or both. This research activity, over a five-year period, allowed me to cull pertinent information about the dynamics of decision making in the Court from the files of Associate Justices William J. Brennan Jr., Thurgood Marshall, and William O. Douglas. It should be noted, again, that the conversations of the justices in all the *DeFunis* and *Bakke* conference sessions I have noted in this book are based solely on the notes taken by Justices Douglas, Brennan, and Marshall. As there are no transcriptions of these secret sessions other than these docket notes, I cannot attest to their accuracy. However, in comparing them, I saw no discrepancies in what the justices jotted down.

Additionally, over the past three decades, I was able to sit down and speak with a number of justices who were sitting at or before the time of *Bakke*, in their chambers in the U.S. Supreme Court building. These conversations provided me with information (1) about the dynamics of Supreme Court decision making and (2) about the *DeFunis* and *Bakke* cases. I spoke with Chief Justice Warren Burger and Associate Justices

Hugo L. Black, Arthur Goldberg, William J. Brennan Jr., Byron R. White, Harry A. Blackmun, Lewis F. Powell, and William O. Douglas.

The Lyndon Baines Johnson Presidential Library, on the campus of the University of Texas at Austin, was a source of much information about the beginnings of federal affirmative action programs. Additional input on the same subject came from my work in the John F. Kennedy Presidential Library, located in Boston, Massachusetts.

There have been some excellent commentators who contributed significantly to the public's understanding of the complexity of the affirmative action debates that took place, publicly and privately, in the Supreme Court. Those who stand out include Professor A. E. Dick Howard, University of Virginia Law School, who provided frequent commentary for the *Washington Post* and National Public Radio as well as for learned journals; the award-winning reporter and columnist for the *New York Times,* Tony Lewis; Fred Graham, *CBS News;* Professor Ronald Dworkin, New York University Law School, who has written occasionally for the *New York Review of Books* on *Bakke* and affirmative action; Joan Biskupic, of the *Washington Post;* the late Meg Greenfield of *Newsweek* and the *Washington Post;* Lou Cannon of the old *Washington Star;* Ethan Bronner of the *Boston Globe;* and Brent Staples, who has contributed some insightful editorial essays for the *New York Times.*

In addition to these informative observers, I drew heavily on the general reporting about these cases from the archives of four major newspapers for information, observations, and interviews with the leading players in the *DeFunis* and *Bakke* cases. These papers are the *New York Times,* the *Washington Post,* the *Los Angeles Times,* and the *Seattle Times.* Mostly from their archives located on the Internet, but also from bleary-eyed examination of microfilm of these media sources, I was able to flesh out the human dynamics of the affirmative action in higher education controversies. In addition, using the Internet I was able to "speak with" Ward Connerly's organization, Californians against Discrimination and Preferences (CADAP), as well as Martin Luther King III's civil rights organization, Americans United for Affirmative Action (AUAA), and a host of other groups who participated in the higher education affirmative action wars.

There are scores of very good secondary sources on the issue of affirmative action in higher education and on Supreme Court decision making. Among the books that I found very helpful are the following: Joel Dreyfuss and Charles Lawrence III, *The Bakke Case: The Politics of Inequality* (New York: Harcourt Brace Jovanovich, 1979); David O'Brien, *Storm Center* (New York: Norton, 1997); John C. Jeffries, *Justice Lewis F. Powell, Jr.* (New York: Scribner's, 1994); Howard Ball, *A Defiant Life: Thurgood Marshall and the Persistence of Racism in America* (New York: Random House, 1999); J. Harvie Wilkinson III, *From* Brown *to* Bakke: *The Supreme Court and School Integration, 1954–1978* (New York: Oxford, 1979); Allan P. Sindler, *Bakke, DeFunis and Minority Admissions: The Quest for Equal Opportunity* (New York: Longman, 1978); Griffin Bell, with Ronald J. Ostrow, *Taking Care of the Law* (New York: Morrow, 1982); Thomas Sowell, *Affirmative Action Reconsidered: Was It Necessary in Academia?* (Washington, D.C.: American Enterprise Institute, 1975); and Terry Eastland and William J. Bennett, *Counting By Race: Equality from the Founding Fathers to Bakke and Weber* (New York: Basic, 1979).

There are, in particular, two very recent publications that are must reading for those interested in examining relevant data on the impact of the *Bakke* precedent on diversification of undergraduate, graduate, and professional schools (especially law and medical schools) since the 1970s. These books are William C. Bowen and Derek Bok, *The Shape of the River: Long Term Consequences of Considering Race in College and University Admissions* (Princeton, N.J.: Princeton University Press, 1999), and Susan Welch and John Gruhl, *Affirmative Action and Minority Enrollments in Medical and Law Schools* (Ann Arbor: University of Michigan Press, 1999). See also a recent essay: Rosemarie Sweeney and Verna L. Rose, "Rate of Minority School Applicants in Some States Declines," 59 *American Family Physician* 746 (March 1999).

Political and social scientists have also made significant contributions to an understanding of the intersection of law, politics, and culture in controversial public policies such as affirmative action. These include the following: Barbara Bardes and Robert W. Oldenick, *Public Opinion: Measuring the American Mind* (Belmont: Wadsworth, 1999); Lee Epstein and Jack Knight, *The Choices Justices Make* (Washington, D.C.: Congressional Quarterly Press, 1998); Philip Cooper and Howard Ball, *The U.S. Supreme Court: From the Inside*

Out (Englewood Cliffs: Prentice-Hall, 1996); and Henry Abraham, *Presidents and Justices* (New York: Oxford, 1993).

Also, there is Lester M. Salamon and Michael S. Lund, eds., *The Reagan Presidency and the Governing of America* (Washington, D.C.: Urban Institute Press, 1984); David G. Savage, *Turning Right: The Making of the Rehnquist Supreme Court* (New York: Wiley, 1992); Steven A. Shull, *American Civil Rights Policy from Truman to Clinton* (Armonk: M. E. Sharpe, 1999); James F. Simon, *The Center Holds: The Power Struggle inside the Rehnquist Court* (New York: Simon and Schuster, 1995); Nancy V. Baker, *Conflicting Loyalties: Law and Politics in the Attorney General's Office, 1789–1990* (Lawrence: University Press of Kansas, 1992); Robert D. Loevy, *The Civil Rights Act of 1964* (Albany: SUNY Press, 1997); Stuart M. Butler, Michael Sanera, and W. Bruce Weinrod, eds., *Mandate for Leadership II* (Washington, D.C.: The Heritage Foundation, 1984); Dilys M. Hill, Raymond A. Moore, and Phil Williams, eds., *The Reagan Presidency: An Incomplete Revolution?* (New York: St. Martin's Press, 1990); Elliot E. Slotnick, "Television News and the Supreme Court: The Case of Allan Bakke" (paper delivered at the 1990 Annual Meeting of the American Political Science Association, San Francisco, August 30–September 2, 1990); Thomas Sowell, *Inside American Education* (New York: Free Press, 1993); and Shirley Ann Warshaw, *The Domestic Presidency: Policy Making in the White House* (Boston: Allyn and Bacon, 1997).

Finally, in the law journals and other magazines, there are hundreds of excellent essays that examine not only the legal strengths and weaknesses but also the associated ethical and social issues that affirmative action litigation has raised. These include Akhil Reed Amar and Neal Kumar Katyal, "Bakke's Fate," 43 *UCLA Law Review* 1745 (1996); A. Leon Higginbotham Jr., "Breaking Thurgood Marshall's Promise," *New York Times Sunday Magazine*, January 18, 1998; Naomi Levine and Lois Waldman, "Marco DeFunis, Justice Douglas and the American Jewish Congress," 41 *Congress Bi-Weekly* (May 24, 1974); Brian C. Eades, "Affirmative Action: The U.S. Supreme Court Goes Color-Blind: *Adarand Constructors, Inc. v. Pena*," 29 *Creighton Law Review*, 771 (1996); and Luke Charles Harris and Uma Narayan, "Affirmative Action and the Myth of Preferential Treatment," 11 *Harvard Blackletter Journal* (1994).

INDEX

White, Byron R., 31, 67, 87, 178
  comments of, in *Bakke*
    conference session, 100
  Title XI argument rejected by, in
    Bakke, 87
  view of Fourteenth Amendment
    held by, 118
Williams, Deborah, 188
Williams, Gregory H., 202
"Willie Horton" issue, 162

Wilson, Pete, 164, 165
Wygant litigation, 177–179
  Court conference session on,
    177–178
*Wygant v. Jackson, Michigan Board
  of Education*, 1986, 177–179,
  200. *See also Wygant* litigation

Yale Law School, 73, 158
Young Americans for Freedom, 77